5<sup>95</sup>/F4

# BOOKS BY DWIGHT D. EISENHOWER

CRUSADE IN EUROPE

PEACE WITH JUSTICE

THE WHITE HOUSE YEARS

Volume I: MANDATE FOR CHANGE
Volume II: WAGING PEACE

AT EASE: Stories I Tell To Friends

# IN REVIEW

## PICTURES I'VE KEPT

### A CONCISE PICTORIAL "AUTOBIOGRAPHY"

# IN REVIEW

PICTURES I'VE KEPT

A CONCISE PICTORIAL "AUTOBIOGRAPHY"

## DWIGHT D. EISENHOWER

1969

DOUBLEDAY & COMPANY, INC.

Garden City, New York

This text is drawn from four books by Dwight D. Eisenhower. They are: *Crusade in Europe*; the two volumes known as *The White House Years*, MANDATE FOR CHANGE and WAGING PEACE; and *At Ease*. It is not a condensation of the entire four books; rather it consists of condensations of certain significant sections of the original books.

The text was condensed by Edwin Corbin, and reviewed, edited, and amended slightly by the author and his Doubleday editors.

Serious students of history, or anyone wishing to quote or cite President Eisenhower, whenever permission is granted by the publishers, should refer to the full texts of the above books.

The assistance of Brig. General Robert L. Schulz and Dr. Kevin McCann in assembling materials for *In Review* is gratefully acknowledged.

Library of Congress Catalog Card Number 68-57660
Copyright © 1969 by Dwight D. Eisenhower
All Rights Reserved
Printed in the United States of America
9  8  7  6  5  4  3  2

# CONTENTS

Heart attack...
Agriculture...
Decision to run again...
The election...

Uprising in Poland...And in Hungary...
Crisis in the Middle East...
Suez and the Aswan Dam...
USIA...
Education and the Congress...
The first civil rights legislation since 1875...
Little Rock...
Trouble in Lebanon...
U.S. landings in Lebanon...Withdrawal...
"Sputnik"...
The Missile program...
Quemoy and Matsu again...

New illness...
The economy...
Alaskan and Hawaiian statehood...
Berlin...
Death of John Foster Dulles...
The Congress...
Visit of Khrushchev...
Disarmament efforts...
Personal diplomacy...
Italy...
India...
Iran...
Morocco...
Home again...

Panama...
Visit to Latin America...
The U-2...
Summit in Paris...
Disruption in Japan...
Elections...
Vice-President Nixon...

Senator John F. Kennedy...
A farewell message to the American people...
Home to Gettysburg...

# LIST OF ILLUSTRATIONS

Photo Credits

All photographs, unless otherwise credited, are from the Dwight D.
    Eisenhower Library.
Alex Gotfryd: Frontispiece
The Kansas State Historical Society, Topeka: 3, 10
Kansas Department of Economic Development, Topeka: 6
Mrs. Ruby Lucier: 11
Department of the Army, U.S. Military Academy, West Point: 16, 17
Author's personal collection: 24, 33, 35, 36, 41, 71, 171
Jeffcoat Studio, Abilene: 33
United Press International: 34, 36, 49, 56, 64, 66, 68, 74, 75, 91, 96, 97,
    115, 121, 124, 125, 130, 132, 146, 154, 172, 179, 187, 199, 208, 209,
    214, 215, 219, 221, 222, 229, 230, 232
Wide World: 47, 48, 82, 114, 146, 183, 187, 198, 219, 235
U.S. Army: 48, 82, 115, 185
Franklin D. Roosevelt Library: 57
Imperial War Museum, London: 64, 66
U.S. Army Signal Corps: 71
U.S. Air Force: 72, 138
Black Star: 88, 89
Manny Warman, Columbia University: 104, 120
Columbia University: 105, 127, 236
Brown Brothers: 125
U.S. News & World Report: 129
Harris & Ewing: 154
Naval Photographic Center: 171, 178
Gilloon Photo Agency: 172, 183
Hungarian Committee: 164, 183
Robert Phillips: 203
George Tames, The New York Times: 208
Wally McNamee, Washington Post: 215
United Nations: 227
Abbie Rowe, White House: 231
CBS News: 234

These are some of the pictures I've kept in my mind or in our family albums. While too many of them show the author, their real value is that many of them contain the likenesses of people who have meant much to me during my lifetime.                                                D.D.E.

---

# PART ONE

O F THE EISENHOWERS who sailed to this country in the good ship *Europa* back in 1741, there was little talk in my boyhood. My father and mother were not heedless of their families' past, to be sure. But they were principally concerned with their present responsibilities and their children's futures. Mine was a cheerful and a vital family. Our pleasures were simple—they included survival—but we had plenty of fresh air, exercise, and companionship.

Two years after I was born in Denison, Texas, on October 14, 1890, my family moved to Abilene, Kansas.

As it must to all small boys, there came a time when we began to comprehend that home was more than just our house and backyard. Once in a while, news of the outside world crept in—a world beyond the limits of Kansas, even.

But before I paid much attention to that distant, outside world, there was a lot to see and learn in the small world around me. Abilene was in those days just another rural town, undistinguishable from scores of others dotting the plains. It looked peaceful and pastoral.

The town was located a mile or two to the north of the Smoky Hill River and lay largely east of a stream which meandered its way through the flat alluvial plain. On a real estate developer's map, the little waterway is entitled "Serpentine Creek"; we, who knew its true character, called it Mud Creek.

It was definitely a small town. Paving was unknown for a long time. Crossings of scattered stone were provided at each corner but after a heavy summer rain the streets became almost impassable because of mud. The police force was one man. The Abilene paper, published the day I was born, offers a sample of the price structure. Eggs were five cents a dozen. Bread was three cents a loaf.

Two or three months before my fifth birthday, I took a long trip to a strange and far off place—Topeka.

When we arrived, it was peculiar to be surrounded by so many strangers. It seemed to me that there were dozens or hundreds of people—all grownups and all relatives—in the house. Even though they were, somehow, my family, I felt lonesome and lost among them.

I began to wander around outside. I noticed a pair of barnyard geese. The male resented my intrusion from our first meeting. Each time thereafter he would push along toward me aggressively and with hideous hissing noises so threatening my security that five-year-old courage could not stand the strain.

Uncle Luther decided that something had to be done. He took a worn out broom and cut off the straw. With the weapon all set, he took me out into the yard. More frightened at the moment of his possible scolding than I was of aggression, I took what was meant to be a firm, but was really a trembling, stand the next time the fowl came close. Then I let out a yell and rushed toward him, swinging the club as fast as I could. He turned and I gave him a satisfying smack right in the fanny.

From thence on, once he found out I had a stick, he would continue his belligerent noises whenever he saw me but he did not again come near me. I never made the mistake of being caught without my weapon. This all turned out to be a rather good lesson because I quickly learned never to negotiate with an adversary except from a position of strength.

Both my parents were against quarreling and fighting. They deplored bad manners. I did discover one day that my Father was far from being a turn-the-other-cheek type. He arrived home early one afternoon as I came in from the school grounds on the run, chased by a belligerent boy of about my own size. My Father called: "Why do you let that boy run you around like that?"

I shouted back, "Because if I fight him, you'll give me a whipping, whether I win or lose!"

"Chase that boy out of here."

This was enough for me. So I did.

I was rapidly learning that domination of others in this world often comes about or is sought through bluff. But it took me some years to learn that pounding from an opponent is not to be dreaded as much as constantly living in fear of another.

Mother and Father maintained a genuine partnership in raising their six sons. Father was the breadwinner, Supreme Court, and Lord High Executioner.

Abilene, Kansas, U.S.A., as recalled by the author and "The 'Gem' of the Plains" as described in the enthusiastic words of a civic promoter of the time. The town was not lacking for frontier spirit but it did lack for sidewalks.

Four of the brothers Eisenhower, at an early stage of development. This photograph, believed to be the first known portrait of Dwight David Eisenhower, was taken when he was three years old, in 1893 or '94. Left to right: Roy, Arthur, Edgar, Dwight.

Mother was tutor and manager of our household. Their partnership was ideal. This may sound unbelievable, and only recollected in tranquility, but I never heard a cross word pass between them. This had its lasting effect on all the boys—Arthur, Edgar, Roy, Earl, Milton, and myself.

Mother took care of minor infractions during the day but anything serious was passed along to Father for settlement. He certainly was never one for spoiling any child by sparing the rod. If the evidence showed that the culprit had offended deliberately, the application of stick to skin was a routine affair.

Father had quick judicial instincts. Mother had, like a psychologist, insight into the fact that each son was a unique personality and she adapted her methods to each.

The year when I was ten, my mother gave permission to Arthur and Edgar, the two older Eisenhower boys, to go out with a group for Halloween "trick or treating." It was upsetting when my father and mother said I as too young to go along. I argued and pleaded until the last minute. Finally, the two boys took off.

I have no exact memory of what happened immediately afterward, but soon I was completely beside myself. Suddenly my father grabbed my shoulders to shock me back into consciousness. What I had been doing was standing by an old apple tree trunk and pounding it with my bleeding fists, expressing resentment in rage. My father legislated the matter with the traditional hickory switch and sent me off to bed.

Perhaps an hour later, my mother came into the room. I was still sobbing into the pillow, my feelings—among other things—hurt, completely abused and at odds with the entire world. Mother sat in the rocking chair by the bed and said nothing for a long time. Then she began to talk about temper and controlling it. Eventually, as she often did, she drew on the Bible, paraphrasing it, I suppose.

This time she said, "He that conquereth his own soul is greater than he who taketh a city."

Hatred was a futile sort of thing, she said, because hating anyone or anything meant that there was little to be gained. The person who had incurred my displeasure probably didn't care, possibly didn't even know, and the only person injured was myself.

In the meantime, she had set about putting salve on my injured hands and then bandaging the worst places.

I have always looked back on that conversation as one of the most valuable moments of my life.

Father understood our wants, in fact our desperate need for playtime's implements and accessories. He allotted each boy a bit of ground out of the land surrounding our house. Each was privileged to raise any kind of vegetables he chose and to sell them.

For my lot, I chose to grow sweet corn and cucumbers. I had made inquiries and decided that these were the most popular vegetables. I liked the thought that I was earning something on my own—and could keep it or spend it on myself.

Each morning before school, there were other items on the agenda—milking cows, feeding chickens and horses, putting the stalls and chicken house shipshape. The legend spread in later years was that I was always the last from bed. This may be true but I doubt it.

All in all, we were a cheerful and a vital family. We would have been insulted had anyone offered us charity; instead my mother was always ready to take home remedies or food and start out to help anyone who was sick. The daily prayers of my parents did not fail to include a plea for the hungry, the weary, and the unfortunates of the world.

Through the first six grades, I attended Lincoln School, directly across from our Fourth Street home. The darkness of the classrooms on a winter day and the monotonous hum of recitations, offset only occasionally by the excitement of a spelling bee or the suppression of a disorderly boy, are my sole-surviving memories. I was either a lackluster student or involved in a lackluster program.

My first love was ancient history. At an early age, I developed an interest in the human record and I became particlularly fond of Greek and Roman accounts. These subjects were so engrossing that I frequently was guilty of neglecting all other. My mother's annoyance at this oblivion to the mundane life of chores and assigned homework grew until, despite her reverence for books, she took my volumes of history away and locked them in a closet.

This had the desired effect for a while. But one day I found the key to that closet. Whenever mother went to town to shop or was out working in her flower garden, I would sneak out the books.

When I got around to the Americans, Washington was my hero. I never tired of reading about his exploits. The qualities that excited my admiration were Washington's stamina and patience in adversity, first, and then his indomitable courage, daring, and capacity for self-sacrifice.

The boys who did the chores assemble. Date: perhaps 1905. Left to right: Dwight, Edgar, Earl, Roy, Arthur.

Family portrait, although not everyone was home for the sitting. With their father, David, and mother, Ida, Milton, Dwight, and Earl present properly sober faces which mirror their father's. Mrs. Eisenhower, and friend Flip (lower right) are more relaxed.

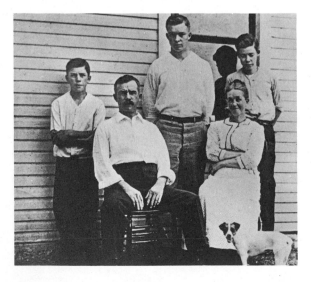

One of the boyhood homes of the future President: 201 Southeast Fourth Street in Abilene.

Reading history was exciting, but nothing could compare with rugged outdoor sports for the Abilene youth.

Friction existed continuously between the north and the south side of town. Those of us from the south, in Abilene's Civil War, were less numerous but we liked to think of ourselves as being tougher. We numbered in our membership all the farm boys who lived south of town.

One time I found myself squared off with another boy. The lad was exactly my age but somewhat smaller and although I cannot recall the cause of the quarrel, we were hitting at each other as hard as we could. Our only hope was for one to outlast the other.

Gradually, I gained an advantage and was pounding my antagonist with satisfying rhythm. Suddenly an avalanche hit me in the back. My opponent's older brother had come racing through the ring of yelling spectators and, striking me right at the shoulders, bore me to the ground. There, he began slamming me all over the place.

Although he was somewhat stronger and larger, I did manage to get up, realizing now that I had two rather than one to try holding my own against. The outlook was dark but I was stubborn enough to keep up the contest.

It happened that Edgar, just coming back from Northside school where he was in the eighth grade, saw what was happening. He pushed his way into the crowd of boys and walking into the center interposed himself between the bigger brother and me. I shall never forget his immortal words: "Now," he said, "you and I will settle this while Dwight finishes the job on this brother of yours."

The bigger boy looked at Ed, turned around and pushed off. The younger boy left too.

By the time I entered high school in 1905, the North-South rivalry had flown out of favor and I cannot recall any further difficulty of any kind. One reason might have been that the South side boasted more than our share of pretty girls.

In high school, plane geometry was an intellectual adventure, one that entranced me. After a few months, my teachers conducted an unusual experiment. The principal and my mathematics teacher called me to the office and told me that they were going to take away my textbook. Thereafter, I was to work out the geometric problems without the benefit of the book. They said that for the remaining months, unless the experiment was terminated by them, I would automatically receive an A-plus grade.

Strangely enough, I got along fairly well.

The town school superintendent visited classrooms regularly. He seemed to be as much concerned with discipline as with academic proficiency. Several times my deportment was reported to him and not as a model.

Although many years later he described me in a newspaper interview as "a typically lively school boy with a very engaging nature and a boyish grin," I cannot recall now any sign on his part that he harbored such feelings.

The most dramatic difference between high schools of today and those of my time is probably not in the curriculum but in the life expectancy of the people. Then, except for the common cold and chilblains, any illness might easily be fatal.

Racing one evening with some of my friends down a wooden platform, I slipped and fell to one knee. The damage seemed slight except for ruining a brand new pair of trousers that I had bought and of which I was exceedingly proud. There was no bleeding of the wound; instead it looked like a raw, red spot on my knee. The next morning there were no ill effects and I went to school.

On the evening of the second day, I did not feel well and I lay down on the sofa in what Mother always called the "front room."

I dropped off, it seems, into delirium. My parents were alarmed and called for the doctor. There ensued a hectic time in our life, lasting two or three weeks. My mother was the day nurse and a friend of hers the night nurse and they stayed constantly at my bedside. The doctor came several times a day and only occasionally was I conscious—usually when he used his scalpel to explore the wound. On one of his visits, I heard him mention the word "amputation."

I became alarmed, and even furious.

When Ed came home, I made him promise to make sure that under no circumstances would they amputate my leg. "I'd rather be dead than crippled, and not be able to play ball."

The doctors—for by that time Dr. Conklin had called in a consultant from Topeka—were baffled by my attitude. But my parents understood. While they were against such contact sports as football, they did give their sons the right to make decisions of this kind.

Sorrowfully, they agreed to accept my decision. After drastic measures, which included the painting of a belt of carbolic acid around my body, the progress of the disease was stopped. I was ill for so long and so seriously that I remained out of school the rest of the spring and had to repeat that year. As a result I did not graduate until 1909.

Abilene citizens and educators took little interest in school athletics. The authorities left the matter to student initiative. We organized the Abilene High School Athletic Association. In my senior year I was elected president of the association. Afterward, I felt I had helped assure its enduring future by a simple device—writing a constitution.

My optimism was more wishful thinking than realistic. Many times since then I have come to realize that a painstakingly written document may be worth no more than the good will and patient cooperation of those who say they subscribe to it. Too often we lay more stress on words than on the stark necessity of deeds to back them up.

The following summer was busy. Edgar's plans for enrollment at Michigan meant that both of us had to work to gather as much money as was possible to get him started. I changed from one job to another, depending upon the prospects for an extra dime an hour. Ed's choice of university looked good to me and I was ready to join him two years later.

I became, for my last year in Abilene, the second engineer in the Creamery's ice plant. The work week was eighty-four hours, from six A.M. until six P.M. and my agreement called for fifty-two weeks a year. But the salary was impressive—$90 per month. I might easily have found myself embedded in this well-paid drudgery except that a new challenge, unplanned and unforeseen, came to me through a friend, Everett Hazlett.

While I was in high school, he attended a private military school. There he acquired an interest in the service academies, particularly the Naval Academy at Annapolis. He applied for an appointment to that institution and took the entrance examination.

It was not difficult to persuade me that this was a good move—first, because of my long interest in military history, and secondly, because I realized that my own college education would not be achieved without considerable delay while I tried to accumulate money.

We immediately began to study together. He wrote to the Navy Department for copies of past examinations which were, incidentally, almost identical to those for entrance to West Point.

Day after day, during that summer, we examined each other on the questions and graded each other by comparing answers with those given in the naval documents provided.

My congressman had no additional vacancy in either military academy. I

One of Dwight Eisenhower's consistent interests, long before he displayed his proficiency in other areas, was sports—and ranking high on the list of all his favorite sports was the All-American one. Here, circa 1907, a young man who would eventually be at the center of many contests, and his teammates present crossed arms and legs for the yearbook or newspaper. (DDE is front row, fourth from left.)

The Belle Springs Creamery in Abilene, in which father David and later son Dwight worked —the first working his way through life, the second working his way toward college.

High school graduation portrait, 1909.

Young Mr. Eisenhower, on his way to West Point, made a short stopover in Chicago to see a friend. "No boy of my acquaintance had ever been overburdened with an extensive wardrobe," he wrote later in *At Ease*. "I traveled light."

wrote to Senator Joseph Bristow requesting appointment as a cadet or a midshipman and asked various influential men in town to write letters to him in support of my application.

Senator Bristow authorized me to participate in a competitive examination for appointment.

After taking the first examination, I learned that because I would be almost twenty-one by the time the next class entered, I was eligible only for entrance to the Military Academy. (The entrance regulations for Annapolis specified an age from sixteen to twenty.)

In the examinations I had come out as number one for the Annapolis appointment but as number two for West Point. The man who ranked above me in the West Point examination failed to meet the physical requirements. I got the appointment from Senator Bristow in the spring of 1911.

This was a great day in my life. The only person truly disappointed was Mother. She believed definitely in the philosophy of turn the other cheek. But, she said, "It is your choice."

I was directed to report to the United States Military Academy on June 14, 1911.

Mother saw me off, and then went back home to her room. [My brother] Milton told me later that for the first time in his life he heard our Mother cry.

The new class of cadet candidates had been instructed to arrive at the Academy before noon on June 14, 1911. Carrying my suitcase, I left the little railway station at West Point and climbed a long hill to the administration building where the initiation process began. My main impression of that first day was one of bewilderment and calculated chaos.

Orders were not given with any serious attempt at instruction or intended for easy comprehension. They were a series of shouts and barks.

By the end of the day we were all harassed and, at times, resentful. Here we were, the cream of the crop, shouted at all day long by self-important upperclassmen, telling us to run here and run there; pick up our clothes; bring in that bedding; put our shoulders back, keep our eyes up, and to keep running, running, running. Everything was on the double. I suppose that if any time had been provided to sit down and think for a moment, most of the 285 of us would have taken the next train out. But no one was given much time to think—and when I did it was always, "Where else could you get a college education without cost?"

Toward evening, all of us were brought together en masse and sworn in as cadets of the United States Military Academy. Whatever had gone before, it was a supreme moment.

The United States of America would now and henceforth mean something different than it ever had before. From here on it would be the nation I would be serving, not myself. Suddenly the flag itself meant something. Across a half a century, I can look back and see a raw-boned, gawky, Kansas boy from the farm country, earnestly repeating the words that would make him a cadet.

Because the summer was a hot one—West Point, New York, could export heat without loss—the experience was strenuous and for some unendurable. It was hardest on those who were not used to exercise or who had been overindulged. My working experience and age came to my rescue.

At times, in the semiprivacy of my room, I could laugh a little at myself and at the system. But whenever an upperclassman saw the sign of a smile, the shouting and nagging started again.

In the first days, when I knew as little as possible about the Army, General Orders had been read and among other instructions, we were required to salute all officers. Ten days later, I was double-timing down the street when I heard a band coming. But before it turned the corner, I encountered the most decorated fellow I had ever seen. I hesitated just a second, then snapped to attention and presented arms but he did not return the salute. I did it again and a third time before realizing that he was a drum major.

The normal life of the cadet has been described many times by numerous and better writers. The most unpleasant phase is the average plebe's assumed awkwardness, clumsiness, and unequaled stupidity.

A classmate and I were not above bedeviling overly serious upperclassmen in their attempts to make us over.

One day, having been found guilty—by a corporal—of a minor infraction of regulations, we were ordered to report to his room in "full dress coats."

At the appointed time, each of us donned full dress coats and with no other stitch of clothing, marched into the corporal's room. We saluted and said solemnly, "Sir, Cadets Eisenhower and Atkins report as ordered."

As usual, the upperclassman had the last word. Dismissing us, he gave us a new order. "Immediately after taps you will report back to my room in complete uniform including rifles and crossbelts and if you miss a single item I'll have you down here every night for a week."

After taps we went back, dressed as instructed, to be braced up against the wall until we left our bodily outlines on it in perspiration. But afterward, we and the other plebes had a lot of laughs—quiet ones—out of the corporal's temporary discomfiture.

One of my reasons for going to West Point was with the hope that I could continue an athletic career. It would be difficult to overemphasize the importance that I attached to participation in sports.

At that time my dimensions, as I recall, were 5′ 11″ in height and 152 pounds in weight. I was muscular and strong but very spare. It was dismaying, then, to find that I was too light in comparison to men who were then on the football team to be taken seriously.

Although I had put on almost twenty pounds by the next season, I was still light for line plunging and line backing. But my enthusiasm made up somewhat for my lack of tonnage. In any event, I always played as hard as I knew how, trying to instill the fear of Eisenhower into every opponent.

Throughout the season, I was used consistently as a varsity player, entitling me to a football letter; and I had every reason to think that I had another two seasons ahead of me with the hope, as weight was added and experience gained, I might make a reputation. But in the Tufts game—only a week or so before the Navy contest, the climax of the entire season—I suffered what I thought was a minor injury. I was plunging, having broken through the line, and a man got his hands on my foot. I twisted and threw my weight against it as I turned. Although my knee swelled rapidly, the inflammation was accompanied by little pain. I was hospitalized for two or three days waiting for the swelling to disappear. Then, discharged, with no warning from the medical men that the joint was permanently weakened and with no instructions to be cautious in using it for at least a while, my only worry was that coaches would keep me benched the next week, depriving me of any chance for glory against Navy. As it turned out, they had no other option.

A few days after release from the hospital, I reported to the riding hall. While taking part in "monkey drill," I leaped off my horse to vault over him as he jumped a low hurdle. The landing shock to my injured knee was more than it could take. I ended on the ground with my leg twisted behind me.

The doctors spent four days straightening my leg, a process so painful that I scarcely slept during the ordeal. I learned to my dismay that rugged sports were denied to me from then on.

Homer and his legendary birthplaces cannot hold a candle to the number of Tufts men who say they caused the original injury.

My activities were now limited to simple gymnastics, walking, and calisthenics. I have often wondered why, at that moment, I did not give increased attention to studies. Instead, as the academic record attests, I gave less, I was almost despondent and several times had to be prevented from resigning by the persuasive efforts of classmates. Life seemed to have little meaning; a need to excel was almost gone.

As my disciplinary record shows, I learned to smoke. Even in this, which was sanctioned to an extent, I managed to be rebellious. Regulations allowed cadets to smoke in their rooms, during study periods, if they used pipes or cigars. Cigarette smoking, if discovered, brought serious penalties. So I started smoking cigarettes.

After I became an upperclassman, I went to cadet dances only now and then, preferring to devote my time to poker. On one of the rare occasions when I did go to a dance, I met a girl, a daughter of one of the professors. We started dancing in a way that the authorities of the time felt was not in accord with the sedate two-step, polka, and waltz that made up the repertoire of cadet dance music. This girl and I liked to whirl; just whirling around the room as rapidly as we could. I suppose the exercise probably showed a little more of the girl's ankles, possibly reaching even to her knees, than the sharp-eye authorities thought was seemly. I was warned not to dance that way any more.

A few months later, it happened that I stopped in at a dance, possibly because it was one of the affairs known as a "Feed Hop" where food was served late in the evening. Often the poker players would take a recess from our Saturday night game, rush over to get sandwiches and a cup of coffee and go back to the game.

I met the same girl again and forgot entirely the warning issued earlier. The exuberant sensation of swinging around the room was too much for me to ignore and so, in due course, I was hailed before the Commandant. He informed me that I not only danced improperly, but had done so after a warning. For this offense I was demoted from the grade of sergeant to that of private.

I was, in matters of discipline, far from a good cadet. While each demerit had an effect on class standing, this to me was a small moment. I enjoyed life at the Academy, had a good time with my pals, and was far from disturbed by an additional demerit or two.

After the tiff with the authorities which took my non-commissioned rank, I regained my chevrons, becoming one of the color sergeants for the Corps. But I never fully reformed.

As I recall, there were about 162 men who finally graduated in my class, and in this list I stood 125th in discipline.

Certain members of the Army football squad, 1913. Cadet Eisenhower was trying a comeback, after an injury. He had won his letter the previous season.

It is interesting to track the careers of these men, as given by the West Point sports historian. (Left to right) Walter W. Wynne, '14, left tackle, was honorably discharged in 1922, and died in an auto accident in Alabama, May 1925. Alexander M. Weyand, '16, right tackle, retired disabled, as a Colonel, in 1946. Alfred E. Larabee, '14, tackle, retired as a Colonel in 1947, died in Oregon in 1959. Charles C. Benedict (to right of DDE), '15, full-back, died at Langley Field, Va., in an air crash, May 1925. Benjamin F. Hoge, '14, captain and left halfback, retired as Colonel in 1951.

The boy between Benedict and Hoge, Richards Vidmer, the son of the post adjutant, was a sort of team mascot. He took a few pointers on to his job when he later became sports editor of the New York *Herald Tribune*.

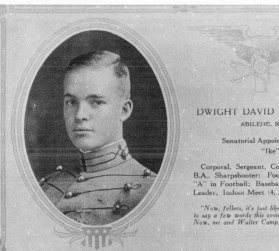

### DWIGHT DAVID EISENHOWER
ABILENE, KANSAS

Senatorial Appointee, Kansas
"Ike"

Corporal, Sergeant, Color Sergeant; A.B.,
B.A., Sharpshooter; Football Squad (3, 2),
"A" in Football; Baseball Squad (4); Cheer
Leader; Indoor Meet (4, 3).

*"Now, fellers, it's just like this. I've been asked
to say a few words this evening about this business.
Now, me and Walter Camp, we think—"*
—*Himself*

THIS is Señor Dwight David Eisenhower, gentlemen, the terrible Swedish-Jew, as big as life and twice as natural. He claims to have the best authority for the statement that he is the handsomest man in the Corps and is ready to back up his claim at any time. At any rate you'll have to give it to him that he's well-developed abdominally—and more graceful in pushing it around than Charles Calvert Benedict. In common with most fat men, he is an enthusiastic and sonorous devotee of the King of Indoor Sports, and roars homage at the shrine of Morpheus on every possible occasion.

However, the memory of man runneth back to the time when the little Dwight was but a slender lad of some 'steen years, full of joy and energy and craving for life and movement and change. 'Twas then that the romantic appeal of West Point's glamour grabbed him by the scruff of neck and dragged him to his doom. Three weeks of Beast gave him his fill of life and movement and as all the change was locked up at the Cadet Store out of reach, poor Dwight merely consents to exist until graduation shall set him free.

At one time he threatened to get interested in life and won his "A" by being the most promising back in Eastern football—but the Tufts game broke his knee and the promise. Now Ike must content himself with tea, tiddledywinks and talk, at all of which he excels. Said prodigy will now lead us in a long, loud yell for— Dare Devil Dwight, the Dauntless Don.

"Thirty years afterward," wrote memoirist Eisenhower, "I found myself in the midst of war. I had occasion to be on the lookout for natural leaders. Athletes take a certain amount of kidding, especially from those who think it is always brawn versus brains. But I noted...how well ex-footballers seemed to have leadership qualifications and it wasn't sentiment that made it seem so..." Here, wearers of the Army's major A include: (back row, left) James A. Van Fleet, (back row, fourth from left) Omar N. Bradley, and (second row, third from left) Dwight D. Eisenhower.

The entry in 1915 *Howitzer*, West Point yearbook.

The knee that kept me from baseball and football eventually came close to changing my life more drastically. As the time neared for graduation, I was called to the office of Colonel Shaw, who was head of the Medical Department. He said that he might find it necessary to recommend that while I be graduated and receive a diploma, I not be commissioned in the Army. The authorities were very careful not to commission anyone who had a serious physical difficulty, one that might cause his early retirement and make him a drain on the government throughout his life because of disability pension.

When Colonel Shaw had finished, I said that this was all right with me. I remarked that I had always had a curious ambition to go to the Argentine (Argentina sounded to me a little like the Old West), and I might go there and see the place, maybe even live there for two or three years.

I may have been the first in his experience who was not seriously upset by the possible termination of all military ambitions. He said he would think the matter over.

Within a few days he sent for me again. "I think, Mr. Eisenhower," he said, "that if you'd apply for service in the Coast Artillery, I would be justified in recommending your commission."

To which I replied, "Colonel, I do not want a commission in the Coast Artillery." A Coast Artillery Corps career—to those outside it—provided a numbing series of routine chores and a minimum of excitement. Colonel Shaw seemed disturbed at my abrupt refusal of his suggestion, perhaps because, as it turned out, he had served with the Coast Artillery himself.

Now I began to seriously consider a trip to South America. I wrote for travel literature and costs.

Once more I was called back by Colonel Shaw. He said he had been going over my entire record and found that my most serious injury had been aggravated by a riding accident. I confirmed this. He said, "Mr. Eisenhower, if you will not submit any requests for mounted service on your preference card, I will recommend to the Academic Board that you be commissioned."

So I told Colonel Shaw that my ambition was to go to the infantry. To which he said, "All right, I'll recommend you for a commission, but with the stipulation that you will ask for no other service in the Army."

When the time came for me to submit my preference card I put down *Infantry,* first, *Infantry* second, and *Infantry* third.

I should add that my West Point record was not all bad. Perhaps I have overstressed my slight differences with the disciplinary code and the academic life. If my nonchalance was a bit offensive, they probably also recognized it as being defensive as well. After my injury I had been a coach and a cheerleader I gave talks to the Corps before games. One report on my early performance even said—it was shown to me years later—that I was "born to command." The man who wrote that was either a reckless prophet or he had relaxed his standards.

After receiving the commission, I finally reached my regiment, with headquarters in San Antonio, Texas.

One Sunday afternoon in October, as Officer of the Day, I walked out of the bachelor officers quarters to make an inspection of guard posts. On the walk across the street was a group of people, including a lady popular with all the second lieutenants of the post. "Ike," she called, "won't you come over here?"

"I have to start an inspection trip," I retorted.

She then turned to one young girl, as I discovered later, and said, "Humph! The woman hater of the post."

Naturally, this caught the attention of the young girl, who said something to Mrs. Harris that caused her to call once more. "We didn't ask you to come over to *stay*. Just come over here and meet these friends of mine."

To this, of course, I hadn't any objection and walked stiffly across the street to say a polite greeting.

The one who attracted my eye instantly was a vivacious and attractive girl, smaller than average, saucy in the look about her face and in her whole attitude. If she had been intrigued by my reputation as a woman hater, I was intrigued by her appearance.

I said that I had to make the rounds of all the guard posts and asked whether she would like to go along. To my astonishment, she turned to her mother, said a few words, and went off with me. That was the entrance into my life of Mamie Geneva Doud.

While it soon became almost routine for me to call on her, I had more time than money to spend on courtship. Except when I was out with Mamie, I lived the life of a hermit. During the late fall, however, I had one very fortunate evening in which there was more income than outgo.

The game had been underway in the Infantry Club for an hour or so when I walked in.

They greeted me joyfully, saying, "Come on, get in here. We're getting everyone's money because we want to give a big party to celebrate."

"I'm sorry," I said. "You fellows don't want me; I've got two silver dollars in my pocket and that's all."

They jeered, good-naturedly, and said, "Every little bit helps."

By dinnertime, I had run my two dollars up to a hundred.

Second lieutenants were a clannish group. Except when we had the money for an evening on the town, we often roamed the post in a rather aimless search for excitement. There were one or two, somewhat more serious than most of us, who spent part of their time going to concerts and museums, and, to our dismay, to lectures. Mostly, we wandered.

A small group of us happened to be standing one evening near the post flagpole, a tall, stately affair with strong supporting cables to hold it straight against the winds of the region. These cables reached from the ground to a point fifty or sixty feet up the pole.

I mentioned that I had once or twice climbed, overhand, similar though somewhat smaller cables just for the fun of it and said that I could easily climb one of these. One of my companions spoke up skeptically. I repeated my assertion that I could climb one of them, using hands only. The skeptic, a man I didn't know well, said that it was tommyrot to talk about overhanding my way to the top.

Although I was the junior second lieutenant of the regiment, I ignored his seniority, grew angry, and retorted, "What would you like to bet?" He had a little bit more money than most of us and he produced five dollars. It happened that I had one lone five-dollar bill in my wallet, so I put it into the hands of one of the other lieutenants, as stake holder.

Next we agreed on the conditions of the contest. I was to climb the slanting cable to the top but without touching it with my feet or legs. A time limit was set. This was satisfactory and I stripped off my regulation blouse and started up. I had no difficulty—at West Point one of my favorite exercises had been rope climbing—and was chuckling cockily about a windfall that would pay for an evening out with my girl when from somewhere below I heard a bellow.

"Who is that up on that cable?"

With a shock, I realized who was talking—our commanding officer, Colonel Waltz.

"Who are you up there?" he demanded.

"Mr. Eisenhower, sir."

"Come down here," he said.

This was disaster. I tried to save my bet, remembering that Colonel Waltz was said to gamble on any sporting event.

"Sir," I called down, "Mr. Adler and I have a bet. He put down five dollars that I cannot overhand my way to the top of this cable. I am almost there—so could I please go on up and touch the pole and then come back down right away?"

*"Do as I say and do it right now. Get down here!"*

Sheepishly, I let myself down along the cable and as quickly as my feet touched the ground came to a stiff salute. First he ordered me to don my jacket, and then he offered a few suggestions for improvement. I was, it seems, foolhardy, undignified, untrustworthy, undependable, and ignorant. He wanted no more of this on his post. Once he had finished taking me over the coals, he stalked off, saying, "There'll be no more of that on the part of anyone."

No sooner was Colonel Waltz out of earshot when Adler spoke up to claim he had won the five dollars.

"Won it?"

"Yes," he said, and he asked the stake holder, Wade Haislip, to turn the money over. I objected flatly and vigorously. The bet was, at the least, a draw because it had been nullified by the intervention of the CO. None of us could have anticipated such an outcome and therefore the bet was null and void. Moreover, I said, everyone could see that I was easily making the ascent and morally I had actually won.

The argument got hot and heavy, growing in intensity, until I suggested that we finish the discussion with fists. One of the others said we could go down behind the barracks where no one would bother us. Adler refused, saying that we'd all get into real trouble. At the same time the majority declared the bet to be a draw and the money returned to each side. Adler kept grousing; he still believed I owed him the five dollars. But now I had my temper under control.

Actually, I was happy that the matter had not gone too far. My knee was still troubling me and I was fearful that Adler, a big, strong fellow, could have helped me fix it so that I would have been nursing a knee again for a week or more.

As the winter wore on, Mamie and I decided to become engaged. I gave her my class ring on Valentine's Day, 1916. She was nineteen. We tentatively agreed to plan on the wedding for the following November, when Mamie would be twenty.

Now, with a more serious attitude toward life, I took a broader look at my future in the military. Possibly I had been prone to lead a carefree if debt-ridden life. Now I would set my sights on becoming the finest Army officer I could, regardless of the branch in which I might serve.

Soon, my fiancée went back with her family to Denver. As a symbol of my new seriousness and sacrifice, I stopped smoking ready-made cigarettes, which were then about $1.00 a carton, and went back to rolling my own.

Throughout the winter of 1915–16 there had been a rising clamor for the United States to act more vigorously against German submarine warfare, in which many of our ships had been sunk.

Many people became impatient with President Wilson. Mamie's concern about my increasingly excellent chances of being plunged into battle developed steadily. Even the reinforcing of the Army by the Congress, which brought the prospect of a relatively rapid promotion for me, did nothing to calm her fear.

I realized that it would make good sense for us to advance our wedding date by a few months.

This began to appear in our correspondence as a definite possibility. A close friend encouraged me to send Mamie a telegram saying that I was ready to go ahead.

I said that I would do my best to get a leave. I asked for twenty days.

To my surprise, I was ordered to report to Department Headquarters to see the general.

I went to the Chief of Staff's office. He didn't say much, but he remarked that the general was busy. While I waited, I thought back to my one other meeting with the general.

One day in the Officers Club when several second lieutenants were having a beer, he looked us over and said, "Is Mr. Eisenhower in the room?"

I stood up and said, "Sir?" I couldn't imagine what he had on his mind. He called me to the bar and said, "Have a drink."

I couldn't say that I was already having one so I took another. "Mr. Peacock tells me that he would like you to coach his team at the Peacock Military Academy."

"Yes, sir."

'It would please me and it would be good for the Army if you would accept this offer."

"Yes, sir," I said.

He indicated that the conversation was over. I saluted and went back to my friends.

Now the Chief of Staff said I could see the general (again).

"I understand you want to get married," the general said immediately.

I confirmed that impression.

Then he looked up at me for the first time. "Oh yes, Mr. Eisenhower. I remember you very well." Then he wanted to know what the rush was about the marriage. I had to tell him a little bit about the circumstances and the change of plan. He smiled and said, "All right, you may have ten days," adding, "I am not sure that this is exactly what the War Department has in mind but I'll take the responsibility."

The train trip from San Antonio to Denver took about fifty-six hours. We were married by a Presbyterian minister from Britain. Our honeymoon was a weekend at a nearby mountain resort, Eldorado Springs.

The post grapevine had given our wedding complete coverage. We reached San Antonio to be greeted by young friends, laden with all sorts of packages.

Mamie, young, full of life and attractive, was the pet of the post. She was showered with attention from officers and ladies of all ages, and thoroughly enjoyed the experience.

I had been advanced one grade in rank on our wedding day (and was now a) first lieutenant.

In mid-winter, the Germans announced that they were going to resume unrestricted submarine warfare. President Wilson warned, in a stern speech, that if they did so, they would bring the United States into the fighting. Sometime later the sinkings began again, and by early April President Wilson went before the Congress and asked for a declaration of war.

The cadre to which I was assigned had only five or six officers including the Colonel, and so all of us had to fill several posts until more officers could be obtained. My job was to be regimental supply officer. And my orders were enough to dismay a young man who had less than two years of commissioned service.

Weeks later I assembled the supply officers and sergeants of the regiment— for a lecture on supply in the field. Needless to say, I had been poring over the textbooks. It was a cloudy day and the officers and enlisted men to whom I was speaking gathered around just outside my tent, under a large tree. A drizzling rain started but we put on raincoats and kept on. While I was talking, the weather became more threatening. Then there was a terrific bolt of lightning, and all that I was conscious of was a sort of ball of fire in front of my eyes.

The next thing I knew I was lying on my back in the mud and an enlisted

Mamie Doud and Dwight D. Eisenhower, San Antonio, Texas, 1916. On the steps of St. Louis College.

Doud Dwight Eisenhower ("Icky") 1918. "Barracks or not, Mamie, Icky, and I had settled down to a fuller family life than we'd ever known." Then…"With his death, a pall fell over the camp. When we started the long trip to Denver, the entire command turned out in respect to Icky. We were completely crushed."

Young mother and young son. Mrs. Dwight David Eisenhower and "Icky" on a sunlit day before tragedy struck.

man was pushing down on my ribs, apparently trying to bring me back from unconsciousness. I did not feel any particular harm except when they picked me up and I shook myself, I had a splitting headache. The Regimental Adjutant had a similar experience.

Colonel Baker often remarked that he was the only regimental commander in the Army whose entire staff had been struck by lightning and lived to tell about it.

Anyhow, the regiment was in good shape. We were sure that we were one of the best outfits in the whole Army and were confident that we were destined for overseas duty. Instead, I got a special order assigning me to the training camp at Fort Oglethorpe, Georgia, to be an instructor of candidates for commission. This was distressing. I wanted to stay with a regiment that would see action soon.

My parting with Mamie was particularly difficult. She couldn't go along because I was going to field duty. Also, she was expecting our first child.

We went to the field and lived in trenches, constructed dugouts, and prepared for warfare on the Western Front. I came out of those trenches on the 26th of September and found a telegram dated the 24th, saying that my son had been born. His name was Doud Dwight.

I tried to recognize that in preparing young officers to lead troops, we were making a constructive contribution. This kind of thinking was small comfort, at times, for a man who had finally decided to make the Army his career. My elation, then, can well be imagined when I received orders in late winter to report to Camp Meade, Maryland, to join the 65th Engineers. This, I was told, was the parent group which was organizing Tank Corps troops for overseas duty.

As soldiers promised a new weapon always will, we convinced ourselves that we would have it in our power to clinch victory. We were sure that within weeks, we'd be in France to dissolve the stagnation of trench warfare with the latest in ultimate weapons.

Within days I was back at Meade. The plan had been changed. My chief said he was impressed by my "organizational ability," I was directed to take the remnants of the 301st, who would not be going overseas, and proceed to an old, abandoned campsite in Gettysburg, Pennsylvania, of all places.

The Tank Corps was new. There were no precedents except in basic training and I was the only regular officer in the command. Now I really began to learn about responsibility.

Although we were part of the Tank Corps, we knew about tanks only from hearsay and newspapers. With the cheerful cynicism of soldiers, we had not expected to see one until we reached Europe. Even at that, we couldn't be sure

whether we would be operating them or facing them. However, someone in the
war zone apparently thought that there might be virtue in letting the Tank
Corps recruits and trainees get a preliminary look at the machine that one day
we were to operate. Three small tanks were sent to us.

During this period, I had the privilege of having my family with me. While
I could not be at home at night, whenever possible I would go there in the evening. My duties required getting up early in the morning but it was fun to have
the chance to see my son growing up and spend the evenings with my wife.

Colonel Welborn called me in to say that if I would agree to give up my
plans for overseas service, he was prepared to recommend me for full colonel.
I declined. "I'm ready to take a reduction in rank to the average of my class—
to major that is—if the lieutenant colonelcy which I have now stands in the way
of my going overseas," I said.

Fate, with its usual bad manners, intervened; I had made no provision for
imminent German defeat.


I had missed the boat in the war we had been told would end all wars. A
soldier's place was where the fighting went on. I hadn't yet fully learned the
basic lesson of the military—that the proper place for a soldier is where he is
ordered by his superiors.

As for my professional career, the prospects were none too bright. I was
older than my classmates, was still bothered on occasion by a bad knee, and
saw myself in the years ahead putting on weight in a meaningless chair-bound
assignment, shuffling papers and filling out forms, hoping to make colonel
before I was retired. If not depressed, I was mad, disappointed, and resented
the fact that life had passed me by.

At times I was tempted, at least faintly, to try my luck as a civilian again.
An Indiana businessman who had been a junior officer at Camp Colt offered
me a position at considerably more pay than a lieutenant colonel and certainly
more than a captain, the grade I would hold as soon as the inevitable demo-
tions came.

But I had little time for reflection. Nothing at West Point or in the forty
months since graduation had prepared me for helping to collapse an Army
from millions to a peacetime corps. The new problem kept me even busier than
we had been.


Major Sereno Brett and I heard that a truck convoy was to cross the country
from coast to coast. To those who have known only concrete and macadam

highways of gentle grades and engineered curves, such a trip seems humdrum. In those days, we were not at all sure it could be accomplished. Nothing of the sort had ever been attempted.

I wanted to go along partly for a lark and partly to learn.

The convoy was then formally directed to proceed overland to San Francisco, via the Lincoln Highway. Delays, sadly, were to be the order of the day.

In an early span of three days, we spent twenty-nine hours on the road and moved one hundred sixty-five miles. This was an average hourly speed of about five and two-thirds miles. Before we were through, however, there were times when the pace of our first three days would seem headlong.

Maintenance crews were constantly on the job to keep the vehicles running. They did good work, as I recall. We lost only two vehicles by accidents and one was beyond their help—it rolled down a mountain.

We reached San Francisco at long last, although most of the time we hardly exceeded a good bicyclist's speed.

In Sacramento, the governor had compared us to the "Immortal Forty-niners." He reminded everyone of the hardship, privation, discouragement, and even death to reach this new land....Their blood is the blood of the western country," he said, "strong—virile—self-reliant...so, in this journey of yours across the plains..." etc.

When I returned to Camp Meade in the autumn, many changes had taken place. Senior officers of the Tank Corps who had seen active operations in France were now back. Among these men the one who interested me most, and whom I learned to like best, was a fellow named Patton. He had two passions, the military service and polo.

*(The two young officers worked closely. Their friendship was a mutual inspiration in their attempts to develop the tank into a more useful piece of war machinery. One idea was to improve the mobility of the light tank by accompanying it with a more powerful vehicle which could, by means of a steel cable, pull the light tank out of difficult situations, such as ravines and steep hills. They decided to experiment, and...)*

...we looked around just in time to see one of the cables part. The front half whirled around like a striking black snake and the flying end, at machine gun bullet speed, snapped past our faces, cutting off brush and saplings as if they had been shaved with a sharp razor.

That evening after dinner, we talked about the incident and George said: "Ike, were you as scared as I was?"

"I was afraid to bring the subject up," I said. We were certainly not more than five or six inches from sudden death.

*(In another experiment they walked in front of their own overheated machine gun and were almost shot down.)*

After the breaking cable and the self-firing gun, we decided that we had about used up our luck. As it turned out, we were to need luck but of another kind entirely—and George Patton, who was to become the finest leader in military pursuit that our Army has known, had little enough.

One of the incalculable benefits I got from my friendship with George Patton was a social invitation to meet a man who was to have a tremendous influence on my life, Brigadier General Fox Conner.

A few months later, General Conner sent word to me that he was going to Panama to command an infantry brigade. Would I like to go along with him as Executive Officer? This was a wonderful chance. General Conner's reputation was splendid; he was one of the Army "brains."

(The young officer's ambition to join Conner was then thwarted—the War Department, as usual, would not go along with the change. But as he noted in 1968, his ambition was "merely delayed, not defeated. The opportunity was renewed later.")

Barracks or not, Mamie, our son Icky and I had settled down to a fuller family life than we'd ever known. Icky, naturally, was in his element, and he thoroughly enjoyed his role as the center of attention. The deafening noise of the tanks enthralled him. And a parade with martial music set him aglow. In his company, I'm sure I strutted a bit and Mamie was thoroughly happy that, once again, her two men were with her.

Possibly we could afford a maid who would help Mamie in our makeshift house that required constant attention. We hired a girl. A chain of circumstances was started, bringing us to a tragedy from which we never recovered.

We learned later that just before we met her, the girl had suffered an attack of scarlet fever. Our young son contracted it from her. We did everything possible to save him. The camp doctor brought in specialists. Hour after hour, Mamie and I could only hope and pray. In those days, before modern medicine eliminated scarlet fever as a childhood scourge, hope and prayer were the only possibilities for parents. At the turn of the year, we lost our firstborn son.

I do not know how others have felt when facing the same situation but I have never known such a blow. During the days of his illness, the doctor had not allowed me into his room. But there was a porch on which I was allowed to sit and I could look into the room and wave to him. Occasionally, they would let me come to the door just to speak to Icky. I haunted the halls of the hospital but within the week he was gone. I didn't know what to do.

My own command had gotten together not long after Icky's arrival and bought him a tank uniform, including overcoat, overseas cap, and all the rest. They would put him in a tank and he was just one of the boys. When we started the long trip to Denver, to bury him, with the others in Mamie's family, the entire command turned out.

Today when I think of it, even as I now write of it, the keenness of my loss comes back to me as fresh and as terrible as it was in that long dark day soon after Christmas, 1920.

Some time after my application for transfer to the Canal Zone had been disapproved, orders came out of the blue for me to proceed to that station. The red tape was torn to pieces, orders were issued, and I was to arrive at the new station by January of 1922.

Our own little car, a Model T Ford, had been sent up to New York for shipment on the transport to Panama.

It was our first trip out of the country. Panama was not the best introduction to life beyond our borders. The houses at our new station were infested with bats and Mamie hated bats with a passion. Frequent thunder showers penetrated roofs and walls and windows and made living there too damp for comfort—except for those black, winged unwelcome visitors who seemed to thrive in the turkish bath our house became after every storm.

It wasn't until I visited Panama in 1946 (or possibly it was 1955), when I flew back and forth across the area, that I saw to my horror that the entire post, where we had once been living, had slid into the Canal and had been laboriously dredged out of the main channel.

I found myself invited to General Conner's quarters in the evening and I saw that he had an extraordinary library, especially on military affairs. We talked for a time and he went through the library and picked out two or three historical novels. "You might be interested in these," he said quietly.

They were stirring stories and I liked them. When I returned the books, the General asked me what I thought. As we talked about them, he said, "Wouldn't you like to know something of what the  armies were actually doing during the period of the novels you've just read?"

Well, that seemed logical enough and I expressed an interest. He took down a few books on the military history of those periods.

The upshot was that I found myself becoming fascinated with the subject. But fascination wasn't enough. After I read the first of these books, General Conner questioned me closely about the decisions made—why they were made and under what conditions. "What do you think would have been the outcome if this decision had been just the opposite?" "What were the alternatives?"

The best chance for such conversations was when we were out on reconnaissance. Usually, we were on horse eight hours a day, most of it at a walk. We would make camp before dark. Close to the equator, the sun sets early and during the long hours before bedtime, between 6:30 and 10:00, we sat around a small campfire and talked about the Civil War or Napoleon's operations.

Our talks went further afield. General Conner was a natural leader and something of a philosopher, both as a student and as a storehouse of axiomatic advice. He was the man who first remarked to me, "Always take your job seriously, never yourself." He was the man who taught me that splendid line from the French, "All generalities are false, including this one." The range and curiosity of his mind was not limited to military affairs.

Excited by these talks and thoughts, I read in the works of authors strange to me: Plato, and Tacitus of the Roman nation, and in historical and philosophical writers among the moderns, including Nietzsche.

It is clear now that life with General Conner was a sort of graduate school in military subjects and in the humanities. I can never adequately express my gratitude to this one gentleman, for it took years before I fully realized the value of what he had led me through. And then General Conner was gone. But in a lifetime of association with great and good men, he is the one more or less invisible figure to whom I owe an incalculable debt.

The most important event during my Camp Gaillard assignment was the news that we were to have another child. Mamie took a steamer, in the early summer, to New Orleans, then she went to Denver. I reached there in time and on August 3 we had another baby boy, one who in appearance so resembled the one we had lost that, for my part, I was thereafter practically unable to see any difference. John did much to fill the gap that we felt so poignantly and so deeply every day of our lives since the death of our first son.

Among other suggestions General Conner made for my professional readiness, he told me that I should try one day for an assignment under Colonel George Marshall. He often said, "In the new war we will have to fight beside allies and George Marshall knows more about the techniques of arranging allied commands than any man I know. He is nothing short of a genius."

*(After Panama DDE was called back to Camp Meade to fill again a position*

*that had haunted him since his leg injury at West Point:* Football Coach. *Then it was back to the Tank Corps.)*

It was high time I was getting to one of the established Army schools, I thought. A strange telegram arrived. It was from Fox Conner, serving as Deputy Chief of Staff to General Hines. The telegram was cryptic in the extreme.

NO MATTER WHAT ORDERS YOU RECEIVE FROM THE WAR DEPARTMENT, MAKE NO PROTEST ACCEPT THEM WITHOUT QUESTION SIGNED CONNER.

For several days I was in a quandary until orders arrived. They detailed me to recruiting duty in Colorado!

To be assigned to the recruiting service, in those days, was felt by most of us to be a rebuke a little less devastating than a reprimand.

*(But it developed that the transfer to recruiting duty was a ruse, a device to get Major Eisenhower out from under the direct command of the Chief of Infantry. Within a short time he received a new order. He had been selected to go to Command and General Staff School at Fort Leavenworth.)*

I was ready to fly—and needed no airplane!

This may seem proof of "It's not *what* you know, it's *who* you know." But a one-minute lecture to any young person who may read these words: Always try to associate yourself with and learn as much as you can from those who know more than you do, who do better than you, who see more clearly than you. Don't be afraid to reach upward.

Anyhow, the order assigned me to a school before I'd had the usual preparatory instruction. And an aide in the office of the Chief of Infantry gave me his felicitations: "You will probably fail."

*(Student Eisenhower decided to study carefully at Leavenworth, working with another officer named Leonard Gerow. In* At Ease *the author simply says that he and Gerow graduated with good marks, separated from each other by two-tenths of one per cent. What he does not add is that he was at the top of his class.)*

Sometime in late May, orders arrived from the Chief of Infantry—I had been retransferred—to go to Fort Benning (in Georgia) to take command of a battalion.

After a few months in that post it developed that General John J. Pershing, the famed "Black Jack" and leader of our AEF in World War I, had designs on me. The new agency he headed, the Battle Monuments Commission, was not only building and beautifying the cemeteries where our war dead were gathered abroad but they were also preparing a battlefield guide. The guidebook writing was assigned to me.

I had been in the job hardly long enough to do any damage when word was sent that I had been selected as a student for the War College. The College was in Washington. To graduate from the War College had long been the ambition of almost every officer and I was anxious to take the assignment.

I was a student at the College until the following June. In the meantime grad uating students had become eligible for assignment to the War Department General Staff and once again a choice was offered me: Did I want the General Staff or to go back to Battle Monuments? When I learned that to complete the work of revising the guidebook written earlier that I would have to go to France to study the battlefields, at first hand, my choice was easy. In June 1928 I saw Paris for the first time. It was a preliminary look at Europe, at countries I would see again.

When I returned from France in 1929, I was available for assignment. It was my hope to go back to troop duty. But there was a new and different role ahead. The Assistant Secretary of War's office beckoned. One of the senior man's principal duties was to study ways of mobilizing American industry in the event of another war. This study became my task.

Finally, General Douglas MacArthur succeeded General Charles Summerall, late in 1930 as Chief of Staff. He was receptive to the ideas we had been advocating.

Assured the friendly cooperation of the Chief of Staff—which of course meant all those serving under him—our work went ahead faster.

General MacArthur, it developed, had need for a personal military assistant other than his Aides, a man who could draft statements, reports, and letters for his signature. He asked me to take the job. I moved over to General MacArthur's office about the 1st of January, 1933, and established a connection with him that was not to end until December 1939.

Douglas MacArthur was a forceful—some thought an overpowering—indi vidual, blessed with a fast and facile mind, interested in both the military and political side of our government.

My office was next to his; only a slatted door separated us. At the time he was fifty-three. He was decisive, personable, and he had one habit that never ceased to startle me. In reminiscing or in telling stories of the current scene, he talked of himself in the third person. "So MacArthur went over to the Senator, and said, 'Senator...'"

In one respect, he was a rewarding man to work for. When he gave an assign-

1925. The family assembles once more in Abilene. (Left to right): Roy, Arthur, Earl, Edgar, father David, Milton, mother Ida and, on the steps, DDE.

A rare and remarkably candid photograph: Dwight D. Eisenhower, on duty and becoming familiar with the corridors of power and decision. Time: early 1930s. Place: Washington, D.C., State-War-Navy building.

At home (temporarily) in Washington: Mamie and Dwight Eisenhower and son, John Sheldon Doud Eisenhower.

General Douglas MacArthur, with aides and attendants, during ceremonies welcoming him to the Philippine Islands. In background, his Chief of Staff, Colonel Eisenhower.

"General MacArthur, it developed, had need for a personal military assistant other than his aides, a man who could draft statements, reports, and letters for his signature."

"Douglas MacArthur was a forceful—some thought an overpowering—individual, blessed with a fast and facile mind... Working with him brought an additional dimension to my experience. My duties were beginning to verge on the political..."

"Because I was learning to fly at the age of forty-six, my reflexes were slower than those of the younger man. Training me must have been a trial of patience...

"The seat of the pants was a surer guide to navigation than the few instruments we had... the pilot depended on his eyes, scanning terrain for landmarks, and on his ears to tell him that all was well under the cowling." By the end of his tour, the author had logged 350 hours.

The infant Filipino air force graduates its air cadets, 1937. To the left of the military advisor in white is General Basilio Valdez; to his right, Lieutenant Anderson, who gave the colonel in civies flying lessons.

One of Mamie Eisenhower's proudest possessions is this photograph showing her pinning a medal on her husband, the new Supreme Commander of the Allied Invasion Forces, when he was a mere Colonel. President Quezon looks on.

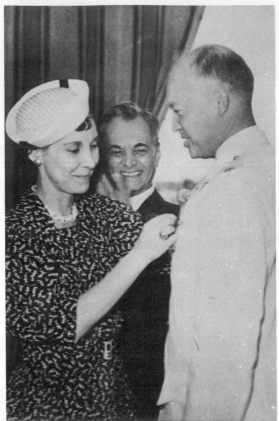

Head shaven, Colonel Eisenhower is at work in the Philippine Islands, summoned frequently for advice to President Quezon's office. "Our conversations became broader and deeper...no longer confined to defense. Taxes, education, honesty in government, and other subjects entered the discussions."

Leaving for San Francisco and World War II, the Eisenhowers faced their future. Son John had been going to school in the mountains in Baguio. Now, "ahead of John lay four years at West Point; for Mamie, premonitions about the future, and long and lonely months when both her son and her husband would be far off.

"I hoped that a field comamnd awaited me..."

ment, he never asked any question; he never cared what kind of hours were kept; his only requirement was that the work be done.

Ordinarily, General MacArthur would have been relieved as Chief of Staff in the fall of 1934. However, reorganization in the War Department was going on and it is possible that the President had not yet chosen the man he wanted to appoint as the next Chief.

Toward the end of this period, a bill had been passed in the Congress bestowing Commonwealth status on the Philippine Islands in ten years. The ten years would give the Philippine government, then headed by Manuel Quezon, an increasing degree of autonomy, as it went about preparing for an independent existence. This included the design and build-up of its security forces.

After two decades, the wheel of fortune had made a full turn. In 1915, forecasting my future, I was sure that the Philippines would be my first assignment. Now, although no hint had ever been raised that I might go there—for one thing there were no football teams to coach—Manila was my next destination. In the happenstance of Army life I had become associated with General MacArthur and the general was a natural candidate for a special role in the Islands. His father, our làst military governor there, was a symbol of American might in battle and American understanding around the conference table.

General MacArthur was still Chief of Staff and was very insistent that I go along with him for a year or so. He said that he and I had worked together for a long time and he didn't want to bring in somebody new.

In the years that followed, I came to understand that in making his request General MacArthur made himself more like most of us. Whatever our position, whatever the power we exercise under the weight of responsibility, we need familiar faces about us as much as we need expert opinion or wise counsel.

Though we worked doggedly through 1936 and 1937, ours was a hopeless venture, in a sense. The Philippines government simply could not afford to build any real security from attack. We had to content ourselves with an attempt to produce a military force adequate to deal with domestic revolt and to provide a least a passive type of defense around the perimeter of the islands to slow up the advance of an aggressor until some friendly nation, presumably the United States, came to our aid.

In the beginning of 1936, we fixed up a field outside the city limits, selected a few students, and started a miniature air force. I decided to be a pilot too. Because I was learning to fly at the age of forty-six, my reflexes were slower than those of the younger men. But it was fun and at the end of the tour, I had 350 hours in my flight log.

In Manila, we noticed in 1938 that there was uneasiness about the possibility of war. The Nazis were in the saddle and riding hard in central Europe. Among other things, they were persecuting the Jews unmercifully and many of the Jewish faith were fleeing Germany, trying to find homes elsewhere in the world.

Out of the Jewish ordeal in Europe, an unusual offer was made to me. Through several Jewish friends, I was asked to take a job seeking in China, Southeast Asia, Indonesia, and every country where they might be acceptable, a haven for Jewish refugees from Nazi Germany. The pay would be $60,000 a year, with expenses. The offer was, of course, appealing for several reasons. But by this time, I had become so committed to my profession that I declined.

I was certain that the United States would be drawn into the whirlpool of the war. I called upon the President of the Philippines and told him I wanted to return home to take part in the work of intensive preparation which I was now certain would begin in the United States.

Manuel Quezon was emphatic in insisting that I remain. He handed me a blank contract for my services and said, "We'll tear up the old contract. I've already signed this one and it is filled in—except what you want as your emoluments for remaining. You will write that in."

"Mr. President," I said, "your offer is flattering. But no amount of money can make me change my mind. My entire life has been given to this one thing, my country and my profession. I want to be there if what I fear is going to come about actually happens."

Mamie, young John, and I departed for San Francisco.

# PART TWO

IN EARLY JANUARY 1940, I was assigned to troop duty with the 15th Infantry at Fort Lewis, Washington. After eight years of desk and staff duty in the rarefied atmosphere of military planning and pleading, I was again in daily contact with the two fundamental elements of military effort—men and weapons.

By the following spring the entire West Coast area was in a state of almost endless movement—men arriving in groups for assignment to units; cadres of men being withdrawn from units to form new organizations; officers and men leaving for and returning from specialist schools; cities of tents and barracks with all the multiple utilities of modern living—hospitals, water systems, light and power plants—springing up overnight where before had been open fields.

In June 1941, I was assigned to Lieutenant General Walter Krueger's Third Army as his chief of staff at San Antonio headquarters.

The Third Army was directed to concentrate in Louisiana for a great maneuver, with Lieutenant General Ben Lear's Second Army as its opponent. Like a vast laboratory experiment, the maneuvers would prove the worth of ideas, men, weapons, and equipment. More than 270,000 men—the largest army ever gathered in the United States for a single tactical operation—were assembled by General Krueger that September. Moving out of Second Army camps at the same time were another 130,000.

During this time I had my first important introduction to the press camera. I was an unknown face to the men who used them. During the critique at Camp Polk a group shot was made of General Krueger, Major A. V. Golding, a British military observer, and me; in the caption my two companions were correctly identified, but I appeared as "Lt. Col. D. D. Ersenbeing."

At the end of the maneuvers I was promoted to the temporary grade of brigadier general.

Although the Washington negotiations with the Japanese Ambassador were nearing their dramatic climax at the beginning of December, a relaxation of tenseness among the civilian population was reflected within the Army. It seemed that the Japanese bluff had been called and war, at least temporarily, averted in the Pacific. On the Russian front the Germans had been stopped before Leningrad, Moscow, and Sebastopol.

On the afternoon of December 7 at Fort Sam Houston, Texas, tired out from the long and exhausting staff work of the maneuvers and their aftermath, I went to bed with orders that under no circumstances was I to be disturbed. My dreams were of a two week leave I was going to take, during which my wife and I were going to West Point to spend Christmas with our plebe son, John. But even dreams like these—and my strict orders—could be shattered with impunity by the aide who brought the news that we were at war.

Within an hour of the Pearl Harbor attack orders began pouring into Third Army Headquarters from the War Department.

Immediacy of movement was the keynote. The normal channels of administration were abandoned. A single telephone call would start an infantry unit across the continent.

Early in the morning of December 12 the telephone connecting us directly to the War Department in Washington began to jangle. I answered and someone inquired, "Is that you, Ike?"

"Yes."

"The Chief says for you to hop a plane and get up here right away. Tell your boss that formal orders will come through later." The "Chief" was General George Marshall, and the man at the other end of the line was Colonel Walter Bedell Smith, who was later to become my close friend and Chief of Staff throughout the European operations.

This message was a hard blow. During the First World War every one of my frantic efforts to get to the scene of action had been defeated—for reasons which had no validity to me except that they all boiled down to "War Department orders." I hoped in any new war to stay with troops. Being ordered to a city where I had already served a total of eight years would mean, I thought, virtual repetition of my experience in World War I. Heavyhearted, I telephoned my wife to pack a bag, and within the hour I was headed for the War Department.

Washington in war time has been variously described in numbers of pungent epigrams, all signifying chaos. This time, however, the War Department had achieved a gratifying level of efficiency before the outbreak of war. This was

As the United States—and her son—moved into war, a mother back in Kansas read the mail.

due to the vision and determination of one man, General Marshall.

I reported to General Marshall early on Sunday morning, December 14, and for the first time in my life talked to him for more than two minutes. Without preamble or waste of time, the Chief of Staff outlined the general situation, naval and military, in the western Pacific.

All the evidence indicated that the Japanese intended to overrun the Philippines as rapidly as possible, and the problem was to determine what could now be done. General Marshall took perhaps twenty minutes to describe all this, and then abruptly asked, "What should be our general line of action?"

I thought a second and, hoping I was showing a poker face, answered, "Give me a few hours."

"All right," he said, and I was dismissed.

Significantly and characteristically, he did not even hint at one of the most important factors in the problem: the psychological effects of the Philippine battle upon people in the United States and throughout the Pacific. Clearly he felt that anyone stupid enough to overlook this consideration had no business wearing the star of a brigadier general.

It was painfully clear that the Philippines themselves could not, at that time, be reinforced directly by land and sea forces.

We had to do whatever was remotely possible for the helpless islands, although the end result might be no more than postponement of disaster. And we simply had to save the air lifeline through Australia, New Zealand, Fiji, and Hawaii.

With these bleak conclusions I marched back to the Chief of Staff. "General," I said, "it will be a long time before major reinforcements can go to the Philippines, longer than the garrison can hold out with any driblet assistance, if the enemy commits major forces to their reduction. But we must do everything for them that is humanly possible. The people of China, of the Philippines, of the Dutch East Indies will be watching us. They may excuse failure but they will not excuse abandonment. Their trust and friendship are important to us. Our base must be Australia, and we must start at once to expand it and to secure our communications to it. In this last we dare not fail. We must take great risks and spend any amount of money required."

He merely replied, "I agree with you." His tone implied that I had been given the problem as a check to an answer he had already reached. He added, "Do your best to save them." With that I went to work.

On my desk memorandum pad, which by accident survived, I find this note, made on January 1, 1942: "I've been insisting that the Far East is critical—and no sideshows should be undertaken until air and ground there are in satisfactory state." Three days later appeared: "At last we're getting some things on the road to Australia. The air plan includes four pursuit groups, and two heavy, two medium, and one light bombardment groups. But we've got to have ships— and we need them now! Tempers are short. There are lots of amateur strategists on the job. I'd give anything to be back in the field."

Strive as we did, we could not save the Philippines. The epic of Bataan came to a tragic end on April 9; Corregidor surrendered on May 6.

President Quezon became the head of yet another government-in-exile. He eventually made his way to the United States. Within a week of his arrival he called at my office. His gratitude to America was profound; he clearly understood all the reasons why more effective help could not be rendered at that moment, but he knew the Philippines would again live under its own flag.

Within the War Department staff basic plans for European invasion began slowly to take shape during January and February 1942. As always, time was the critical element in the problem. Yet everywhere delay was imposed upon us! It profited nothing to wail about unpreparedness. It is a characteristic of military problems that they yield to nothing but harsh reality; things must be reduced to elemental simplicity and answers must be clear, almost obvious. Everywhere men and materials were needed. The wave of Japanese aggression had not then reached full tide, and everything upon which we in the United States could lay our hands had necessarily to go to the Southwest Pacific to prevent complete inundation. Aside from preserving lines of air and sea communications to Australia, we had to hold the Indian bastion at all costs; otherwise a junction between Japanese and German forces would be accomplished through the Persian Gulf. Prevention of this catastrophe became the chief preoccupation of our British partners.

Already we had learned the lesson that, while air power alone might not win a victory, no great victory is possible without air superiority. Consequently the need for airplanes in vast numbers competed with all other needs—shipping, cannon, tanks, rifles, ammunition, food, clothing, heavy construction material, and everything from beeswax to battleships that goes to make up a nation's fighting power.

We had to do the best we could, with almost nothing to distribute but deficits, in stemming the onslaughts of our enemies, but plans for victory had to look far ahead to the day when the airplanes, the battle fleets, the shipping, the landing craft, and the fighting formations would allow us to pass to the offensive and to maintain it. It was in this realm of the future—a future so uncertain as to be one almost of make-believe—that the projected plan for European invasion had to take its initial form.

Early in January 1942 the Chief of Staff had announced a determination to reorganize the War Department for the efficient waging of war. There would have to be an agency which could assemble and concentrate the sum total of strategic information for General Marshall's attention and direct operations under his general supervision. The creation of the Operations Division of the War Department General Staff was the answer to this need.

On March 9, I became the first chief of OPD. Almost simultaneously I was promoted to a temporary major generalcy.

As I remember it, I was far too busy then to take the time to thank General Marshall for the advancement to the grade which, in our prewar Army, represented the virtual apex of a professional military career.

The question before the War Department resolved itself into the selection of the exact line of operations along which the potential power of the United States would be best directed against the European Axis.

Already much was known of the tremendous effort the German was making to insure integrity of his Atlantic wall. Moreover, a considerable amount of the German Air Force could still be disposed in those areas, and important elements of his fleet were lying in the harbors of northern France, in Norway, and in the Baltic Sea. The coastline was crowded with U-boat nests, while undersea mining was rapidly covering every possible approach.

Many held that attack against this type of defense was madness, nothing but military suicide.

A very few, initially a very, very few—took a contrary view. General Marshall, who had already been informed of the basic conception on which we were working, was one of the believers.

We felt we were bringing a new concept, almost a new faith, to strategic thinking, one which envisioned that the air-arm, co-ordinated with ground operations to the extent that an effective ground-air team could be developed, would tend to multiply the effectiveness of both.

Basically the plan provided for amphibious landings in northwest Europe, with buildup in the beachheads, to be followed by major advances to destroy Hitler's forces.

The Chief of Staff listened patiently through long presentations and at the end said, "This is it. I approve." He immediately conferred with Admiral Ernest J. King and General Henry ("Hap") Arnold, who also approved. The next step was to secure the approval of the President. Then our Allies would have to be convinced. It was manifest that the wholehearted support of the British Government must be obtained or the scheme would fall of its own weight. Without unstinted co-operation by the British there was no possibility of turning that country into an armed camp of Americans, much less of obtaining British naval, air, ground and logistic support. President Roosevelt directed General Marshall to proceed to London.

He came back with the agreement between the British and American governments to make the attack across the English Channel the principal offensive effort of the two governments in Europe. This decision was made in April 1942.

History has proved that nothing is more difficult in war than to adhere to a single strategic plan. Unforeseen and glittering promise on the one hand and unexpected difficulty or risk upon the other present constant temptation to desert the chose line of action in favor of another. This one was no exception—realization of the plan was far removed from its making, and countless occasions were to arise when argument, blandishment, and exhortation would seek its abandonment. But the war in Europe was finally won because through every trial and every temptation—in spite of difficulty, delay, pressure, and profitable preliminary operations in the Mediterranean which themselves offered a temptation to forsake the original concept—the President, General Marshall, and many others never wavered from their purpose of launching a full-out invasion of Europe across the English Channel at the earliest practicable moment.

Marshall directed me to visit London and to bring back recommendations involving future organization and development of our European forces.

Our inspection team spent ten days in the United Kingdom. I returned home to report that the individual in charge of the American effort in Europe should be someone thoroughly indoctrinated in the plans of the United States Government, with a working knowledge of our capabilities in the production of land, air, and naval units and materials to support them in offensive fighting. In his quick way General Marshall asked me who should take the job, and this time I had my answer ready. I recommended General Joseph T. McNarney. The Chief of Staff rejected this recommendation. He had just appointed McNarney Deputy Chief of Staff for the War Department.

On June 8, I submitted to the Chief of Staff a draft of a "Directive for the Commanding General, European Theater of Operations," which provided for unified command of all American forces allocated to the European area. I remarked to General Marshall that this was one paper he should read in detail before it went out because it was likely to be an important document in the further waging of the war. His reply still lives in my memory. "I certainly do want to read it. You may be the man who executes it. If that's the case, when can you leave?" Three days later General Marshall told me definitely that I would command the European theater.

It is difficult now to recapture the sober, even fearful, atmosphere of those days: the state of the public mind which was reflected in the thinking of so many people in and out of the service. Except for the early June defeat of the Japanese fleet at Midway, Allied fortunes were at low ebb. Prospects were bright only in their long-range aspect, and were contingent on Russia's maintaining herself in the war with the material help that could be given her while the United States developed her latent power. Moreover, it was essential that Great Britain hang on grimly in India and the Western Desert in order to keep our two principal enemies divided and to deny them the Middle East oil.

It became increasingly doubtful to the American headquarters in London that a full-out attack could be launched in the early spring of 1943, and because it would be extremely hazardous to begin a major operation across the English Channel in the fall of the year, we began to realize that a large-scale invasion might not be possible before the spring of 1944.

It was determined to proceed with the planning for the invasion of northwest Africa with an Allied force, to be carried out under an American commander. The operation received the name Torch. Both governments agreed that the whole venture should have, initially at least, a completely American complexion. The hope was that French North Africa would receive the invading troops with no more than a nominal show of resistance, and the chances of this favorable development were considered to be much brighter if the operation was advertised as purely American. British standing in France was at a low ebb because of Oran, Dakar, and Syrian incidents, in which British forces had come into open conflict with the French.

In his headquarters in the Claridge Hotel, General Marshall informed me that I was to be the Allied commander in chief of the expedition.

This violent shift in target, timing, and the circumstances of attack might have had a serious psychological effect on all those who were convinced that victory could not be attained except by an offensive aimed directly at the enemy's continental vitals. But fortunately the decision to attack Africa definitely did not constitute or imply any abandonment by the Combined Chiefs of Staff of their determination to carry out, when practicable, the invasion of Europe across the English Channel. The African venture was looked upon as diversionary in character but necessitated by the circumstances of the moment. The least

Sent to command all Allied operations in North Africa, the now-General Eisenhower is bundled into a knitted cap and warm uniform as he heads for the Tunisian front.

of the results was that northwest Africa would be denied to the Axis for a submarine and aircraft base. Next, it was expected that through an advance to the eastward Malta would be succored. The final hope expressed at that early date was that all North Africa might be cleared of the Axis; and that the Mediterranean, at least along its southern shores, could be used by the convoys of the Allied nations, thus eliminating the long route around the Cape of Good Hope to reach both the Middle East and India.

My first task was to select American and British officers to fill key positions in the command and staff organizations. We tried to include in every section individuals of both nationalities.

The whole basis of our higher organization was new. Time and time again during the summer old Army friends warned me that the conception of Allied unity which we took as the foundation of our command scheme was impracticable and impossible; that any commander placed in my position was foredoomed to failure and could become nothing but a scapegoat to carry the odium of defeat for the whole operation.

In the early days officers of the two nationalities were apt to conduct their business in the attitude of a bulldog meeting a tomcat, but as time went on their own discoveries of mutual respect and friendship developed a team that in its

### The Top Men

British General Sir Harold Alexander (left), Allied Deputy Commander in North Africa, and Lieutenant General George Patton, task force commander, confer with the commander-in-chief of that theatre.

A dangerous and delicate mission complete. General Henri Giraux with General Eisenhower at a ceremony marking the transfer of American equipment to the new French Army in Algeria, North Africa, May 8, 1943.

Try for an assignment under a Colonel Marshall, the young Eisenhower was advised by his mentor, General Fox Conner. "In the new war we will have to fight beside allies and Marshall knows more about the techniques of arranging allied commands than any man I know." This prophetic advice was followed when General Marshall reached out to bring Dwight Eisenhower to Washington at the war's outset—gave him the task of forging plans for allied operations and then put him in charge for Europe.

In a group portrait grained with that special quality of wartime documentary photographs, an Allied planning conference in North Africa looks toward the next steps. Seated center, in white, Prime Minister Winston Churchill. From left to right: Anthony Eden, British Foreign Secretary; General Sir Alan Brooke, Britain's Chief of the Imperial General Staff; British Air Chief Marshall Sir Arthur Tedder, Air commander-in-chief in the Mediterranean; Admiral Sir Andrew B. Cunningham, British Naval commander-in-chief in the Mediterranean; Britain's General Sir Harold L. Alexander, Deputy commander-in-chief of Allied Forces in North Africa; U. S. General George C. Marshall, Chief of Staff; U. S. General Dwight D. Eisenhower, Commander-in-chief, Allied Forces in North Africa, and General Sir Bernard L. Montgomery, Chief of the British 8th Army (standing, extreme right).

unity of purpose, devotion to duty, and absence of friction could not have been excelled if all its members had come from the same nation and the same service.

At Gibraltar our headquarters was established in a dismal setting. The subterranean passages under the Rock provided the sole available office space, and in them was located the signal equipment by which we expected to keep in touch with the commanders of the three assault forces. The eternal darkness of the tunnels was here and there partially pierced by feeble electric bulbs. Damp, cold air in block-long passages was heavy with a stagnation that did not noticeably respond to the clattering efforts of electric fans. Through the arched ceilings came a constant drip, drip, drip of surface water that faithfully but drearily ticked off the seconds of the interminable, almost unendurable, wait which occurs between completion of a military plan and the moment action begins. . . . Every day we expected a major attack by hostile bombers; as each day went by without such an attack we went to bed puzzled, even astonished.

During those hours that we paced away in Gibraltar's caverns, hundreds of Allied ships, in fast- and slow-moving convoys, were steaming across the North Atlantic toward a common center on the coast of northwest Africa. To attack Algiers and Oran, most of these ships would pass through the narrow Strait of Gibraltar, flanked by guns that might at any moment speak up in favor of the Nazis. Other ships, coming from America, were to proceed directly against Casablanca and port towns to its north and south.

The three main expeditions were plowing through seas infested with U-boats. At Gibraltar most of our separate convoys would enter an area where they would come under the threat of enemy bombers. Our troops had been only hastily trained for this complicated type of landing operation and, for the most part, had never participated in battle. Available shipping did not permit us to carry along all the forces and equipment necessary to assure success. Of course we were tense.

We had three days to wait. Finally the leading ships steamed in at night through the narrow strait and we stood on the dark headlands to watch them pass. Still no news of air or submarine attack!

At no time during the war did I experience a greater sense of relief than when, on the following morning, I received a meager report to the effect that beach conditions were not too bad and the Casablanca landing, under General Patton, was proceeding as planned. I said a prayer of thanksgiving.

The afternoon of November 7 brought one of my most distressing interviews of the war.

Both the British and American governments believed that North African public opinion favored the Allies, and naturally desired to make the invasion appear as an operation undertaken in response to a popular desire for liberation from the Vichy yoke. Not only did we definitely want to avoid adding France to our already formidable list of enemies; we wanted, if possible, to make it appear that we had come into Africa on invitation rather than by force.

Because of the earnest conviction held in both London and Washington that General Henri Giraud could lead the French of North Africa into the Allied camp, we had started negotiations in October to rescue the general from virtual imprisonment in southern France. The general, with but three personal aides and staff officers, came by submarine to my headquarters during the afternoon of November 7.

It was quickly apparent that he had come out of France laboring under the grave misapprehension that he was immediately to assume command of the whole Allied expedition. Upon entering my dungeon he offered himself to me in that capacity. I could not accept his services in such a role. I wanted him to proceed to Africa, as soon as we could guarantee his safety, and there take over command of such French forces as would voluntarily rally to him.

Fortunately a night's sleep did something to change General Giraud's mind and at the next morning's meeting he decided to participate on the basis we desired.

During the course of the night and in the early morning hours of November 8 operational reports began to come in that were encouraging in tone. As anticipated, the landings at Algiers (under General Charles W. Ryder) met almost no opposition and the area was quickly occupied.

At Oran we got ashore, but the French forces in that region, particularly the naval elements, resisted bitterly.

We immediately turned all our attention to the greater mission assigned us of co-operating with General Sir Harold Alexander's desert forces, then twelve hundred miles away at the opposite end of the Mediterranean. Between us we would destroy all Axis forces in northern Africa and reopen the sea for the use of Allied shipping. There were available to Hitler and Mussolini only the ports lying between Bone in Algeria and Tripoli in northwest Libya, from which to support Rommel. Every advance by the Allies from either flank would tend to squeeze the Axis channel of supplies and with continuation of this process eventual strangulation would result. Our main strategic purpose was, therefore, the speedy capture of northern Tunisia.

(*Months of bitter fighting ensued while the American and French forces struggled to overcome the combination of enemy, weather, and terrain. By the middle of January Eisenhower placed General Anderson in charge of the entire battle line on the West, while Alexander and Montgomery were pushing their way across the desert from the East. By early spring the desert advance had covered a distance equal to that between New York and Chicago. As the Allied forces converged upon Tunis in April of 1943, it became evident that the Axis forces were doomed. By the 13th of May, except for a few stragglers in the mountains, the only living Germans left in Tunisia were safely within prison.)*

The sudden capture of 275,000 Axis military men caused me rather ruefully to remark... "Why didn't some staff college ever tell us what to do with a quarter of a million prisoners?"

Rommel himself escaped before the final debacle... but the myth of his and Nazi invincibility had been completely destroyed. Von Arnim surrendered the German troops, and Field Marshal Messe, in nominal command of the whole force, surrendered the Italian contingent. When Von Arnim was brought through Algiers on his way to captivity, some members of my staff felt that I should observe the custom of bygone days and allow him to call on me.

The tradition that all professional soldiers are really comrades in arms has, in tattered form, persisted to this day.

For me World War II was far too personal a thing to entertain such feelings. Daily as it progressed there grew within me the conviction that as never before in a war between many nations the forces that stood for human good and men's rights were this time confronted by a completely evil conspiracy with which no compromise could be tolerated. Because only by the utter destruction of the Axis was a decent world possible, the war became for me a crusade in the traditional sense of that often misused word.

In this specific instance, I told my Intelligence officer to get any information he possibly could out of the captured generals but that, as far as I was concerned, I was interested only in those who were not yet captured.

The Tunisian victory was hailed with delight throughout the Allied Nations. It clearly signified to friend and foe alike that the Allies were at last upon the march. The Germans, who had during the previous winter suffered also the great defeat of Stalingrad and had been forced to abandon their other offensives on the Russian front in favor of a desperate defense, were compelled after Tunisia to think only of the protection of conquests rather than of their enlargement.

Within the African theater one of the greatest products of the victory was the progress achieved in the welding of Allied unity and the establishment of a command team that was already showing the effects of a growing confidence and trust among all its members.

During the final weeks of the Tunisian campaign, particularly after the outcome could be definitely foreseen, major staffs were busy planning our next campaign. As directed by the Casablanca Conference, this was to be the capture of Sicily.

The broad outline of the Sicilian campaign was announced to our press representatives one month before it took place. This unprecedented step was taken, paradoxically, to maintain secrecy.

During periods of combat inactivity reporters have a habit of filling up their stories with speculation, and since after some months of experience in a war theater any newsman acquires considerable skill in interpreting coming events, the danger was increased that soon the enemy would have our plans almost in detail. Because of the confidence I had acquired in the integrity of newsmen in my theater, I decided to take them into my confidence.

The experiment was one which I would not particularly like to repeat, because such revelation does place a burden upon the man whose first responsibility is to conceal the secret. But I did succeed in placing upon every reporter in the theater a feeling of the same responsibility that I and my associates bore. Success was complete. From that moment onward, until after the attack was launched, nothing speculative came out of the theater and no representative of the press attempted to send out anything that could possibly be of any value to the enemy.

Up to that moment no amphibious attack in history had approached this one in size. Along miles of coastline there were hundreds of vessels and small boats afloat and antlike files of advancing troops ashore. Overhead were fights of protecting fighters.

The point we wanted to capture at the earliest possible moment was Messina, the enemy port in the northeastern end of the island, directly across the narrow strait from the Italian mainland. Through this port almost all enemy supplies would have to flow, and once it was secured the position of the garrison on the island would be hopeless.

By the end of July the Italian garrison, except for a few small elements under the direct domination of their German overlords, had entirely quit, but along the great saw-toothed ridge of which the center was Mount Etna the German garrison was fighting skillfully and savagely. Panzer and paratroop elements here were among the best we encountered in the war, and each position won was gained only through the complete destruction of the defending elements.

Nevertheless, by the time the Seventh and Eighth Armies had closed up into position for their final assault against the Mount Etna bastion the Germans saw that the game was up and began the evacuation across the Strait of Messina. Our bombers operated against this line of escape, but the narrowness of the strait allowed the enemy to get out most of the badly battered German garrison during hours of darkness.

It was during this campaign that the unfortunate "slapping incident" involving General Patton took place. Patton, on a visit to base hospitals to see the wounded, encountered, in quick succession, two men who had no apparent physical hurts. Of the first one he met, Patton inquired why he was a patient in the hospital. To this the man replied, "General, I guess it's my nerves." Patton flew into a rage. He had, himself, been under a terrific strain for a period of many days. Moreover, he sincerely believed that there was no such thing as the "battle fatigue" or "battle neurosis."

Within a matter of moments he met a second soldier under somewhat similar circumstances. This time his emotions were so uncontrollable that he swung a hand at the soldier's head. He struck the man's helmet, which rolled along the ground, and by this time doctors and nurses, overcoming their natural timidity in the presence of the commanding general, intervened between Patton and the soldier.

The story spread throughout the hospital and among neighboring units with lightning speed. I soon received an unofficial report from the surgeon commanding the hospital, a report that was soon elaborated by a group of newsmen.

The question became, what to do?

Patton's offense, had it been committed on the actual front, within an assaulting platoon, would not have been an offense. His emotional tenseness and his impulsiveness were the very qualities that helped to make him, in open situations, such a remarkable leader of an army.

But because of the time and place of his action Patton's offense was a serious one, more so because of his rank and standing.

I first wrote him a sharp letter of reprimand in which I informed him that repetition of such an offense would be cause for his instant relief. I informed him, also, that his retention as a commander in my theater would be contingent upon his offering a public apology to the two men whom he had insulted.

After the incident was all over my old friend George sent me a long letter in which the following appeared: "I am at a loss to find words with which to express my chagrin and grief at having given you, a man to whom I owe everything and for whom I would gladly lay down my life, cause to be displeased with me."

The results of the Sicilian campaign were more far-reaching than the mere capture of the enemy garrison. The bombastic Mussolini was thrown out. Evidence of unrest and dissatisfaction throughout the Italian nation became more and more pronounced and it was obvious that Italy was seeking the easiest way out of the war. Mussolini's place as Premier was taken by old Field Marshal Pietro Badoglio. The initial pronouncements of the latter indicated his government's purpose to continue in the war, but it was clear that this statement was made in the hope of placating the Germans and giving the Italians a chance to escape punishment from their arrogant ally.

The Italians wanted frantically to surrender. However, they wanted to do so only with the assurance that such a powerful Allied force would land on the mainland simultaneously with their surrender that the government itself and their cities would enjoy complete protection from the German forces.

Finally it was agreed that the surrender would be effective on the evening of September 8 and that Badoglio and I should simultaneously announce the capitulation.

Everything was proceeding according to plan when, at noon on September 8, I received a message through clandestine channels to the effect that Badoglio had reversed his decision on the ground that we were too hasty and that the result would merely mean complete domination of Italy by the Germans and the sanguinary punishment of the individuals involved. The matter had proceeded too far for me to temporize further. I replied in a peremptory telegram that regardless of his action I was going to announce the surrender at six-thirty o'clock as previously agreed upon and that if I did so without simultaneous action on his part Italy would have no friend left in the war.

I announced the surrender at six-thirty that evening and Badoglio, in fear and trembling, finally decided an hour and a half later that he had to follow suit.

This action did not by any means change our invasion plans. For some days we had known that the Italian garrison in the Salerno Bay area was being replaced by the best of the German troops and our Intelligence sections predicted a hard battle in the beachhead culminating in strong counterattacks.

When General Mark Clark led the Fifth Army into Salerno he had not previously participated in any of the fighting of World War II. He proved to be a fine battle leader and fully justified the personal confidence that had impelled me to assign him to such an important position.

The two great initial objectives of the Italian invasion were the capture, first, of Naples as a satisfactory port from which to supply our troops, and, second,

From the Tunisian front, and a spot of C rations, to the Italian front.

Italy: Generals Eisenhower and Mark Wayne Clark talk with British soldiers riding in a Bren gun carrier. On one visit to the front, the two generals (and friends) were sitting under trees when a shell came in overhead and landed nearby. It seemed to them just a stray shell so they continued to talk. "A day or two afterward we saw accounts written up that said the two generals were so green they didn't realize that when shelling started, one took cover behind a tree or went flat on the ground. I wonder whether the writer would have been so sure about our nonchalance if he had seen us in the early days of Africa, ducking for the ditches every time we saw a plane in the air."

(Above) on a trip to Tehran, FDR and DDE bring their respective smiles to bear on a war that is beginning to give some reason for optimism. And (left) the President awards the General the Legion of Merit.

of the airfields at Foggia from which to supplement the air bombardment of central Europe, which up to that moment had been conducted almost exclusively from the British bases.

All later fighting in that area would have a principal objective: pinning down German forces far from the region of the major assault that was to take place the following year across the English Channel.

The Italian campaign thereafter became a distinctly subsidiary operation, though the results it attained in the actual defeat of Germany were momentous, almost incalculable. It was obvious, however, that the Italian avenue of approach did not in itself offer a favorable route from which to attack decisively the German homeland. That could be done only across the English Channel and through France and the Low Countries.

While the summer and fall fighting was in full swing we received word that the President and the Prime Minister and their staffs were preparing to hold a joint meeting near Cairo.

The Prime Minister preceded the President into our area and I met Mr. Churchill at Malta, where we had a lengthy conference.

He dwelt at length on one of his favorite subjects—the importance of assailing Germany through the "soft underbelly," of keeping up the tempo of our Italian attack and extending its scope to include much of the northern shore of the Mediterranean. He seemed always to see great and decisive possibilities in the Mediterranean, while the project of invasion across the English Channel left him cold. (How often I heard him say: "We must take care that the tides do not run red with the blood of American and British youth, or the beaches be choked with their bodies.")

Several days later, accompanied by my principal commanders, we proceeded to Cairo to present our views concerning the forces in the Mediterranean.

My own recommendation, then as always, was that no operation should be undertaken in the Mediterranean except as a directly supporting move for the Channel attack and that our planned redeployment to England should proceed with all possible speed. Obviously a sufficient strength had to be kept in the Mediterranean to hold what we had already gained and to force the Nazis to maintain sizable forces in that area.

This was the program adopted by the Cairo Conference, and our shipment of troops and equipment to England continued without abatement.

Again I had an opportunity for private talks with the President, at one of which he informally presented me with the Legion of Merit.

One evening General Marshall asked me with some others to dinner. It was a splendid American dinner with turkey and all that goes with it. As the guests were leaving, one guest said to General Marshall, "Thank you very much for a fine Thanksgiving dinner." I turned around in complete astonishment and said, "Well, that shows what war does to a man. I had no idea this was Thanksgiving Day."

With our command of the sea and our communications firmly anchored in Naples it was much easier for us to sustain active operations in southern and central Italy than it was for the enemy, who had to bring in everything he used over the long, tortuous, and exposed lines through the Alps.

Carefully planned minor offensives, with success assured in each, comprised the campaign I expected to use during the winter; it was dictated by the objective and by the need to sustain morale amidst the inescapably miserable conditions of the Italian mountains.

To the soldier at the front the high command's designation of an operation as "secondary" makes little difference. In this case it certainly meant no amelioration of his hardships. Heavy rains fell and the streams were habitually torrents. The weather grew colder day by day. Men and vehicles sank in the mud. But the dogged fighting was constant. The enemy's emplacements, often dug into solid rock, covered every approach—every foot of ground was gained only by weary maneuvers over mountain slopes and by blasting and digging the hostile gunners out of their shelters.

The methods employed by successful leaders in developing morale differ so widely as to defy any attempt to establish rules. One observation, however, always applies; in any long and bitter campaign morale will suffer unless all ranks thoroughly believe that their commanders are concerned first and always with the welfare of the troops who do the fighting. A human understanding and a natural ability to mingle with all men on a basis of equality are more important than any degree of technical skill.

In early December, I had received word the President would return to the United States through our area. I went to Tunis to meet him.

The President arrived in midafternoon and was scarcely seated in the automobile when...he said, "Well, Ike, you are going to command Overlord."

Because I had to discuss with him, at once, details of his next day's plans, we had no opportunity to talk further about the new assignment, but I did manage to say, "Mr. President, I realize that such an appointment involved a difficult decision. I hope you will not be disappointed."

There was much to do. In addition to my Allied responsibilities I was, of course, the commander of American forces in the theater. Administration of such a force, with its eternal questions of supply, maintenance, replacement, promotion, demotion, and a voluminous correspondence with the War Department, is a very intricate and sometimes very personal process. While engaged in all of these details and counting on getting away to England about the tenth of January, I received a Christmas telegram from General Marshall. He urged me to come immediately to Washington for short conferences with him and the President and for a brief breather before undertaking the new assignment.

I protested, on the ground that time was vital and that, moreover, I could accomplish little by a visit to Washington until I had been in London at least long enough to familiarize myself with the essentials of the problems there. General Marshall did not agree. He advised me to "allow someone else to run the war for twenty minutes," and to come to Washington.

Upon arrival in the United States I met with the War Department staff and later with the President. Mr. Roosevelt was temporarily ill with influenza but seemed quite cheerful and kept me at his bedside for more than an hour.

He took occasion to brief me on his post-hostilities occupational plans for Germany. He definitely wanted the northwest section as the United States area but listened attentively as I voiced my objection to dividing Germany into "national sectors." I admitted all the difficulties of true joint occupation but said we should insist upon that plan as the only practicable one—and one, moreover, which would quickly test the possibilities of real "quadripartite action." I urged, again, that occupied territories be turned over, as quickly as possible, to civil authority. He seemed impressed but did not commit himself.

As I left the President I said, "I sincerely trust that you will quickly recover from your indisposition." He quickly replied, "Oh, I have not felt better in years. I'm in bed only because the doctors are afraid I might have a relapse if I get up too soon." I never saw him again.

During my short stay in the United States I had a treasured opportunity of going with my wife to see our son at West Point. Later I made a hasty trip to see my mother and brothers, my wife's parents, and a few other members of our families, all gathered for the occasion in the town of Manhattan, Kansas. These family visits were a rejuvenating experience.

I left the United States on January 13 to undertake the organization of the mightiest fighting force that the two Western Allies could muster. On the evening of the second day I was back in London.

Immediate subordinates included Air Chief Marshal Sir Arthur Tedder, Lieutenant General Omar Bradley, General Sir Bernard Montgomery, Lieutenant General Carl Spaatz, and Admiral Sir Bertram Ramsay, all tested battle leaders and all experienced in the problems of developing real allied unity in a large operation. Air Chief Marshal Sir Trafford Leigh-Mallory was assigned to the Allied forces, with the title of Air Commander in Chief.

It was desirable that for the preparatory stages of the assault and for proper support during the critical early stages of the land operation—until we had established ourselves so firmly that danger of defeat was eliminated—all air forces in Britain, excepting only the Coastal Command, should come under my control. Some opposition quickly developed, partly from the Prime Minister and his chiefs of staff.

My insistence upon commanding these air forces at that time was influenced by the lesson so conclusively demonstrated at Salerno: when a battle needs the last ounce of available force, the commander must not be in the position of depending upon request and negotiation to get it. It was vital that the entire sum of our assault power, including the two Strategic Air Forces, be available for use during the critical stages of the attack. I stated unequivocally that so long as I was in command I would accept no other solution.

Plans called for the early establishment of separate British and American army groups on the Continent and it was logical that, when these were in sufficient force to accomplish a decisive breakout and begin a rapid advance through western Europe, the land force in each natural channel of march should have its own commander, each reporting directly to my headquarters. This plan would apply also to the army group which was later to invade France from the south. It would be completely confusing—a case of too many cooks—to place any headquarters intermediate between these three principal ground commanders and my own.

There were long discussions but the general outline of the operation we intended to conduct was:

Land on the Normandy coast.

Build up the resources needed for a decisive battle in the Normandy-Brittany region and break out of the enemy's encircling positions. (Land operations in the first two phases were to be the tactical direction of Montgomery.)

Pursue on a broad front with two army groups, emphasizing the left to gain necessary ports and reach the boundaries of Germany and threaten the Ruhr. On our right we would link up with the forces that were to invade France from the south.

Build up our new base along the western border of Germany, by securing ports in Belgium and in Brittany as well as in the Mediterranean.

While building up our forces for the final battles, keep up an unrelenting offensive to the extent of our means, both to wear down the enemy and to gain advantages for the final fighting.

Complete the destruction of enemy forces west of the Rhine, in the meantime constantly seeking bridgeheads across the river.

Launch the final attack as a double envelopment of the Ruhr, again emphasizing the left, and follow this up by an immediate thrust through Germany, with the specific direction to be determined at the time.

Clean out the remainder of Germany.

This general plan, carefully outlined at staff meetings before D-day, was never abandoned, even momentarily, throughout the campaign.

In order to obtain the maximum length of good campaigning weather, the earlier the attack could be launched the better. Another factor in favor of an early attack was the continuing and frantic efforts of the Germans to strengthen his coastal defenses. Because of weather conditions in the Channel, May was the earliest date that a landing attempt could be successfully undertaken and the first favorable combination of tides and sunrise occurred early in the month. Thus early May was the original and tentatively selected target date.

Two considerations, one of them decisive in character, combined to postpone the target date. The first and important one was our insistence that the attack be on a larger scale than that originally planned by the staff in London.

Another was the degree of dependence on the preparatory effort of the air force. The month of May would give them much more time and better opportunity to impede the movement of German reserves and demolish German defenses along the coastline.

After the abandonment of the May target date, the next combination of moon, tide, and time of sunrise that we considered practicable for the attack occurred on June 5, 6, and 7.

If none of the three days should prove satisfactory from the standpoint of weather, consequences would ensue that were almost terrifying to contemplate. Secrecy would be lost. Assault troops would be unloaded and crowded back into assembly areas enclosed in barbed wire, where their original places would already have been taken by those to follow in subsequent waves. Finally, always lurking in the background was the knowledge that the enemy was developing new, and presumably effective, secret weapons on the French coast. What the effect of these would be on our crowded harbors, especially at Plymouth and Portsmouth, we could not even guess.

It was a tense period, made even worse by the fact that the one thing that could give us this disastrous setback was entirely outside our control. Some soldier once said, "The weather is always neutral." Nothing could be more untrue. Bad weather is obviously the enemy of the side that seeks to launch projects requiring good weather, or of the side possessing great assets, such as strong air forces, which depend upon good weather for effective operations. If really bad weather should endure permanently, the Nazi would need nothing else to defend the Normandy coast!

During all this period my personal contacts with the Prime Minister were frequent and profitable.

Mr. Churchill clearly and concretely explained his attitude toward and his hopes for Overlord. He gradually became more optimistic than he had earlier been, but he still refused to let his expectations completely conquer his doubts. More than once he said, "General, if by the coming winter you have established yourself with your thirty-six Allied divisions firmly on the Continent, and have the Cherbourg and Brittany peninsulas in your grasp, I will proclaim this operation to the world as one of the most successful of the war." And then he would add, "And if, in addition to this, you have secured the port at Le Havre and freed beautiful Paris from the hands of the enemy, I will assert the victory to be the greatest of modern times."

Always I would reply, "Prime Minister, I assure you that the coming winter will see the Allied forces on the borders of Germany itself. You are counting only on our presently available thirty-six divisions. We are going to bring in ten additional from the Mediterranean, and through the ports we capture we shall soon begin to rush in an additional forty from the United States."

He doubted that we could get the elbow room to do all this in the summer and fall of 1944 and often observed. "All that is for later; my statement still holds." In reply to my insistence that the picture I painted him was not too rosy, even if the German continued to fight to the bitter end, he would smile and say, "My dear General, it is always fine for a leader to be optimistic. I applaud your enthusiasm, but liberate Paris by Christmas and none of us can ask for more."

By the time the operational staffs had moved to Portsmouth, I felt that the only remaining great decision to be faced before D-day was that of fixing, definitely, the day and hour of the assault. However, the question of the wisdom of the airborne operation into the Cherbourg peninsula was not yet fully settled in Air Chief Marshal Leigh-Mallory's mind. Later, on May 30, he came to me to protest once more against what he termed the "futile slaughter" of two fine

The honors (or honours) go, in due course, to an ally. Here, on 29 August, 1943, Generals Patton, Eisenhower, and Montgomery, at the latter's villa, are seated on the steps after DDE has invested Montgomery with the Order as Commander of the Legion of Merit.

To London, and new and unprecedented, sweeping authority, as Supreme Commander, Allied Expeditionary Forces. (FDR asked General Eisenhower what he thought of the title. "I acknowledged that it had the ring of importance, something like 'Sultan,'" he wrote later. "He wished me adios. It was our last meeting.")

divisions. He believed that the combination of unsuitable landing grounds and anticipated resistance was too great a hazard to overcome.

To protect him in case his advice was disregarded, I instructed the air commander to put his recommendations in a letter and informed him he would have my answer within a few hours. I took the problem to no one else. Professional advice and counsel could do no more.

I went to my tent alone and sat down to think. Over and over I reviewed each step. I realized, of course, that if I deliberately disregarded the advice of my technical expert on the subject, and his predictions should prove accurate, then I would carry to my grave the unbearable burden of conscience justly accusing me of the stupid, blind sacrifice of thousands of the flower of our youth. Outweighing any personal burden, however, was the possibility that if he were right the effect of the disaster would be far more than local: it would be likely to spread to the entire force.

But a prompt decision was necessary: Leigh-Mallory's estimate was just an estimate, nothing more, and our experience in Sicily and Italy did not, by any means, support his degree of pessimism. Bradley, with Ridgway and airborne commanders, had always supported me and the staff in the matter, and I was encouraged to persist in the belief that Leigh-Mallory was wrong.

I telephoned him that the attack would go as planned and that I would confirm this at once in writing. When, later, the attack was successful he was the first to call me to voice his delight and to express his regret that he had found it necessary to add to my personal burdens during the final tense days before D-day.

All southern England was one vast military camp, crowded with soldiers awaiting final word to go. The mighty host was tense as a coiled spring, and indeed that is exactly what it was—a great human spring, coiled for the moment when its energy should be released and it would vault the English Channel in the greatest amphibious assault ever attempted.

When the commanders assembled on the morning of June 4 the report we received was discouraging. Low clouds, high winds, and formidable wave action were predicted to make landing a most hazardous affair. The meteorologists said that air support would be impossible, naval gunfire would be inefficient, and even the handling of small boats would be rendered difficult. Admiral Ramsay thought that the mechanics of landing could be handled, but agreed with the estimate of the difficulty in adjusting gunfire. His position was mainly neutral. General Montgomery, properly concerned with the great disadvantages of delay, believed that we should go. Tedder disagreed.

Weighing all factors, I decided that the attack would have to be postponed.

Pre-invasion moves in England:
1941. The Supreme Commander
and Sir Arthur Tedder.

Allies—and comrades. The Prime
Minister and the General have
just inspected allied troops who
will take part in the long planned
invasion of Europe. Mr. Churchill here demonstrates an important piece of military equipment,
the speedy zipper of his "siren
suit."

This decision necessitated the immediate dispatch of orders to the vessels and troops already at sea and created some doubt as to whether they could be ready twenty-four hours later in case the next day should prove favorable for the assault.

The conference on the evening of June 4 presented little, if any, added brightness to the picture of the morning, and tension mounted even higher because the inescapable consequences of postponement were almost too bitter to contemplate.

At three-thirty the next morning our little camp was shaking and shuddering under a wind of almost hurricane proportions and the accompanying rain seemed to be traveling in horizontal streaks. The mile-long trip through muddy roads to the conference at naval headquarters was anything but a cheerful one, since it seemed impossible that in such conditions there was any reason for even discussing the situation.

When the conference started the first report given us by Group Captain Staff and the Meteorologic Staff was that the bad conditions predicted the day before for the coast of France were actually prevailing there and that if we had persisted in the attempt to land on June 5 a major disaster would almost surely have resulted. This they probably told us to inspire more confidence in their next astonishing declaration, which was that by the following morning a period of relatively good weather, heretofore completely unexpected, would ensue, lasting probably thirty-six hours.

The prospect was not bright because of the possibility that we might land the first several waves successfully and then find later build-up impracticable, and so have to leave the isolated original attacking forces easy prey to German counteraction. However, the consequences of the delay justified great risk and I quickly announced the decision to go ahead with the attack on June 6. The time was then 4:15 A.M., June 5. No one present disagreed and there was a definite brightening of faces as, without a further word, each went off to his respective post of duty to flash out to his command the messages that would set the whole host in motion.

A number of people appealed to me for permission to go aboard the supporting naval ships in order to witness the attack. Every member of a staff can always develop a dozen arguments why he, in particular, should accompany an expedition rather than remain at the only post, the center of communications, where he can be useful. Permission was denied to all except those with specific military responsibility and, of course, the allotted quotas of press and radio representatives.

Back home, John Eisenhower graduates from West Point, is allowed to visit Allied Headquarters, and asks an assignment to troops immediately. His father advised against it, telling the young lieutenant that being sent into "action would lay him open to charges of favoritism."

Among those who were refused permission was the Prime Minister. His request was undoubtedly inspired as much by his natural instincts as a warrior as by his impatience at the prospect of sitting quietly back in London to await reports. I argued, however, that the chance of his becoming an accidental casualty was too important from the standpoint of the whole war effort and I refused his request. He replied, with complete accuracy, that while I was in sole command of the operation by virtue of authority delegated to me by both governments, such authority did not include administrative control over the British organization. He said, "Since this is true it is not part of your responsibility, my dear General, to determine the exact composition of any ship's company in His Majesty's Fleet. This being true," he rather slyly continued, "by shipping myself as a bona fide member of a ship's complement it would be beyond your authority to prevent my going."

All of this I had ruefully to concede, but I forcefully pointed out that he was adding to my personal burdens in this thwarting of my instructions. Even, however, while I was acknowledging defeat in the matter, aid came from an unexpected source. I later heard that the King had learned of the Prime Minister's intention and, while not presuming to interfere with the decision reached by Mr. Churchill, he sent word that if the Prime Minister felt it necessary to go on the expedition he, the King, felt it to be equally his duty and privilege to participate at the head of his troops. This instantly placed a different light upon the matter and I heard no more of it.

Nevertheless, my sympathies were entirely with the Prime Minister. Again I had to endure the interminable wait that always intervenes between the final decision of the high command and the earliest possible determination of success or failure in such ventures. I spent the time visiting troops that would participate in the assault. A late evening trip on the fifth took me to the camp of the U.S. 101st Airborne Division, one of the units whose participation had been so severely questioned by the air commander. I found the men in fine fettle, many of them joshingly admonishing me that I had no cause for worry, since the 101st was on the job and everything would be taken care of in fine shape. I stayed with them until the last of them were in the air, somewhere about midnight. After a two-hour trip back to my own camp, I had only a short time to wait until the first news should come in.

The first report came from the airborne units I had visited only a few hours earlier and was most encouraging in tone. As the morning wore on it became apparent that the landing was going fairly well. Next morning we went to the beaches in a destroyer and upon arrival found that the 1st and 29th U.S. Divisions, assaulting on Omaha, had finally dislodged the enemy and were proceeding swiftly inland.

The first critical objective of the Normandy campaign, which was to establish a secure beachhead with adequate avenues of supply in the area between Cherbourg and the mouth of the Orne, was fully accomplished by the end of June.

From the beginning it was the conception of Field Marshal Montgomery, Bradley, and myself that eventually the great movement out of the beachhead would be by an enormous left wheel, bringing our front onto the line of the Seine, with the whole area lying between that river and the Loire and as far eastward as Paris in our firm possession.

By July 2, 1944, we had landed in Normandy about 1,000,000 men, including thirteen American, eleven British, and one Canadian divisions. In the same period we put ashore 566,648 tons of supplies and 171,532 vehicles. It was all hard and exhausting work but its accomplishment paid off in big dividends when finally we were ready to go full out against the enemy. During these first three weeks we took 41,000 prisoners. Our casualties totaled 60,771, of whom 8975 were killed.

The July battling all along the front involved some of the fiercest and most sanguinary fighting of the war. On the American front every attack was channelized by swamps and streams and the ground was unusually advantageous to the defense.

Just after the middle of July the U.S. First Army attained, on its portion of the front, the line St. Lô to the west coast of the Cherbourg Peninsula—from which it could launch a powerful assault. General Bradley slashed his way downward to the base of the peninsula, passing through the bottleneck at Avranches, and launched his columns against the rear of the German forces.

As the enemy saw the American First Army attack gather momentum to the southward, his reaction was swift and characteristic. Chained to his general position by Hitler's orders as well as by the paralyzing action of our air forces, he immediately moved westward all available armor and reserves from the Caen area to counterattack against the narrow strip through which American forces were pouring deep into his rear.

The Air co-operation against the enemy attack was extraordinarily effective. The United States Ninth Air Force and the RAF destroyed hundreds of enemy tanks and vehicles.

When I assured Bradley that even under a temporary success by the German counter-attack he would have extensive supply support, he unhesitatingly determined to retain only minimum forces at Mortain, and to rush the others on south and east to begin an envelopment of the German spearheads.

Another factor that justified this very bold decision was the confidence that both Bradley and I had now attained in our principal battle commanders. In Patton, who took command of the Third Army on the right immediately after the breakout was achieved, we had a great leader for exploiting a mobile situation. On the American left we had sturdy and steady Hodges to continue the pressure on the Germans.

The enveloping movement from the south therefore had as its first objective the destruction or capture of the German forces in the Mortain-Falaise region, while at the same time there remained the opportunity for sweeping up remaining portions of the German First and Seventh Armies by directing an even wider employment toward the crossings of the Seine River. The operation assumed this over-all picture: Montgomery's army group was attacking generally southward against the old Normandy beachhead defenses, while Bradley's forces, with their left anchored near the position of the initial break-through, were carrying out the great envelopments intended to trap the entire German force still between his marching columns and the front of the British Twenty-first Army Group.

A well-known photograph. The Supreme Commander talks with U. S. paratroopers, whose faces are blackened in preparation for the drop into occupied France. The time: June 1944.

Inspection, just prior to D-Day.

The D-Day invasion.

"Mr. Churchill gradually became more optimistic than he had been, but he still refused to let his expectations conquer his doubts. More than once he said, 'General, if by the coming winter you have established yourself with your thirty-six Allied divisions firmly on the Continent...I will proclaim this operation to the world as one of the most successful of the war. And, if, in addition, you have secured the port at Le Havre and freed beautiful Paris from the hands of the enemy, I will assert the victory to be the greatest of modern times.'"

"Always I would reply, 'Prime Minister, the coming winter will see the Allied forces on the border of Germany itself.'"

In the meantime the Allied air forces kept up an incessant battering against any possible crossings of the Seine so as to impede the escape of any German forces that might try to cross to the north of that river before the trap could be closed.

By late July the enemy was bringing reinforcements across the Seine as rapidly as he could. Five divisions entered the battle area during the week August 5-12 but, as before, they were unable to affect the outcome.

In the face of complete disaster the enemy fought desperately to hold open the mouth of the closing pocket so as to save as much as he could from the debacle. German commanders concentrated particularly on saving armored elements, and while a disappointing portion of their Panzer divisions did get back across the Seine, they did so at the cost of great proportion of their equipment. Eight infantry divisions and two Panzer divisions were captured almost in their entirety.

The battlefield at Falaise was unquestionably one of the great "killing grounds" of any of the war areas. Roads, highways and fields were so choked with destroyed equipment and with dead men and animals that passage through the area was extremely difficult. Forty-eight hours after the closing of the gap I was conducted through it on foot, to encounter scenes that could be described only by Dante. It was literally possible to walk for hundreds of yards at a time, stepping on nothing but dead and decaying flesh.

When the Allied armies finally completed their envelopment of the German forces west of the Seine the eventual defeat of the German in western Europe was a certainty. The question of time alone remained.

The initial break out brought up one of the longest-sustained arguments that I had with Prime Minister Churchill throughout the period of the war. The discussions involved the wisdom of going ahead with Dragoon, the code name for the operation that was to bring in General Jacob L. Devers' forces through the south of France.

One of the early reasons for planning this attack was to achieve an additional port of entry through which the reinforcing divisions already prepared in America could pour rapidly into the European invasion. The Prime Minister held that we were now assured of early use of the Brittany ports and that the troops then in the Mediterranean could be brought in via Brittany, or even might better be used in the prosecution of the Italian campaign with the eventual purpose of invading the Balkans via the head of the Adriatic.

To any such change I was opposed, and since the United States Chiefs of Staff, following their usual practice, declined to interfere with the conclusions of the commander in the field, I instantly became the individual against whom the Prime Minister directed all his argument.

Although I never heard him say so, I felt that the Prime Minister's real concern was possibly of a political rather than a military nature. He may have thought that a postwar situation which would see the Western Allies posted in great strength in the Balkans would be far more effective in producing a stable post-hostilities world than if the Russian armies should be the ones to occupy that region. I told him that if this were his reason for advocating the campaign through Jugo-slavia he should go instantly to the President and lay the facts, as well as his own conclusions, on the table. I well understood that strategy can be affected by political considerations, and if the President and the Prime Minister should decide that it was worth while to prolong the war, thereby increasing its cost in men and money, in order to secure the political objectives they deemed necessary, then I would instantly and loyally adjust my plans accordingly. But I did insist that as long as he argued the matter on military grounds alone I could not concede validity to his arguments.

As usual the Prime Minister pursued the argument up to the very moment of execution. As usual, also, the second that he saw he could not gain his own way, he threw everything he had into support of the Dragoon operation. He flew to the Mediterranean to witness the attack and I heard that he was actually on a destroyer to observe the supporting bombardment when the attack went in.

Another interesting, if less pressing, discussion took place with Secretary Henry Morgenthau, on the subject of Germany's future and I expressed myself roughly as follows:

"These things are for someone else to decide, but my personal opinion is that, following upon the conclusion of hostilities, there must be no room for doubt as to who won the war. Germany must be occupied. More than this, the German people must not be allowed to escape a sense of guilt, of complicity in the tragedy that has engulfed the world. Prominent Nazis, along with certain industrialists, must be tried and punished. Membership in the Gestapo and in the SS should be taken as prima facie evidence of guilt. The General Staff must be broken up, all its archives confiscated, and members suspected of complicity in starting the war or in any war crime should be tried. But I flatly disagreed with the proposal that Germany should be reduced to a pastoral state.

These views were presented to everyone who queried me on the subject, both then and later. They were eventually placed before the President and the Secretary of State when they came to Potsdam in July 1945.

The liberation of Paris on the twenty-fifth of August had a great impact on people everywhere. Even the doubters began to see the end to Hitler. By this time enemy losses were enormous. Since our landings three of the enemy's field marshals and one army commander had been dismissed from their posts or incapacitated by wounds. Rommel was badly wounded by one of our strafing planes on July 19. Later he committed suicide to escape trial for alleged complicity in the July 20 murder plot against Hitler. One army commander, three corps commanders, and fifteen division commanders had been killed or captured. The enemy had lost 400,000 killed, wounded, or captured. Half the total were prisoners of war, and 135,000 of these had been taken in the month subsequent to July 25.

German materiel losses included 1300 tanks, 20,000 other vehicles, 500 assault guns, and 1500 pieces of artillery. In addition the German air forces had suffered extensively. More than 3500 of his aircraft had been destroyed and this in spite of the fact that the Luftwaffe had been seriously depleted before the invasion began.

With the capture of Paris we were substantially on the line that had been predicted before D-day as the one we would attain three to four months after our landing. Thus, in long-term estimate, we were weeks ahead of schedule.

Immediately after the capture of Paris, I notified General Charles de Gaulle that I hoped he, as the symbol of French resistance, would make an entrance before I had to go in or through it.

All along the front we pressed forward in hot pursuit of the fleeing enemy. In four days the British spearheads, paralleled by equally forceful American advances on their right, covered a distance of 195 miles, one of the many fine feats of marching by our formations in the great pursuit across France. By September 5, Patton's Third Army reached Nancy and crossed the Moselle River between that city and Metz. General Courtney Hodges' First Army came up against the Siegfried defenses by the thirteenth of the month and was shortly thereafter to begin the struggle for Aachen. Pushed back against the borders of the homeland, the German defenses showed definite signs of stiffening. On September 4, Montgomery's armies entered Antwerp. Marseilles had been captured on August 28 and this great port was being rehabilitated.

In the south Devers' Sixth Army Group became operational and came under my command on September 15. The continuous front under control of SHAEF (Supreme Headquarters Allied Expeditionary Force) now extended from the Mediterranean in the south to the mouth of the Rhine, hundreds of miles to the north.

During the three months beginning September 1, I spent much of my time in travel. The front was constantly broadening and distances were getting greater, so that every visit was time-consuming.

At times I received advice from friends, urging me to give up or curtail visits to troops. They correctly stated that, so far as the mass of men was concerned, I could never speak, personally, to more than a tiny percentage. They argued, therefore, that I was merely wearing myself out, without accomplishing anything significant, so far as the whole Army was concerned. With this I did not agree.

There is an old expression, "the nakedness of the battlefield." It is descriptive and full of meaning for anyone who has seen a battle. The feeling that pervades the forward areas is loneliness. There is little to be seen; friend and foe, as well as the engines of war, seem to disappear from sight when troops are deployed for a fight. Loss of control and cohesion are easy, because each man feels himself so much alone, and each is prey to the human fear and terror that to move or show himself may result in instant death. Here is where confidence in leaders, a feeling of comradeship with and trust in them, pays off.

My own direct efforts could do little in this direction. But I knew that if men realized they could talk to "the brass" they would be less inclined to be fearful of the lieutenant.

As we pushed rapidly across western Europe the wildest enthusiasm greeted the advancing Allied soldiers. In France, Belgium, Holland, Luxembourg the story was everywhere the same. The inhabitants were undernourished and impoverished, but the regaining of their individual liberty, of their right to talk freely with their neighbors and to learn of the outside world, seemed to overshadow, at least for the moment, their hunger and their privation. The people had lived in virtual captivity for more than four years.

In general, the liberated peoples were startlingly ignorant of America and the American part in the war. Our effort had been so belittled and ridiculed by Nazi propaganda that the obvious strength of the American armies completely amazed and bewildered the populations of western Europe.

The fall period was to become a memorable one because of a series of bitterly contested battles, usually conducted under the most trying conditions of weather and terrain. Walcheren Island, Aachen, the Hurtgen Forest, the Roer dams, the Saar Basin, and the Vosges Mountains were all to give their names during the fall months of 1944 to battles that, in the sum of their results, greatly hastened the end of the war in Europe. Each was of a size to compare with the largest of our Civil War battles or to Waterloo in the Napoleonic wars. In addition to the handicap of weather there was the difficulty of shortages in ammunition and supplies. The hardihood, courage, and resourcefulness of the Allied soldier were never tested more thoroughly and with more brilliant results than during this period.

A 5-day storm in mid-June had established a forty-year record for severity. Again in the autumn the floods broke another meteorological record extending back over decades. By November 1 many of the rivers were out of their banks and weather conditions along the whole front slowed up our attacks.

Capture of the approaches to Antwerp was a difficult operation. The Scheldt Estuary was heavily mined, and German forces on Walcheren Island and South Beveland Island completely dominated the water routes leading to the city.

Bradley wrote to me on September 21: "... all plans for future operations always lead back to the fact that in order to supply an operation of any size beyond the Rhine, the port of Antwerp is essential." He never failed to see that logistics would be a vital factor in the final defeat of Germany.

The amphibious assault against Walcheren, on November 1, was carried out against some of the strongest local resistance we met at any coast line during the European operation.

Final German resistance on the island was eliminated by November 9, by which time some 10,000 enemy troops had been captured, including a division commander. The cost was high. For the entire series of operations in the area our own casualties, almost entirely Canadian and British, numbered 27,633. This compared to less than 25,000 in the capture of Sicily, where we defeated a garrison of 350,000. In spite of all difficulties, Antwerp quickly became the northern bulwark of our entire logistical system.

The fighting throughout the front, from Switzerland to the mouth of the Rhine, descended during the late fall months to the dirtiest kind of infantry slugging. Advances were slow and laborious. Gains were ordinarily measured in terms of yards rather than miles. Operations became mainly a matter of artillery and ammunition and, on the part of the infantry, endurance, stamina, and courage. In these conditions infantry losses were high, particularly in rifle platoons.

Through late November and early December the badly stretched condition of our troops caused constant concern, particularly on Bradley's front. In order to maintain the two attacks that we then considered important we had to concentrate available forces in the vicinity of the Roer dams on the north and bordering the Saar on the south. This weakened the static, or protective, force in the Ardennes region.

I personally conferred with Bradley about it at various times. Our conclusion was that in the Ardennes region we were running a definite risk but we believed it to be a mistaken policy to suspend our attacks all along the front merely to make ourselves safe until all reinforcements arriving from the United States could bring us up to peak strength.

The German Sixth Panzer Army, which had appeared on our front, was the strongest and most efficient mobile reserve remaining to the enemy within his whole country. When the American attacks on that front had to be suspended early in December, we lost track of the Sixth Panzer Army and could not locate it by any means available.

Soon, it would show itself again.

On December 16, 1944, General Bradley came to my headquarters to discuss ways and means of overcoming our acute shortages in infantry replacements. Just as he entered my office a staff officer came in to report slight penetrations of our lines in the Ardennes region.

I was immediately convinced that this was no local attack; it was through this same region that the Germans launched their great attack of 1940 which drove the British forces from the Continent, and France out of the war. That first attack was led by the same commander we were now facing, Field Marshal Karl Von Rundstedt. We had always been convinced that before the Germans acknowledged final defeat in the West they would attempt one desperate counteroffensive. It seemed likely to Bradley and me that they were now starting this kind of attack.

The morning of December 17 it became clear that the German attack was in great strength. Two gaps were torn through our line . . . it was clear that the enemy was employing considerable armor and was progressing rapidly to the westward.

For the assault Von Rundstedt concentrated three armies. These were the Fifth and Sixth Panzer Armies and the Seventh Army. Included were ten Panzer and Panzer Grenadier divisions and the whole force totaled twenty-four divisions with their supporting troops.

Surprised as we were by the timing and the strength of the attack, we were not wrong in its location, nor in the conviction that it would eventually occur.

Developments were closely examined and analyzed all during December 17 and 18. By the night of the eighteenth I felt we had sufficient information of the enemy's strength, intentions, and situation, and of our own capabilities, to lay down a specific plan for our counteraction. On the early morning of December 19, accompanied by Air Marshal Tedder and a small group of staff officers, I went to Verdun, where Generals Bradley, Patton and Devers had been or-

From a little known essay on morale: "The army should not be coddled or babied, for that does not produce morale. But the army should be taught to respect itself..." A General who respected his men talks with a number leaving for a reinforcement center from Le Havre, France.

A U.S. Infantryman fights through snow and crawls under a wire fence toward surrounded U.S. forces in Bastogne...

dered to meet me. As the conference started, with everyone around a long table, I remarked: "The present situation is to be regarded as one of opportunity for us and not of disaster. There will be only cheerful faces at this conference table." True to his impulsive nature, General Patton broke out with, "Hell, let's have the guts to let the —— — ——— go all the way to Paris. Then we'll really cut 'em off and chew 'em up." Everyone, including Patton, smiled at this one, but I replied that the enemy would never be allowed to cross the Meuse.

I had already determined that it was not essential for our counterattack to begin on both flanks simultaneously. In the north, where the weight of the German attack was falling, we would be on the defensive for some days. But on the south we could help the situation by beginning a northward advance at the earliest possible moment.

I issued verbal orders for these arrangements to be undertaken on 22 December. The only way of achieving the necessary control on both flanks was to place Montgomery temporarily in command of all the northern forces and direct Bradley to give his full attention to affairs on the south.

The German attack had quickly gained the popular name of "Battle of the Bulge," because of the rapid initial progress made by the heavy assault against our weakly held lines, with a resulting penetration into our front that reached a maximum depth of some fifty miles.

Early in the battle, on December 22, I issued one of the few "Orders of the Day" I wrote during the war. In it I said:

> By rushing out from his fixed defenses the enemy may give us the chance to turn his great gamble into his worst defeat. So I call upon every man, of all the Allies, to rise now to new heights of courage, of resolution and of effort. Let everyone hold before him a single thought—to destroy the enemy on the ground, in the air, everywhere—destroy him! United in this determination and with unshakable faith in the cause for which we fight, we will, with God's help, go forward to our greatest victory.

Bastogne lay in the general path of the sector of advances of the German Fifth Panzer Army.

The defense of Bastogne was not only a spectacular feat of arms but had a definite effect upon the outcome of the entire battle.

One of the breaks in our favor occurred December 23. This was a sudden, temporary clearing of the weather in the forward areas which released our air forces to plunge into the battle. From that moment onward, with some interruptions owing to bad weather, our battle-tested ground-air tactical team began again to function with its accustomed efficiency. The air forces bombed sensitive spots in the German communications system, attacked columns on the road, and sought out and reported to us every significant move of the hostile forces.

On December 26, Patton had established tenuous contact with the garrison of Bastogne, while on the north the Germans had just been repulsed from a very determined, and what proved to be their final, major attack on that flank. By this time the garrison at Bastogne was proving to be a serious thorn in the side of the German high command. As long as it was in our hands, the German corridor to the westward was cut down to the narrow neck lying between Bastogne on the south and Stavelot on the north.

On January 3, the First Army, spearheaded by the VII Corps, began its attacks on the northern flank and all danger from the great German thrust had disappeared. From that moment on it was merely a question of whether we could make sufficient progress through his defenses and through the snowbanks of the Ardennes to capture or destroy significant portions of his forces.

The losses on both sides in the Battle of the Ardennes were considerable. Field commanders estimated that in the month ending January 16 the enemy suffered 120,000 serious casualties.

In addition to personnel losses the enemy suffered heavy casualties in tanks, assault guns, planes, and motor transport. These we estimated at the time as 600 tanks and assault guns, 1600 planes, and 6000 other vehicles.

Altogether, we calculated our losses at a total of 77,000 men, of whom about 8000 were killed, 48,000 wounded, and 21,000 captured or missing. Our tank and tank destroyer losses were 733.

I wanted to pass to the general offensive as quickly as possible because I was convinced that in the Battle of the Bulge the enemy had committed all of his remaining reserves. I counted on a greatly weakened resistance from that moment onward, both because of losses suffered by the Germans and because of the widespread discouragement that I felt sure would overtake his armies. Moreover—and this was very important—the Russians had opened their long-awaited and powerful winter offensive on January 12.

Operations were planned in three general phases, beginning with a series of attacks along the front to destroy the German armies west of the Rhine. The next phase would comprise the crossing of that river and establishment of major bridgeheads. Thereafter we would initiate the final advances that we were sure should carry us into the heart of Germany and destroy her remaining power to resist.

Somewhere during this final advance we would meet portions of the Red Army coming from the east.

The Rhine itself presented a very strong defensive front, and strategists believed that the difficult Allied crossing would not become possible until May. However, by March 7th the rapid central advance of the United States First Army under General Bradley brought the assaulting troops of the 111 Corps to the Ludendorff Bridge at Remagen.

The Germans had, of course, made elaborate advance preparations to destroy the Rhine bridges. The Ludendorff Bridge was no exception. However, so rapid was the advance of the American troops and so great was the confusion created among the defenders that indecision and doubt overtook the detachment responsible for detonation of the charges under the bridge. Apparently the defenders could not believe that the Americans had arrived in force and possibly felt that destruction of the bridge should be delayed in order to permit withdrawal of German forces which were still west of the river in strength.

Bradley instantly telephoned me. I was at dinner in my Reims headquarters with the corps and division commanders of the American airborne forces when Bradley's call came through. When he reported that we had possession of a permanent bridge across the Rhine I could scarcely believe my ears. He and I had frequently discussed such a development as a remote possibility but never as a well-founded hope.

I fairly shouted into the telephone: "How much have you got in that vicinity that you can throw across the river?"

He said, "I have more than four divisions but I called you to make sure that pushing them over would not interfere with your plans."

I replied, "Well, Brad, we expected to have that many divisions tied up around Cologne and now those are free. Go ahead and shove over at least five divisions instantly, and anything else that is necessary to make certain of our hold."

His answer came over the phone with a distinct tone of glee: "That's exactly what I wanted to do but the question had been raised here about conflict with your plans, and I wanted to check with you."

That was one of my happy moments of the war. Broad success in war is usually foreseen by days or weeks, with the result that when it actually arrives higher commanders and staffs have discounted it and are immersed in plans for the future. This was completely unforeseen. We were across the Rhine, on a permanent bridge; the traditional defensive barrier to the heart of Germany was pierced.

The French First Army under Devers had already pushed up to the Rhine in the South. Shortly thereafter Allied forces in the north had equal success, leaving only the important Saar basin in German control west of the Rhine by March 10th. This too was eliminated at a great cost to the Germans by March 25th.

In retrospect it is difficult to understand why the German, as he saw his armies north of the Moselle undergo complete collapse and destruction, failed to initiate a rapid withdrawal of his forces west of the river in order to remove them from their exposed position and employ them for defense of the Rhine.

More than once in prior campaigns we had witnessed similar examples of what appeared to us sheer tactical stupidity. I personally believed that the cause was to be found in the conqueror complex: the fear of a military dictator that to give up a single foot of ravished territory would be to expose the rotten foundation on which was built the myth of invincibility.

During the month-long campaign our captures of German prisoners averaged 10,000 per day. This meant that the equivalent of twenty full divisions had been subtracted from the German Army, entirely aside from normal casualties in killed and wounded. The enemy suffered great losses in equipment and supplies, and in important areas of manufacture and sources of raw materials.

Just to the north of the Remagen bridgehead ran the Sieg River, which flanked the Ruhr region on the south. So vital was the safety of the Ruhr to the German warmaking capacity that the enemy hastily assembled along the Sieg all of the remaining forces that he could spare from other threatened areas in the west.

Montgomery was always a master in the methodical preparations of forces for a formal, set-piece attack. In this case he made the most meticulous preparations for crossing the river north of the Ruhr.

His assault was planned on a front of four divisions. Supporting these divisions was an airborne attack. Normal use of airborne forces was to send them into battle prior to the beginning of ground attack so as to achieve maximum surprise and create confusion among defending forces before the beginning of the ground assault. In this instance Montgomery planned to reverse the usual sequence. He decided to make the river crossing under cover of darkness, to be followed the next morning by the airborne attack.

The assault, on the night of March 23-24, was preceded by a violent artillery bombardment. I remained with the forward troops during the night. With the arrival of daylight I went to a convenient hill from which to witness the arrival of the airborne units, which were scheduled to begin their drop at ten o'clock. The airborne troops were carried to the assault in a total of 1572 planes and 1356 gliders; 889 fighter planes escorted them during the flight, and 2153 other fighters provided cover over the target area and established a defensive screen to the eastward.

Fog and the smoke of the battlefield prevented a complete view of the airborne operation but I was able to see some of the action.

Operation Varsity, the name given to the airborne phase of this attack, was the most successful airborne operation we carried out during the war.

During the morning I met the Prime Minister with Field Marshal Brooke. Mr. Churchill always seemed to find it possible to be near the scene of action when any particularly important operation was to be launched. On that morning he was delighted, as indeed were all of us. He exclaimed over and over, "My dear General, the German is whipped. We've got him. He is all through." The Prime Minister was merely voicing what all of us felt and were telling each other.

Even Hitler, fanatic that he was, must have had lucid moments in which he could not have failed to see that the end was in sight. He was writing an ending to a drama that would far exceed in tragic climax anything that his beloved Wagner ever conceived.

On March 31, I issued a proclamation to the German troops and people, urging the former to surrender and the latter to begin planting crops. I described the hopelessness of their situation and told them that further resistance would only add to their future miseries.

My purpose was to bring the whole bloody business to an end. But the hold of Hitler on his associates was still so strong and was so effectively applied elsewhere, through the medium of the Gestapo and SS, that the nation continued to fight.

Field Marshal Model commanded the German forces in the Ruhr pocket. He first attempted to break out of the encirclement by an attack toward the north, and he was defeated. A similar attempt toward the south was equally abortive, and the German garrison had nothing to look forward to except eventual surrender. Bradley kept hammering back the enemy lines and on April 14 the Americans launched a local attack that split the pocket in two. Within eighteen days of the moment the Ruhr was surrounded it had surrendered with an even greater number of prisoners than we had bagged in the final Tunisian collapse almost two years earlier.

The end of the war brought jubilation but not before some of its most hideous scenes were stamped indelibly in the mind of mankind. At a concentration camp at Ohrdurf, the Supreme Commander and a party of senior officers, including Generals Bradley and Patton, inspect evidence of the Nazi treatment of prisoners. Russian and Polish prisoners shot by their captors cover the ground.

Unconditional surrender. General Eisenhower with Soviet General Suslaparov at Rheims.

General Patton's army had overrun and discovered Nazi treasure, hidden away in the lower levels of a deep salt mine. A group of us descended the shaft, almost a half mile under the surface of the earth.

At the bottom were huge piles of German paper currency, apparently heaped up there in a last frantic effort to evacuate some of it before the arrival of the Americans. In one of the tunnels was an enormous number of paintings and other pieces of art.

In another tunnel we saw a hoard of gold, tentatively estimated by our experts to be worth about $250,000,000, most of it in gold bars.

Crammed into suitcases and trunks and other containers was a great amount of gold and silver ornaments obviously looted from private dwellings through-out Europe. All the articles had been flattened by hammer blows, to save storage space, and then merely thrown into the receptacle, apparently pending an opportunity to melt them down into gold or silver bars.

The same day I say my first horror camp. It was near the town of Gotha. I never felt able to describe my emotional reactions when I first came face to face with indisputable evidence of Nazi brutality and ruthless disregard of every shred of decency.

I have never at any other time experienced an equal sense of shock.

I visited every nook and cranny of the camp because I felt it my duty to be in a position from then on to testify at first hand about these things in case there ever grew up at home the belief or assumption that "the stories of Nazi brutality were just propaganda." Some members of the visting party were unable to go through the ordeal. I not only did so but as soon as I returned to Patton's headquarters that evening I sent communications to both Washington and London, urging the two governments to send instantly to Germany a random group of newspaper editors and representative groups from the national legisla-tures. I felt that the evidence should be immediately placed before the American and British publics in a fashion that would leave no room for cynical doubt.

In the north Montgomery's Twenty-first Army Group advanced toward Bremen and Hamburg and pushed a column forward to the Elbe to protect the northern flank of Bradley's advance.

When Bradley's army group was firmly established on the Elbe, the stage was set for the final Allied moves of the campaign. The enemy was split into independent commands in the north and south and had no means of restoring

A toast to victory. Left to right: Field Marshal Bernard Montgomery, General Dwight D. Eisenhower, Soviet Marshal Gregori Zhukov, British Air Chief Marshal Sir Arthur Tedder.

a single front against the Russians or ourselves. With his world collapsing about him, the German soldier lost most of his desire to fight. During the first three weeks of April the Western Allies captured more than a million prisoners.

Our troops were everywhere swarming over western Germany and there were few remaining targets against which the air force could be directed without danger of dropping their bombs on either our own or the Russian troops.

The first direct suggestion of surrender that reached SHAEF came from Himmler, who approached Count Bernadotte of Sweden in an attempt to get in touch with Prime Minister Churchill. On April 26, I received a long message from the Prime Minister, discussing Himmler's proposal to surrender the western front. I regarded the suggestion as a last desperate attempt to split the Allies and so informed Mr. Churchill. I strongly urged that no proposition be accepted or entertained unless it involved a surrender of all German forces on all fronts.

However, until the very last the Germans never abandoned the attempt to make a distinction between a surrender on the western front and one on the eastern. With the failure of this kind of negotiation German commanders finally had, each in his own sector, to face the prospect of complete annihilation or of military surrender.

The first great capitulation came in Italy. Alexander's forces had waged a brilliant campaign throughout the year 1944 and by April 26, 1945, had placed the enemy in an impossible situation. Negotiations for local surrender began and on April 29 the German commander surrendered. All hostilities in Italy were to cease May 2.

Montgomery's forces arrived in Lubeck May 3. By then, a great change in the governmental structure of Germany had taken place. Hitler had committed suicide and the tattered mantle of his authority had fallen to Admiral Karl Doenitz. The admiral directed that all his armies everywhere should surrender to the Western Allies. Thousands of dejected German soldiers began entering our lines.

On May 5 a representative of Doenitz arrived in my headquarters. At the same time we were informed that the German Government had ordered all of its U-boats to return to port. I at once passed all this information to the Russian high command who had designated a Red Army officer to come to my headquarters as the Russian representative in any negotiations that Doenitz might propose. I informed them that I would accept no surrender that did not involve simultaneous capitulation everywhere.

Doenitz at last saw the inevitability of compliance and the surrender instrument was signed by Jodl at two forty-one in the morning of May 7. All hostilities were to cease at midnight May 8.

After the necessary papers had been signed by General Jodl and General Smith, with the French and Russian representatives signing as witnesses, General Jodl was brought to my office. I asked him through the interpreter if he thoroughly understood all provisions of the document he had signed.

He answered, "*Ja.*"

# PART THREE

So FAR AS I can now recall, the earliest serious suggestion that I might become a presidential candidate one day was made by Virgil Pinkley, a newspaper correspondent in the North African theater, in 1943.

To say that I was astonished by Pinkley's suggestion is far from an exaggeration; my reaction was that he was something of a humorist.

"Virgil," I said, "you've been standing out in the sun too long."

From that date onward similar suggestions came periodically, but thereafter, on guard, I merely laughed them off, until one day when President Harry Truman, riding with General Bradley and me in Berlin after the European armistice in 1945, abruptly said that he would help me get anything I might want, including the presidency in 1948.

After that conversation I began to realize the necessity of expressing replies to queries about personal political possibilities in something more than jocular retort.

A few months afterward, late in 1945, I was ordered back to the United States and assigned as Chief of Staff of the United States Army, and this subject was so often brought up to me so to grow more than tiresome.

Shortly before the scheduled date for the 1948 nominating primaries in New Hampshire, a newspaper publisher in that state, Leonard V. Finder, wrote me a long letter urging that I allow my name to be entered on the Republican slate there. Having thus been given a fine opportunity to clarify my position, I drafted a reply....

"My decision to remove myself completely from the political scene is definite and positive. I know you will not object to my making this letter public to inform all interested persons that I could not accept nomination even under the remote circumstances that it were tendered me."

Several months earlier General Bradley had reported that he could soon leave the Veterans Administration, and in February 1948 I turned the office of Chief of Staff over to him. I promptly began terminal leave and in the spring of 1948 went to Columbia University as its president.

I continued to turn a deaf ear to those who refused to give up their attempts to make me a political figure.

This attitude did not mean that I was unconcerned about national affairs, including those with pronounced political overtones. Indeed, I was disturbed by what seemed to be a trend in thinking among our people, particularly the young, which held that problems—all problems—confronting us fell within the purview and responsibility of the federal government; that hard work on the part of the individual was no longer the key to his own social and financial betterment. I protested, in a casual although public talk, against a tendency to think that we, regardless of our earning capacity, should all eat caviar and drink champagne throughout our lives, where hot dogs and beer might be more appropriate. For this homely observation I was, much to my amusement, taken severely to task in an editorial in the Columbia College newspaper, *The Spectator*.

But the drift toward federal paternalism was not the only thing that disturbed me. The panic with which the public had demanded—and our political leaders had acceded to—rapid demobilization of America's armed forces after World War II presaged the possibility of a new wave of isolationism similar to that which followed World War I. Though we did not fully succumb to our traditional faith in isolation—largely because of the continuation of the Soviet conspiracy to achieve world domination—we were reducing our military forces drastically. There were too many who did not yet understand that without strength we could neither choose isolation nor be honorably involved in world councils.

My feelings about such issues had long since convinced me that it would be impossible for me ever to adopt a political philosophy so narrow as to merit the label "liberal," or "conservative," or anything of the sort. I came to believe, as I do to this day, that an individual can only examine and decide for himself each issue in a framework of philosophic conviction dedicated to responsible progress—always in the light of what he believes is good for America as a whole—and let the pundits hang the labels as they may.

Again I began receiving a volume of mail from people with politics on their minds—so voluminous, approximately twenty thousand letters, cards and wires in a single week, that at times it overwhelmed the university's postal facilities.

The 1948 Republican Convention took place earlier than the Democratic. When the Republican delegates assembled in Philadelphia in late June, it became clear that Governor Thomas E. Dewey would probably be nominated. Except for one devoted friend, who had been badgered to come as a messenger from the Philadelphia scene by those who did not think Dewey could be elected, I refused to see anyone, to answer any telephone call, or to reply to any telegram or letter coming from that city. I asserted that my New Hampshire letter spoke for itself and still expressed my fixed decision.

Upon the nomination of Governor Dewey the bombardment took an unexpected turn. Many Democrats decided that my letter to Mr. Finder, refusing to enter the political arena, referred only to the Republican party; they apparently assumed that in their case my answer would be different. Just before the Democratic Convention in mid-July, a renewed rush of messages, telephone calls, and visitors engulfed me. It became clear that another public statement was necessary. "I...could not accept nomination for any public office or participate in a partisan political contest."

This solved the difficulty through the 1948 presidential election. Until November of that year my mind was free of the subject. But almost within hours after Truman's defeat of Dewey, the process began once again; now the pleas were that I should seek the Republican nomination in 1952.

My preference, whenever had I thought of a retirement career, inclined me toward a small school in a rural setting. In such a place, where friendly ties with students and faculty could be easily developed, I felt I might hope to share with them some lessons in hindsight from a reasonably full life. Possibly I visualized myself as a campus character whose lack of scholarly achievements would be offset by an ability to talk freely and fully about the world. Such a role I would have loved and it would have been easy. Columbia, on the other hand, was a formidable challenge.

Located in the world's greatest city, Columbia University was an international mecca for students and scholars. All sorts and conditions of men and women walked the campus. Its twenty-six or so acres, crowded with buildings, a self-contained and even self-centered community, were a microcosm of the intellectual world, as Abilene had been of small-town America.

Famed philosophers, scientists, historians were familiar figures on the sidewalks. "Names" in every field of human knowledge and research studded the University directory. The students, who in the undergraduate and graduate

Back home. With their mother (from left) Arthur, Earl, Milton, standing and Dwight and Edgar, seated.

President Harry S. Truman has just appointed DDE Army Chief of Staff.

And a happy wedding day at Fort Monroe, Virginia.

General and Mrs. Eisenhower, whose own marriage and devotion will come to shine in the nation's memory, look on at the newlywed Captain John S. D. Eisenhower and his lovely bride, the former Barbara Jean Thompson.

schools numbered around thirty thousand, were variety itself, in race, dress, speech. In all this diversity, a single concern—the search for knowledge and its dissemination—gave the Columbia community homogeneity. As everywhere, Columbia had its share of freeloaders, of students who were happy just to get by, of faculty and staff members who cherished the shelter of a rut to the windy and dangerous slopes leading up to peaks. But these were a small minority. Most were concerned with intellectual excellence.

Above all, I saw in Columbia, because of its standing among American educational institutions and its influence on the educational process, opportunities as large and rewarding as the environment might be strange and difficult. If the faculty could stand me, I decided, I could stand the job.

When Mamie and I first saw our future residence on Morningside Heights, I was a little disturbed by the mansion-like appearance of the place. Sixty Morningside Drive, in all its weight of marble and dark oak, was a grand and formal structure architecturally. It could be brightened, even warmed up, and Mamie immediately took on that task with Elizabeth Draper, the decorator. Even at that point, I saw that there was no room in which I could hope to flee grandeur. If there had been an attic I could have remodeled, I might have designed such a room. But there was no attic and the basement was beyond redemption. On the roof, which had once housed a watertank as insurance against collapse of public supply, was a sort of "penthouse." From it, you could see all Harlem and on clear nights the lights of Long Island.

In this room, even as in the barn loft of my boyhood, I could find high above the street escape from the insistent demands of official life. Into the redone water tank room, Mamie and I moved furniture utterly ineligible for a place in the gracious rooms below but dear from long association and worn by the years. A piano dominated one corner.

Access to the retreat was by a tiny elevator, unpredictable in operation, in which four passengers were a crowd. Up there, we were as cut off from the great city about us as we would have been on a remote island, and it was the one place where I could be myself ... daubing at a canvas and covering myself with paint. My career as an alleged artist in oils had begun at Fort Myer shortly before I left the Army for Columbia.

An artist, Thomas E. Stephens of New York, began a portrait of Mamie. I was an interested spectator. Having completed a sitting for the day, he asked Mamie to go with him through the house so that they could agree on a proper place for the portrait, when finished. Sitting alone after the two of them left, it occurred to me that I might as well make use of the paints remaining on his palette to try poking away on my own. The problem was to find anything on which to begin. It happened then that my old companion, Sergeant Moaney, came into the room and I had an idea. "Sergeant," I said, "in my room there is a little box about twelve inches on each side. Will you please knock out the sides, take any kind of white cloth you can find, and stretch it on the board by tacking the edges?" Within a matter of minutes, Moaney was back with a clean dustcloth and the bottom of the box. Together, we fastened the cloth to the board.

The only subject I could think of was right before me—Mamie's unfinished portrait. So I started out and kept going until the two explorers came back about forty-five minutes later. I displayed my version of Mamie, weird and wonderful to behold, and we all laughed heartily. Tommy Stephens, for some reason, urged me to keep on trying. I did not even bother to argue; painting was beyond me. So when he said that he wanted my "painting" as a keepsake, I was glad to give it to him, this product of my first grand venture into "art."

A few days later a package arrived. Opening it, I found a present from Mr. Stephens: everything I could possibly need—except ability—to start painting. I looked upon the present as a wonderful gesture and a sheer waste of money. I had never had any instruction in painting; the only thing of possible help was a working knowledge of linear perspective, a subject we had studied at West Point.

I left the open package in my room. Each day I seemed to develop a little more curiosity about painting a picture. The result was that I took the plunge, to find that in spite of my complete lack of talent, the attempt to paint was absorbing. My most urgent need at the start was a generous-sized tarpaulin to cover the floor around the easel. The one thing I could do well from the beginning was to cover hands, clothes, brush handles, chair, and floor with more paint than ever reached the canvas. With the protection provided by the tarp, and with my painting clothes always stored in a dark recess of a closet, I succeeded in avoiding total domestic resistance to my new hobby.

The penthouse retreat at Columbia was an ideal studio. A professional might have objected to its lack of north exposure and a skylight. But privacy and quiet were more important to me than lighting. After all these years, I am still messy; my hands are better suited to an ax handle than a tiny brush. I attempt only simple compositions. My frustration is complete when I try for anything delicate. Even yet I refuse to refer to my productions as paintings. They are daubs, born of my love of color and in my pleasure in experimenting, nothing else. I destroy two out of each three I start. One of the real satisfactions is finding out how closely I come to depicting what I have in mind—and many times I want to see what I am going to do and never know what it will be.

In the White House, in bad weather, painting was one way to survive away from the desk. In a little room off the elevator on the second floor, hardly more than a closet, the easel, paints, and canvases were easy to use. Often, going to lunch, I'd stop off for ten minutes to paint. In Gettysburg, I've tried many landscapes and still lifes but with magnificent audacity, I have tried more portraits than anything else. I've also burned more portraits than anything else.

I arrived at Columbia determined to enjoy a first hand association with the students and faculty. I insisted on a change in the location of the president's office. Nicholas Murray Butler had worked on the second floor of Low Library, reaching it by a private elevator from the office of the University's secretary. This protected him against intrusion by the crowds that often thronged the rotunda, usually sightseers; it also made him inaccessible to visitors who had not gone through the red tape of appointment-making. The office was moved to the first floor. There, I hoped, both students and faculty might have direct and easy access to their President and I would not feel immured in a remote citadel.

Duties and responsibilities, whose scope I had not fully realized before I arrived, soon sealed me off from all but formal or brief association with the students. This fact became a source of vast annoyance to me. Students, the chief reason for a university's being, and for me the paramount appeal and attraction in campus life, were in danger of becoming numerical figures on forms and passing, unknown faces on campus.

Supervising the management of a vast endowment that included one of the largest real estate empires in New York; administrating an economic enterprise that employed more maintenance people, to mention just one category, than most colleges had students; satisfying the demand for speeches, alumni appearances, ceremonial functions; correcting an appalling deficit that threatened academic standards, salary scales, and Columbia's traditional objective of excellence—all these, as ravenous of energy as they were of time, fast became a moat against communications with the young men and women.

In the Army, whenever I became fed up with meetings, protocol, and paper work, I could rehabilitate myself by a visit with the troops. Among them, talking to each other as individuals, and listening to each other's stories, I was refreshed and could return to headquarters reassured that, hidden behind administrative entanglements, the military was an enterprise manned by human beings. As a university president, perhaps less sure of myself, I did not at first permit myself as much freedom as I enjoyed in Army command. The invisible and intangible rules of academic propriety and procedure were partial shackles on my personal inclinations.

With the advantages of hindsight, I know now that I should have tossed the rules into the trash can, abandoning my office and its minutiae more frequently. In one period, I did set myself the goal of visiting every classroom, office, and laboratory. Under the guidance of deans and faculty, I spent a morning or an afternoon each week dropping in on lectures, poking into corners, and occasionally getting a chance to chat briefly with students or teachers. Climbing stairs was good exercise, I suppose; at least I was usually a little tired once back in the office, and I did come to know more than I had before. But a guided tour is seldom fun and often profitless; you are apt to see only what the guide deems proper.

There were countless ways, on the other hand, in which I might have enjoyed myself and possibly done some good. I never succeeded in liberating myself from the traditional decorum and occasional pomp of the university president's role although eventually I think I would have burst my way into thoroughly enjoying life there. But I remained chief officer of everything from ritual to rentals.

During the years as an army officer, I had met many outstanding men; my command in World War II had brought me into association with great men. Columbia was a concentration of outstanding characters and superior intellects. Here and there was a bore, to be sure. But most of the men and women who make up that complex of culture and learning and buildings called Columbia were brilliant in their talk, profound in their thoughts, and enthusiastic about the university and its work. They immensely broadened my horizons. Among them, I felt myself a student who learned more from them than I could ever hope to give in return.

At Columbia, I not only made friends but was fortunate to be able to take several there with me. Certain men were invaluable to me during my time at the Pentagon. One of these was Kevin McCann, whose interest in education was deep and who was sharply sensitive to the rapidly changing conditions of the postwar years. Another was my administrative aide, Major Robert Schulz, who had joined me in the Pentagon shortly after the war. The others were Master Sergeant John Moaney and his wife Delores, who are regular members of our household, and Sergeant Leonard Dry, my principal driver.

Two trusted confidants in university affairs were Albert Jacobs, the provost, and Kevin, who as assistant to the president, was tireless in his efforts to help me, a man whose background was completely governmental and military, understand the needs and sensitivities of a faculty and others in our educational institution. Learning how to take a place in academic life was not simple but learning to like the people of Columbia was; I conceived an instant liking for many faculty members and administrators. I had only known one, Lou Little, before my arrival.

When Lou was football coach at Georgetown University, back in the twenties, I was coaching an Army team that lost to Georgetown by one point. While I was still Chief of Staff, and on the eve of my departure to take up duties at Columbia, I was given the mission of saving Lou for the university. He had been offered the head coaching job at Yale. Columbia alumni panicked. They decided that only I could persuade Lou to stay on. A group of them, headed by Bill Donovan, of the OSS in World War II, and Frank Hogan, the New York District Attorney, escorted Lou to Fort Myer for a talk. I had no professional or financial arguments to offer. I was reduced to a personal appeal. It was not at all eloquent:

"Lou, you cannot do this to me," I said. "You're one of the reasons I am going to Columbia."

The coach seemed a little flustered. But he recovered quickly and, asking for time to consider his future, we talked football, reminisced, and had a general discussion of the state of the game. For once all the years that I had spent coaching football in the Army seemed to make sense.

I continued to be uneasy about Lou's decision. And then I learned that immediately on his arrival at his hotel in Washington, he called his wife, Loretta, and said:

"Stop packing. We're not going!"

To the alumni, that success in saving Columbia from depredation by Yale might have been my largest contribution to Columbia's stature. At least I am told that whenever the alumni got together during my time there, my triumph was cited as convincing proof that I had leadership potential. Those of the Columbia family who were less concerned with football may have assessed it with a colder eye. Nevertheless, there was, I think, a substantial academic by-product, one that not everyone could see at the time.

More important than bricks and mortar was the moral and intellectual strength of Columbia, a power for good throughout the country and the Western World. To extend this strength, to channel it better to serve the nation, new growth—I thought—should be rooted in the chief asset of any university, its faculty.

The Columbia faculty, I believed, was capable of taking the lead in studying and analyzing the national viewpoint on the vast social, political, and economic problems thrust upon us after World War II. With such a venture, they would amplify the university's role so that its influence would not be restricted to campus classrooms or scholarly conferences. Among the nationwide problems that concerned us at the time were:

First—The mental and physical health of our young people. Weakness of mind and body among far too many of them had been startlingly revealed during the war years when hundreds of thousands were rejected from the country's service because they were below minimal educational and physical standards.

Second—The role of pressure groups in every area of our social and economic life. I would later make this the subject of my last address as President of the United States but even then the aggressive demands of various groups and special interests, callous or selfish, or even well intentioned, contradicted the American tradition that no part of our country should prosper except as the whole of America prospered. Unless there were changes, I felt that eventually only the promises of the extreme right and the extreme left would be heard in public places.

Third—There was a sort of torpor about individual responsibility and a disbelief that an enlightened and dedicated individual could, on his own, accomplish much for the good of all. This seemed to suggest a disregard for the meaning of American citizenship, and its obligations as well as its rights, or an ignorance of the opportunities for self-expression and self-development in our country.

For examining these and other problems, I saw on the Columbia faculty an immense pool of talent, scholarly and humane in its comprehension of human needs and aspirations, above the bias of sect and party. At first I thought of it as a sort of intellectual Supreme Court which could search through the entanglements of the problems before us and by dispassionate study, and with imaginative and profound thought, propose solutions that would win acceptance. I found that when I began to speak out on this point, many—even within the faculty itself—thought my notions were too idealistic. They may well have been right.

In any case, with Dean Philip Young of the Graduate School of Business, I began to elaborate the idea of a truly national assembly where we could mobilize in addition to the university's educational and intellectual resources other experts from every walk of life. Gathered together, free from telephone calls and urgent summons to make instant decisions, they might examine the larger problems, find a common ground of agreement about answers, and arrive at working conclusions.

There was little or no co-ordination or joint effort among the schools within

The first person to greet the new president of Columbia University was nine-year-old David Syrett. He was toting a tommy gun but his chief objective was an autograph. He got it, and a handshake, along with the comment, "Young man, this is the dirtiest hand I ever shook." Young David, wrote the older Dwight David in *At Ease,* "symbolized for me the idea that humanity would be present among the humanities and sciences."

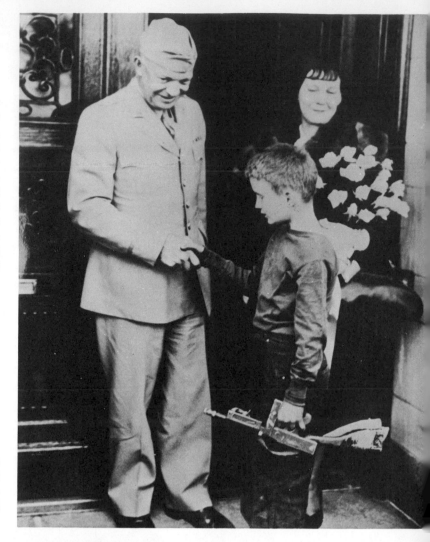

Moving men puzzle over the crates of belongings as the new President moved in. This one sent from Belgium is, a bit prematurely, labeled with "IKE"s and elephants.

Caught in a cheerful bind, the University President and Army man at a Columbia-Army game exhibits the art of alliance.

A new and better battlefield. Columbia Coach Lou Little accepts—or at least listens to—a little advice from an ex-coach.

the university at that time. The real co-ordination was with the student himself, who picked out courses, and drew on the various disciplines. But the various faculties did little together. Young and I got them working on problems and drafting papers, and then brought in businessmen, encouraging an atmosphere of the free exchange of ideas. My own education at Leavenworth and at the War College had been in the "case method" and I understood its usefulness.

Working toward this idea became an absorbing pursuit for me through most of 1949. I talked about it, thought about it almost incessantly. Till late in the year, I got no farther than a name—The American Assembly. Then, Averell Harriman became interested. He offered the family home, Arden House, with superb surrounding acreage, high on a ridge near the Hudson as a site for the Assembly. I visited the place and found it a mansion of delightful drawing rooms and endless corridors. I was enthusiastic and the property was soon transferred to Columbia.

Now known as the Harriman campus of Columbia University, the old mansion has witnessed scores of meetings concerned with almost every aspect of human society. Throughout the years, its influence, although difficult to measure, has been far reaching beyond my dreams of almost two decades ago. Much of the time I think its beginnings were my principal success as university president. The American Assembly, however, was not the only venture that meant much to me during my short academic career.

Another project undertaken at Columbia, called the Conservation of Human Resources, had its beginnings, too, in my wartime realization that we had seriously neglected the full education and preparation of our young people to be vigorous and productive members of society. This neglect was tragically tabulated, among young men, in the Armed Forces rejection records of the years 1940–45. I suspected that a fair study of these records, while they were still easily available, could produce guideposts for our future conduct as a nation. Dr. Eli Ginzberg, whose profound scholarship did not in the slightest blunt an almost boyish enthusiasm about any proposal for the betterment of human living, took over this project with a passion. The support I was able to produce in furthering his research and advancing his proposals is still one of my proudest memories of life at Columbia.

The Institute for the Study of War and Peace, the new Engineering Center headed by Dean John Dunning, the Citizenship Education Project were innovations we worked out during my Columbia years. One innovation was less a matter of intellect than of the senses. It reflected the distaste for concrete and macadam of a big-city university president who had started out as a country boy.

Our campus of twenty-six acres or so was, by New York standards, an immense real estate holding. The original planners probably thought they had ample room for buildings and open lawn. They had not foreseen an enrollment of thirty thousand. By the time I arrived, despite a few trees and small patches of grass, we were a "campus" of buildings and paving.

The factory yard appearance distressed me most of all. Leaving my office by the front entrance of Low Library on a hot day, I looked down the long flight of stone steps, across 116th Street crowded with parked cars and creeping traffic, over the gray gravel and clay of tennis courts to Butler Library, grassless, treeless. This was the physical center and heart of the university. It should be a green oasis. In my eye, I could see the hot and noisy street converted into lawn, with automobiles forever barred.

An improvement would take a little time and only a small expenditure of money, I thought. When I first presented the idea to city officials, all of them, including Mayor William O'Dwyer, were sympathetic. I quickly learned that stopping the flow of traffic through a single block of a main artery on Manhattan Island presents the city authorities with problems they think appalling and unsolvable. For one thing, New Yorkers through generations had been accustomed to free movement on 116th Street. To restrict their use of it would provoke an outraged reaction expressed in meetings and at the polls. I countered that most of the traffic was university-centered and our people would adjust their driving patterns for the sake of an attractive park.

The second objection was that fire equipment could not be barred from the street. Although I suspected that such equipment did not use 116th Street once a year, I suggested that the barrier to other traffic would be the flimsiest sort of fencing which, in an emergency, would be no obstacle to any public vehicle. At times it seemed that settling one problem spawned two or three more. The project that I thought could be accomplished within a very few months dragged on eternally. I was living in the White House, surrounded by lawn, before the dream became reality and 116th Street a pleasant mall.

All the ideas I had for changes, all the projects for advancing Columbia, were so different from the tasks of my earlier years, so novel and fresh in their appeal, that I found the work fun—or would have, if only I could have concentrated without the distraction of other demands.

Instead, I found myself caught up in a whirl of additional duties. My life at the university, exhausting enough for a neophyte in education, was complicated by a presidential summons in the fall of 1948. I was asked to go to Washington regularly to serve as senior adviser to the Secretary of Defense.

When these new duties were first presented to me, the usual assurances were made that they could be done in my spare time. Politicians thought the academic life was marked by an abundance of that! I was assured that even if my new task called for long hours occasionally, the work would still be compatible with my university role and even profitable to Columbia.

In the first flush of my arrival on campus, knowing that the trustees would expect me to be an active spokesman for the university, I had accepted numerous invitations to speak during the winter months. On the campus itself, I had become involved in enough developments to consume all my waking hours when I was not in front of a microphone. Now, the "part-time" duty in Washington turned out to be no less than a major role in the reconstruction of the military establishment.

Sometimes I was an umpire between disputing services; sometimes a hatchet-man on what Fox Conner used to call Fool Schemes. It was true that both my jobs, at the university and in Defense, were somewhat compatible; each was concerned with the expanding future and security of the nation. Most of the time they were a tolerable load, and frequently inspiring and rewarding.

But commuting by plane and train between Washington and New York ate up a good many hours. Making half a dozen speeches a week was something of a burden although, to be sure, if prepared texts were not required, the speeches were harder on the audience than on the speaker. And the ride between New York and Washington, although a soon-familiar monotonous and dreary process through familiar train yards and past endless billboards, did offer occasional leisure for relaxation, reading, or a nap.

Both Mamie and I were becoming very comfortable at Columbia, certain that ahead of us lay no sudden summons which would take us away from university life. We were so sure, in fact, that after more than a third of a century of married life, we began to think about buying a house and farm to which we could retire when my campus days were over.

While I was Chief of Staff, Mamie and I frequently discussed the sort of home that would fit us best, if we ever got one. On several occasions, we actually began making specific plans. These never got beyond sketchy scratchings. We knew that years would pass before we could do anything more than dream and talk. Now, after leaving the military and moving into Columbia, we started thinking again about a place of our own. The topic recurred regularly at Morningside Heights. For my part, I wanted an escape from concrete into the countryside. Mamie, who had spent a lifetime adjusting herself to other people's housing designs, or the lack of them, wanted a place that conformed to her notions of what a home should be. In the fall of 1950, we finally did something about it.

George and Mary Allen had recently bought a small farm in the Gettysburg area, a mile or so south of the battlefield. On it was a stone house dating back to the eighteenth century which Mary planned to restore. They urged us to consider the same sort of move. We would be within easy traveling distance of Washington and New York and we could reach any spot in the United States quickly. The idea was attractive. After all, Gettysburg had been significant in the early years of our married life* and our sentimental attachments to it were reinforced by its significance in American, as well as our personal, history.

So, one weekend, we left New York with the Allens on a farm hunting expedition. Of all the properties we saw, the one most appealing was a farm of not quite 190 acres. The house, dwarfed by an immense barn, was located at the end of a private dirt lane a half mile long.

The buildings had seen better days. So had the soil. It would take work and money to modernize it. But the view of the mountains to the west was good.

Mamie had found the place she wanted. To complete the story, I must move ahead in time. Shortly after we bought the property, we were ordered back to Europe and once again our plans for the home we had in mind were deferred. And later, entering the White House in 1953, Mamie said, "I still have no home of my own." This had become such a touchy point with her that she had made up her mind, come what may, to build her own.

She started off by deciding to restore the old farmhouse located on the ground we had bought. I had an engineering survey made and found, much to Mamie's dismay, that she could not really rebuild. While the house had a face of brick, much of it was actually a log cabin, with a brick veneer covering its walls. The logs were moldy and worm-eaten, about two hundred years old. There was nothing to do but tear the place down.

So anxious was Mamie to retain even a fragment of the original structure, that when she found one portion of the wall and a Dutch oven in which no logs had been used, she built a complete house around them. We could not enlarge the basement because the house stood on a rocky ridge, precluding blasting that would destroy the Dutch oven. This meant that to a certain extent the pattern of the house was already predetermined.

I went to a builder, Charles Tompkins, a friend of ours, and asked whether

*Cadet Eisenhower had visited the town while still at West Point and later the Eisenhowers were posted to duty there during World War I.

he would undertake construction of the building on a cost-plus basis. He said that his own work was largely in heavy construction, but he would be delighted to take on the job and would do it without charging us for company overhead.

Because he had no prepared architectural plans, the house had to be built step by step, according to Mamie's ideas. Building this way, work frequently had to be redone. Mamie occasionally forgot a detail or two. For example, when the walls were going up, we discovered that no plans had been made for central air-conditioning. Part of the walls had to be torn down so that air ducts could be installed. We found that electric switches were not in the proper places. Other work had to be done over because of our improvised design. But the work was done well and the house, although not completely convenient, did conform largely to her ideas.

Before the building began, Charlie Tompkins asked me whether I wanted to use union labor or local labor, which was not unionized but which he considered competent. I told him that as President of the United States, I would be dealing with unions and I thought it only proper to use union labor. When the house was finished, he told me that he had kept two sets of books—one of costs actually incurred and the other of what the cost had been if we had used local labor. The additional expense was $65,000.

This involved much more than a mere difference in wages, of course. It was caused by the transport of laborers, in some instances from Washington, requiring us to pay for an eight-hour day for four hours' work, with the other hours spent in traveling to and from the job. Then jurisdictional strikes in Pennsylvania delayed the work and finally, when the costs were added up, they amounted to $215,000. This did include $45,000 for projects and improvements on other than the house itself.

This was considerably more than Mamie had thought of spending at the outset. But during construction, we began to scrape the barrel. I had some savings, made after leaving the army; Mamie had some money accumulated through the years and helped by her mother, she willingly participated in meeting the costs. By mid-1955, we had a place that we could call home—and it was paid for.

From that time onward, whenever Mamie saw a piece of furniture or an article that she wanted to own, she had a place to send it rather than depending on storage facilities in Washington or elsewhere. We have now lived in our home for eleven years—counting the time spent in it on weekends during the latter part of my presidency. While it is beautiful to us, like other home builders, we have found things we would like to change. But we have learned to live with our mistakes.

And we have learned, too, that one room can constitute a home. All the others are hardly more than support or embellishment. At Gettysburg, the important room is a glassed-in porch, not much larger than a modest living room, where we spend hours. Facing east, with the morning sun brightening it and in shadow through the heat of a summer day, the furnishings casual and designed for comfort, both Mamie and I find it an oasis of relaxation. I don't expect that we will ever again attempt to build a house. Were we to do so, I think it would be built around such a porch.

Naturally, because George Allen was involved, at least at the start, there is a small story to go with this case history. When we first went down to Gettysburg to look at property, there was no place for us to stay and we decided to go to a motel. George made the reservation, signing the ledger "George Allen and party." We waited in the car. We had dinner, went to a drive-in movie (the only one I have ever been in), and went back to the motel. The man waved the registration book at us. "You can't come in until you all register," he said.

For years, ever since my name came to have a certain currency, others have registered for me. And while we were shopping for property, there was reason not to let it be known that I was the prospective purchaser. But he said, "When there are ladies involved, everyone must be registered."

I went in, signed, and when he saw my name, he seemed reassured. It has always amused this pair of old married parties, who have made their temporary homes in all parts of the world, that we had to really measure up for one night in a Pennsylvania motel.

World events determined that my career at Columbia University would be short. On the evening of December 18, 1950, while on a trip to Heidelberg College in Ohio, my wife and I were sitting comfortably in a Pullman car on the sidetracks in Bucyrus, Ohio. There a railway employee reached us with a message that a telephone call would be coming through from the President of the United States. Since, to reach the station, I was compelled to wade several hundred yards in snow more than a foot deep, it took me a considerable time to reach the little freight office where the telephone was located, but President Truman's call came through almost instantly. After giving me a background of pertinent events in Europe, he said that he had just received, from the other nations of the North Atlantic Treaty Organization, notification of their unanimous preference for a military commander. They wanted me. He said that he agreed with the choice. Would I accept the nomination?

The request caused me an initial sense of disappointment. Such a change would inevitably mean a radical disruption in the life of which Mamie and I were becoming so fond, and I hated the idea of leaving. But I believed in the NATO concept; to my mind, the future of Western civilization was dependent on its success. Furthermore, I could understand why the nations of NATO would want to have as their commander an officer familiar with Europe and whose name, because of the Allied campaign in World War II, had become associated with victory. In any event, since I was still an officer in the Army, I replied that if the President, as Commander-in-Chief, felt that I could undertake the assignment with a better chance of success than any other soldier of his choice, my affirmative answer was inevitable.

During the months after arriving in Paris I was extremely busy with many problems. One of the time-consuming tasks was to obtain agreement among the NATO nations on a plan for bringing West German forces into our security organizations.

The plan I supported was known as the European Defense Community. EDC was a plan, originated by France, in which all western European countries were to participate, including Britain, to set up a supranational army with a common uniform and agreed allocations of forces.

In addition to these politico-military matters, we had, of course, problems of a more strictly military complexion. Complete, integrated plans had to be drawn up for the defense of Western Europe against invasion from the east— as realistically as possible with the forces then existing. In February of 1951 only one American division (plus three armored cavalry regiments, computed as equivalent to a second) was stationed in Europe.

*(General Eisenhower traveled extensively, explained the advantages, negotiating differences, and persuaded heads of state, and finally secured the agreements needed to make NATO a reality.)*

During all this time a stream of visitors from the United States was flowing into my headquarters with politics almost the single subject on their minds.

Senator Henry Cabot Lodge came on Tuesday, September 4, 1951, for a visit which turned out to be, for me, significant. While many had preceded him throughout the year, he was different in that he said he was reflecting the known views of numerous large groups, many of whom now wanted to start organizing a nationwide movement to present my name before the 1952 Republican convention. Cabot, an associate and friend of mine from wartime days, presented his plea with the ardor of a crusader. Thinking to put him on the defensive at once, I asked, "You are well known in politics; why not run yourself?" Without pause his answer came back, "Because I cannot be elected."

And then Cabot put forward the point of his presentation. "You," he said flatly, "are the only one who can be elected by the Republicans to the Presidency. You *must* permit the use of your name in the upcoming primaries."

To this I was not prepared to agree. But despite my protests he argued with the tenacity of a bulldog and pounded away on this theme until, as he left, I said I would "think the matter over."

The turn of the year brought about a second and important break in my hope of remaining forever outside the political world. The New Hampshire primary was scheduled for March 11, 1952, and a candidate's party affiliation had to be known by the authorities of that state before his name could be entered in the primary.

I had, up to this time, refused to make any public move that would even imply a personal choice between the two major political parties; but events now answered this question. Earlier, Senator Lodge had been informed on an authoritative basis, by General Lucius Clay, that I was a Republican and had consistently voted the Republican ticket since I had left active military service in 1948. With the pressure building up on Lodge and the others cooperating with him to enter my name in the primary, he finally, in early January, took it upon himself to say that he could assure the New Hampshire officials that I was a Republican. He made the announcement without consulting me, probably to save me embarrassment. This done, the reporters in Paris clamored for corroboration, and I felt that, in the circumstances, I had to give it.

On February 10 Miss Jacqueline Cochran arrived on a special mission. Two days earlier there had been a mass meeting at midnight in New York's Madison Square Garden, arranged by supporters who were hoping by this means to add weight to their argument that I should become a candidate. The entire proceedings were put on film. As soon as the film was processed, Miss Cochran flew the Atlantic and brought it immediately to Paris.

Fifteen thousand people had assembled in Madison Square Garden. It was a moving experience to witness the obvious unanimity of such a huge crowd—to realize that everyone present was enthusiastically supporting me for the highest office of the land.

It was becoming clearer, every day, that I could not much longer remain actively in command of military forces in such an atmosphere.

From the beginning I had felt that I could consider completion of my job the signing of the EDC treaty by the French, and I could return to Columbia

The Koreans flee before the Chinese Communists, crowding and crawling over a bridge across the Taedong River.

A photograph taken in mid-April, 1950, which reached New York on July 7, was taken by a photographer who accompanied the Chinese Communist troops as they invaded Hainan.

General Douglas MacArthur enters his Tokyo headquarters after being informed that the President has just relieved him of his Far Eastern command.

A final visit to Germany as he prepares to relinquish his NATO command. Besieged for weeks by those who urged him to return to the U.S. and run for office, he decides that "I would abide by the decisions of my party and of the electorate if I were nominated.

"We looked around us, said good-bye to Europe, and turned toward home. Once again, Mamie and I began packing."

One of the most expressive photographs of the author, catches him—now commander of Atlantic Pact forces—as he learns that General MacArthur has been relieved.

University. This, I judged, should be accomplished by June 1. Accordingly, I requested relief from my command as of that date, while doubling my efforts to expedite the French government's agreement to the treaty.

Sometime later a letter written by George Washington on May 5, 1789, to Edward Rutledge, was presented to me by Mr. St. John Terrell. On reading it I was struck by the solemn concern expressed by Washington as he proceeded "to embark again on the tempestuous and uncertain Ocean (sic) of public life.

"Though I flatter myself the world will do me the justice to believe that at my time of life and in my circumstances, nothing but a conviction of duty could have induced me to depart from my resolution of remaining in retirement; yet I greatly apprehend that my countrymen will expect too much from me. I fear if the issue of public measure should not correspond to their sanguine expectations, they will turn the extravagant (and I may say undue) praises that they are heaping upon me at this moment into equally extravagant (though I will finally hope unmerited) censures. So much is expected, so many untoward circumstances may intervene in such a new and critical situation, that I feel an insuperable diffidence in my own abilities."

It was with much the same feeling expressed by General Washington, but also with the expectation of new experiences and new opportunities for service, that my wife and I now turned toward the future that loomed before us.

No individual can be completely or fully prepared for undertaking the responsibilities of the presidency; possibly no one can even be fully aware of their weight and difficulty, except one who had borne them. It is generally assumed, I think, that any person seriously considered by the public as a possible nominee for the office will be the possessor of a satisfactory education and competence in rather traditional fields. Certainly his ability in handling and understanding people would be of interest to the average voter, as would his training and experience in making tough and significant decisions. The basic features of his political philosophy should be fully exposed to the public and his lively interest in fundamental issues of his time should be obvious.

I was, of course, a political novice.

But because of special experiences in my past life, I was probably more acutely aware than the average citizen of the complexities, anxieties, and burdens of the life led by a head of government.

In varying assignments, over a period of many years, I had had a chance to observe and work with, among others, Prime Minister Winston Churchill;

President Franklin Delano Roosevelt; and the chief executives of the Philippines, an "emerging nation" (the term was not used then), and of France, an old nation.

In any event, while perforce recognizing the public impression that I was at last a declared candidate, there was one more condition to be satisfied before I could accept the Republican nomination, if offered: the convention would have to adopt a platform with which I could agree. I would not become the party's nominee, I told my intimates emphatically, unless I was prepared to carry out its basic campaign promises. In my view, the policies and programs of the party should be the vital factor in the decision of the American people.

After Mamie and I arrived in New York from Paris, we took off for Abilene, the Kansas town in which I spent my boyhood, to lay the cornerstone for the Eisenhower Foundation, an institution initiated in 1945 by Kansans to honor the fighting men of World War II and to promote citizenship training in the United States.

Although I was in Abilene on a political errand, it would be callous to think that the nostalgic memories of childhood there did not cross my mind. On the afternoon of June 4, 1952, I was slated to deliver a televised outdoor speech, scheduled as the first of a series of personal appearances in which I was expected to outline to the public my basic positions on current American problems.

Rain began about noon. It was no Kansas spring shower; it was a drenching downpour, the kind we used to call, fifty years ago in that region, a "gully washer."

At five o'clock the time came for me to mount the rostrum. A raincoat was still a necessity, and to negotiate the mud and puddles of the open field between the car and the stand, I had to roll my trousers to the knees.

Because the talk was the first of what was planned as a series between the time of my homecoming and the opening of the Republican National Convention, it was general in its tenor. I called attention again to the need for alertness and firmness in our attitude toward the ambitions of world Communism, and the utter futility of any policy of isolation.

I spoke also of a series of internal dangers besetting us. The first of these I listed was the increasing trend toward unreasonable antagonisms among different economic groups in our country. I put myself on record as an enemy of inflation and expressed the conviction that excessive taxation could destroy the incentive to excel.

I spoke once more against the evil of centralization of government and against dishonesty or corruption on any of its levels.

The next morning we confirmed, both from newspapers and telephone calls from friends, that the reaction to my afternoon performance were far from flattering. Criticisms were voiced about the weather, my appearance, my delivery and, finally, the substance of my speech. One rabid Taft supporter, Congressman B. Carroll Reece of Tennessee, said, "It looks like he's pretty much for home, mother and heaven."

That morning I was scheduled to meet with the press at the local theater, which in my youth we used to call the "Opry House."

And of course there was the inevitable question: "Did you ever dream someday when you left Abilene you would come back, running for the Presidency of the United States?" I told them that as a young boy I had great difficulty in determining whether I wanted to be a railroad conductor or another Hans Wagner, a baseball hero. Later that day an Abilene friend called my attention to a youthful prophecy by a classmate writing in our high school yearbook of 1909. I would grow up, he predicted, to be a professor of history at Yale; my older brother Edgar would be President of the United States.

Unlike the verdict on my first-day appearance in Abilene, friends and most of the press gave me a satisfactory grade on the morning's meeting. This was possibly because I have always enjoyed the give and take of the questions and answers of a press conference far more than I do the delivery of a set speech, even though it is easier in a prepared talk to present in more exact fashion a specific attitude on a difficult question than it is in an off-the-cuff answer.

My Abilene visit was, for me, the beginning of new kind of life.

*(The next month was filled with the politics and complicated processes of nomination, trips about the country and meetings with visiting delegates, all of which culminated at the Republican Convention in Chicago on July 12.)*

At the end of the first ballot I had 595 votes—9 short of victory. Taft had 500, Warren 81. Suddenly the head of the Minnesota delegation, Senator Edward Thye, leaped to his feet, demanding the floor. He had earlier cast 19 votes for his state's favorite son, Harold Stassen. The chair recognized him.

"Minnesota," he said, "wishes to change its vote to Eisenhower."

It was all over.

My acceptance speech did not attempt to reach for eloquence or to become a vehicle for displaying any fancied oratorical ability. It was meant to be a serious, sober exposition of the problems before the Republican party and the purposes we hoped to achieve through a November victory at the polls.

I said that I accepted their summons to lead a crusade, a "crusade for freedom in America and freedom in the world..."

That evening Mr. and Mrs. Richard Nixon, Mamie, and I went before the convention, and I delivered my acceptance speech. The events of seven and one-half months now seemed to completely contradict and belie everything I had been saying since leaving Europe in 1945. I learned again that the word "never" is rarely used correctly in expressing human intentions. My arguments, protestations, and sincere belief for years had now become as nothing.

The earliest national election that I can recall was that of 1896, in which William McKinley opposed William Jennings Bryan. As a little boy in Abilene, I had helped campaign that year by marching in a nighttime parade with a flaming torch made of a rag soaked in coal oil. Now, fifty-six years later, my own name was at the head of the Republican ticket.

Once we began active compaigning, I decided, there would be no letup; the fight would be carried on to midnight of election eve at high intensity.

"Right after Labor Day, I'll really start swinging," I told a group of political and labor representatives who came to see me on August 28.

Only people who have lived and worked on a whistle-stopping train can fully grasp the urgent, whirling grind that is the daily and hourly portion of such a barnstorming organization. Though the airplane and television have worked to make this kind of campaign a thing of the past, the memories of my experience in 1952, the last year in which whistle-stopping was the major mode of electioneering, still remain with me.

The train pulls into a station for a scheduled seven-minute stop, for example. The instant the wheels cease turning, the candidate, who lives in the rearmost section of the last car on the train, steps blithely out to face the crowd, doing his best to conceal with a big grin the ache in his bones, the exhaustion in his mind. Armed with a card on which he—or an assistant—has written three or four words to remind him of the particular subjects he must mention, and the local candidates for whom he wants to express support at this stop, he awaits cessation of the crowd's clamor—which he fervently prays will consume at least two minutes of his alloted seven. Then he launches into a talk that he is convinced, by his battered memory, must certainly fail because it has been delivered over and over again, never-ending and tiresome.

But quickly he feels within himself a transformation. Although as he came out to the platform he was bored, resentful, or even sorry for himself, invariably the excitement generated by the crowd buoys him up—suddenly he is anxious

Much of the U.S. decides that it "Likes Ike" and the slogan abounds, including those in a (peaceful) demonstration at Columbia University.

After the candidate's wife responded with her own button ("IKE LIKES ME"), he seemed to have the last word.

Campaigning. In Salisbury, North Carolina, the candidate and his wife were serenaded— at 2 A.M. by a crowd of students. In Austin, Texas, at 5:30 A.M., a crowd called to them. "More than once we had to appear on the platform tousled, sleepy-eyed, and wearing old bathrobes. Because one enterprising photographer caught them in his garb early in the morning, other photographers on the campaign train, who had been asleep, besieged press secretary Jim Hagerty to have the incident re-staged. "Because of our friendship with the photographic group, we complied." The Eisenhowers dutifully donned bathrobes and waved. "Their gratitude was satisfying," wrote the author in *Mandate for Change*. "Every man implied they were going to vote Republican."

to make his planned points; he strives for new thoughts; he speaks enthusi-astically of Congressman Blank; he seeks for lucidity, conciseness, and logic in the exposition of his policies. He seems to feel that he owes it to these people to expose to them his beliefs, his convictions, his hopes and aspirations for our country. He almost wishes he could have those two minutes back, to share his wisdom more generously with his audience.

At the appointed time the train slowly moves out. Now, as he calls his good-bys, he feels a genuine regret that his stay has been so short. Then, out of sight once more, he stumbles back into the car, to an inviting couch where he tries, for a moment to revitalize himself for the next chore.

Throughout the day, whenever there was a moment, I was always writing and correcting—at times missing a meal as a a result. Only at the last possible minute was any speech ever finished, to be turned over to the typists and hur-riedly mimeographed for the press.

The moment this happened, I normally began the process of preparing the next address. And about the time I could settle down to this, the whistle would blow for the next stop.

And every night there was a platform talk to be delivered, formal or informal.

Occasionally our train would be parked for brief periods in switching yards, and invariably this would become known to people in the neighborhood, who would promptly gather around the car where Mamie and I lived. When this happened at unseemly hours, my wife and I would find ourselves either asleep or otherwise unprepared for greeting well-wishers. More than once we had to appear on the back platform tousled, sleepy-eyed, and wearing old bathrobes, just to give a wave and a greeting.

Though the routine, repeated day after day, was grueling, there were too many unusual happenings along the way, serious or amusing, to class the expe-rience as monotonous.

One time a teleprompter operator, failing to notice I was extemporizing, got so far ahead of me that I never could catch up. On another occasion a motor-cycle policeman, eager to get me to my hotel, took me on a short cut—away from my own motorcade.

In a Detroit speech on October 24 I announced my intention, if elected, to go to Korea before the following January to determine for myself what the conditions were in that unhappy country. A few days earlier, C. D. Jackson, a friend and adviser, had come to me to express the hope that I would announce such a purpose.

My feeling about the idea was the need for making the trip if elected; his was on the effect a public announcement of this intention would have on the election.

On the final day of campaigning I returned to Boston where, in addition to a long motorcade through its narrow, crowded street, a rally was held in the Boston Garden. Later, at 11 P.M., a nationwide television program was broadcast in which Dick and Pat Nixon participated with Mamie and me. In the final minutes Dick and I urged all citizens to vote and conveyed our grateful thanks to all the people who had participated in this renewal of America's great quadrennial competition. On the stroke of midnight the campaigning was to end.

But there was one more wholly unscheduled, insignificant, but unforgettable incident to complete the day.

Hank Griffin, a photographer, had an idea that he thought would be interesting to his paper. He wanted to make a picture that would show the Republican nominees, with their wives, under a large clock, at the second midnight arrived.

To set up the photograph he had secured a large wall clock, but encountered great difficulty in finding a method of mounting it immediately over our heads for the desired composition. Finally he found a tall cloak stand and, using adhesive tape, fastened his clock to the upper hooks.

With everything ready, and the hour and second hands pointing to twelve, he asked, with a big smile, "Please look this way!" With this, bang! the clock fell, striking a sharp blow on my bald head and producing a cut from which the blood flowed for several seconds. The poor photographer. Never had I seen anyone suffer more embarrassment and chagrin than Hank Griffin.

There was little for us to do until the votes were counted and the election decided at some point during the following night.

The verdict: we had taken about 55 percent of the popular vote and 442 to 89 electoral votes, winning by a landslide margin of more than six and a half million votes.

When Mamie and I left the hotel we were made sharply aware, through a very simple occurrence, of a complex change in our lives. As we walked out to Park Avenue, bent to get into our car, we found in the front seat, instead of our own driver, two complete strangers. There was a moment's pause—then we knew. From that moment on we were to be transported, guarded, and protected by the United States Secret Service.

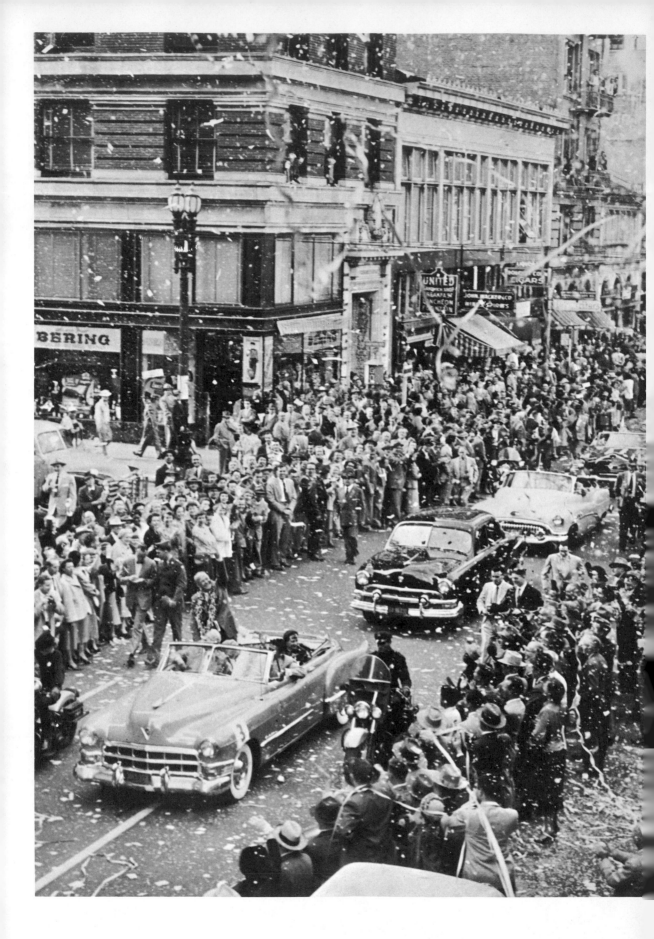

Into San Francisco for the convention, and the nomination.

And a 39-year-old Californian, Senator Richard M. Nixon and his wife show their reaction to the Senator's place on the ticket as running mate.

On January 21, 1953, shortly after 7:30 A.M., I entered the oval room of the West Wing of the White House, destined to be my office for the next eight years. The office of the President of the United States, as compared to the sumptuous quarters of many business leaders and of most Cabinet officials, is a surprisingly plain room. I had been in it many times before; its simplicity seemed to me most appropriate for the American head of state.

Remembering my beginnings, I had to smile. If my chances of walking into this room had been calculated when I was born in Denison, Texas, in 1890, they would have been approximately zero. And yet the homely old saw had proved to be true: in the United States, any boy can grow up to be President.

I sat down at the massive desk. One drawer was locked. I rang for William Simmons, the White House Office receptionist.

"Mr. Simmons," I asked, "is there a key to this desk? I can't get into this drawer." He produced the key; there in the drawer lay a small pile of confidential reports left by President Truman.

As I left my office late on the evening of January 22, I paused for a moment to write to myself:

My first full day at the President's Desk. Plenty of worries and difficult problems.... The result is that today just seems like a continuation of all I've been doing since July '41—even before that.

This attitude did not last long. One tiny incident that helped shatter it was nothing more than a telephone call from General Omar Bradley, then Chairman of the Joint Chiefs of Staff.

Hanging up the receiver, I turned to my secretary, Mrs. Ann C. Whitman. "I've just learned a lesson from Omar Bradley," I said. "He addressed me over the phone as 'Mr. President.'"

My telephone conversation was not with a stranger or short-time acquaintance—it was with a man who for forty years had called me "Ike," as I had called him "Brad." His salutation put me on notice: from then onward, for as long as I held the office, I would, except for my family, to a very definite degree be separated from all others, including my oldest and best friends. I would be far more alone now than when commanding the Allied forces in Europe in World War II.

Of the problems confronting me early in 1953 none required more urgent attention than the war in Korea. By election time in 1952 American casualties

In a belated resignation,
the man gives up one
Presidency for another.

had reached a total of 21,000 killed, 91,000 wounded, and 13,000 missing, making this the fourth most costly conflict in United States history, ranking only behind the Civil War and two World Wars.

Like every other American, I deeply resented the unprovoked and cold-blooded attack against South Korea (on that June day in 1950) and believed that we could not afford to yield an inch to the Communist aggression there. My trip to Korea as President-Elect gave me some personal knowledge of the situation, including the terrain, the combat conditions, and the leaders involved.

The United States entered the Korean War to carry out a "police action," with no objective more ambitious than the expulsion of Communist forces from the Republic of Korea. It is quite probable that the Communists expected, when they made their attack, a cheap and easy victory, believing that neither the United States nor any other Western power would assume the risk of general war in order to defend that newly independent country.

But now, in the spring of 1953, I was President and the war had dragged on for more than two and a half years. I considered several possible lines of action. First of all would be to let the war drift without a change in policy. If a satisfactory armistice could not be quickly achieved, continuing this way seemed to me intolerable. We were sustaining casualties for little, if any gain.

If we decided upon a major, new type of offensive, the present policies would have to be changed and new ones agreed to by our allies. Foremost would be the possible use of small atomic weapons. But an American decision to use them at that time would have created strong disrupting feelings between ourselves and our allies.

Of course, there were other problems, not the least of which would be the possibility of the Soviet Union entering the war. In nuclear warfare the Chinese Communists would have been able to do little. But we knew that the Soviets had atomic weapons in some quantity and estimated that they would soon explode a hydrogen device. Of all the Asian targets which might be subjected to Soviet bombing, I was most concerned about the unprotected cities of Japan.

The lack of progress in the long-stalemated talks—they were then recessed—and the nearly stalemated war demanded, in my opinion, definite measures on our part to put an end to these intolerable conditions. One possibility was to let the Communist authorities understand that, in the absence of satisfactory progress, we intended to move decisively without inhibition in our use of weapons, and would no longer be responsible for confining hostilities to the Korean Peninsula. We would not be limited by any world-wide gentleman's agreement. In India and in the Formosa Straits area, and at the truce negotiations at Panmunjom, we dropped the word, discreetly, of our attitude. We were sure it would reach Soviet and Chinese Communist ears.

Soon the prospects for armistice negotiations seemed to improve.

On April 9 Korean President Syngman Rhee wrote me a frank letter of protest criticizing the Communists' recent offer for resumption of peace negotiations. If a peace agreement should be arranged that would allow the Chinese to remain in Korea, Rhee wrote, South Korea would feel justified in asking all her allies to get out of the country except those who would be willing to join in a drive northward to the Yalu.

The Rhee letter was extreme. I answered promptly, in an effort to restrain and reassure him.

I expressed sympathy with his aspirations and those of the Korean people to bring an end to the artificial and unnatural division of their country, and with their desire to expel the Chinese invader. We would seek a settlement of the problems confronting Korea but such an effort would be nullified if the Rhee government should take actions which could not be supported by the

Inauguration. "Custom decreed that the outgoing and incoming Presidents ride down Pennsylvania Avenue together." The incoming Eisenhower asked the outgoing Truman who had ordered his son, John Eisenhower, back from Korea for the Inauguration. "I did," said the President. And a grateful father thanked him sincerely.

Fulfilling a campaign promise, President-elect Eisenhower goes to Korea. An inspection tour brings him face to face with his son, serving on the Korean front with the 15th Infantry in the same battalion that DDE had commanded as a Lieutenant Colonel, only twelve years earlier.

And with South Korean President Syngman Rhee.

United States and others of the United Nations in Korea's defense.

On June 8 the Communists agreed to voluntary repatriation of prisoners of war, for months the biggest thorn in the side of negotiators. The next day the negotiators at Panmunjom began dealing with the question of a final cease-fire line.

World reaction to progress in the armistice negotiations was universally favorable.

On the 17th of June, Rhee sent me a letter in which he reiterated his old argument on the fatal nature of the truce about to be signed. He expressed his gratitude for the help that the United States had given to Korea, but there was no doubt that he was highly emotional. His attitude caused us much uneasiness.

The ink was scarcely dry on all this correspondence when a bombshell exploded. Twenty-five thousand North Korean non-Communist prisoners had somehow escaped from the stockades in which they were being held.

Shortly thereafter, Rhee's government admitted complicity in the incident.

The Communists asked at this juncture—and, I must confess, with some right—whether the United States was able to live up to any agreement to which the South Koreans might be a party.

This situation required immediate action. That day I dispatched a message to Rhee:

> Persistence in your present course of action will make impractical for the UN Command to continue to operate jointly with you under the conditions which would result therefrom. Unless you are prepared immediately and unequivocally to accept the authority of the UN Command to conduct the present hostilities and to bring them to a close, it will be necessary to effect another arrangement. Accordingly, the UN Commander-in-Chief has now been authorized to take such steps as may become necessary in the light of your determination.

Meanwhile, as might be expected, the feeling on the home front was one of bewilderment. There seemed to be some confusion in the minds of many people as to the identity of the real enemy, and I found it necessary in a news conference on July 1 to remind a questioner, "The enemy is still in North Korea." I said we were witnessing an acute example of the difficulties that arise when allies, dedicated to the same principles and the same basic ideas, draw apart on the means of attaining their objectives. This was the history of coalitions, I said, and we should not be too discouraged about it. In this case the differences were very real. Moreover, when people were emotionally upset—as President Rhee was—they were apt to overstate their cases and become extraor-

"We cannot surrender," said Syngman Rhee, even as a war which had dragged on was stalemated in negotiations which had dragged on. "The lack of progress in the talks demanded, in my opinion," wrote President Eisenhower, "definite measures to put an end to these intolerable conditions. One possibility was to let the Communist auhorities understand that, in the absence of satisfactory progress, we intended to move decisively without inhibition in our use of weapons...We dropped the word, discreetly, of our intention. Soon the prospects for armistice negotiations seemed to improve."

Then Rhee allowed twenty-five thousand North Korean non-Communist prisoners to "escape..."

"When people were emotionally upset," said DDE mildly, "—as President Rhee was—they become extraordinarily difficult while others are trying for calm solutions."

dinarily difficult when others were trying for calm solutions.

In spite of seemingly favorable progress toward an armistice, I soon found myself writing a memorandum in near exasperation. "There has been so much backing and filling, indecision, doubt and frustration engendered by both Rhee and the Communists that I am doubtful that an armistice even if achieved will have any great meaning."

Fortunately, I was wrong. The truce was signed three days later, on July 27, 1953. Three years of heroism, frustration, and bloodshed were over.

Our nation, born because of the dedication of its people to liberty and justice, has sought consciously to achieve a just and universal peace in freedom for all people. Hope ran high when, in 1945, many nations' representatives met in San Francisco to establish the United Nations Organization and a world in which law would supplant force as the arbiter in international disputes. That was hope's high point; from then onward every attempt to advance even a single step toward world peace encountered one unsurmountable obstacle—the implacable purpose of the men in the Kremlin to achieve Communist domination of the world.

The answer to Communist ambitions had to be in some form of collective defense. Formal and specific recognition of this need was given expression in the formation of the North Atlantic Treaty Organization, by which, in 1949, most of the nations of Western Europe had come together for security purposes with Canada and the United States.

Soviet propaganda against this organization began at once; it has never ceased. Stalin was responsible for the anti-NATO propaganda. Before I assumed office he had hinted in one of his rare interviews that he would like to meet with me. I had last met him on a trip to Moscow in August 1945. In long conversations he revealed himself to be what most people suspected: the ironhanded boss of the Soviet Union. He was also a man completely devoid of a sense of humor. For hours I had stood with him in a reviewing stand on top of Lenin's tomb watching Russian male and female athletes demonstrate their prowess in gymnastics.

"This develops the war spirit," Stalin said stolidly. "Your country ought to do more of this."

Even at a movie in the evening he was unable to unbend. We watched a Soviet picture on the capture of Berlin, featuring my old friend Marshal Zhukov, with ranks of medals glittering on his best dress uniform. At the movie Stalin sat between Zhukov and me. At one point, I leaned over and said to our interpreter, who was seated directly behind Stalin, "Tell Marshal Zhukov that if he ever loses his job in the Soviet Union he can surely get one in Hollywood."

Stalin listened to the translation in silence. "Marshal Zhukov," he informed me in a flat tone, "will never be without a job in the Soviet Union."

Now, more than seven years later, I doubted whether much that was productive could come out of meeting with such a man. Nonetheless, at a news conference on February 25, when a reporter asked if I would agree to leave the United States to meet with Stalin, I answered, "I would meet anybody, anywhere, where I thought there was the slightest chance of doing any good, as long as it was in keeping with what the American people expect of their Chief Executive."

The question became academic. Within ten days Stalin was dead.

The new leadership in Russia, no matter how strong its links with the Stalin era, was not completely bound to blind obedience to the ways of a dead man. The future was theirs to make. Consequently, a major preoccupation of my mind through most of 1953 and despite the grave, and justifiable doubts concerning Communist pledges I had held for a quarter century was the development of approaches to the Soviet leaders that might be at least a start toward the birth of mutual trust.

Given any progress in the development of such trust, we could "proceed concurrently and constructively with the next great work—the reduction of the burden of armaments now weighing upon the world." The words are from a speech of mine before the American Society of Newspaper Editors on April 16, 1953.

"Every gun that is made, every warship launched, every rocket fired signifies, in the final sense, a theft from those who hunger and are not fed, those who are cold and are not clothed.

"The cost of one modern heavy bomber is this: a modern brick school in more than thirty cities.

"We pay for a single fighter plane with a half-million bushels of wheat.

"We pay for a single destroyer with new homes that could have housed more than eight thousand people.

"The new Soviet leadership now has a precious opportunity to awaken, with the rest of the world, to the point of peril reached and to help turn the tide of history.

"This government is ready to ask its people to join with all nations in devoting a substantial percentage of the savings achieved by disarmament to a fund for world aid and reconstruction...

"The monuments to this new kind of war would be these: roads and schools, hospitals and homes, food and health.

"We are ready, in short, to dedicate our strength to serving the needs, rather than the fears, of the world...

"What is the Soviet Union ready to do?"

Whatever the answer was, let it be plainly spoken, I said. The hunger for peace was too great, the hour in history too late, for any government to mock men's hopes.

"If we strive but fail and the world remains armed against itself, it at least need be divided no longer in its clear knowledge of who has condemned humankind to this fate."

Seven months later I stood before the General Assembly of the United Nations, in New York.

The core of the speech, after a recital of the calamitous horror all the world faced in a nuclear war, came in these paragraphs:

> To hasten the day when fear of the atom will begin to disappear from the minds of people...there are certain steps that can be taken now.
> I therefore make the following proposals:
> The governments principally involved, to the extent permitted by ele-

mentary prudence, to begin now and continue to make joint contributions from their stockpiles of normal uranium and fissionable materials to an International Atomic Energy Agency. We would expect that such an agency would be set up under the aegis of the United Nations...

The important responsibility of this Atomic Energy Agency would be to devise methods whereby this fissionable material would be allocated to serve the peaceful pursuits of mankind. Experts would be mobilized to apply atomic energy to the needs of agriculture, medicine, and other peaceful activities. A special purpose would be to provide abundant electrical energy in the power-starved areas of the world. Thus the contributing powers would be dedicating some of their strength to serve the needs rather than the fears of mankind...

Underlying all this, of course, was the clear conviction that as of that moment, the world, as it still is, was courting disaster in the armaments race, that something must be done to put a brake on this momentum.

In the circumstances of that time the proposals were revolutionary. At home and overseas, editorial and public reaction to the speech was good. Though the Soviet Union did not immediately give the world its final answer, I had achieved most of my short-term purposes. The United States had set the stage for a practical approach to the development of confidence among the great powers of the world—if the Kremlin so desired.

The press spontaneously gave the proposal a fitting title, "Atoms for Peace."

In the congressional session of 1953 we were obligated to redeem promises made in the Republican platform of 1952. Stern facts influenced our approach. The Republicans had a majority of only eleven votes in the House. In the Senate the Republican margin consisted of just one man.

Another relevant fact was the unfamiliarity of legislative Republicans with either the techniques or the need of cooperating with the Executive. Not since 1931—nearly a quarter of a century before—had a Republican President had a Republican majority in both houses of the Congress. Not a single Republican senator arriving in Washington in January of 1953 had ever served with a President of his own party. Of the 221 Republicans in the House, only fifteen had served with a Republican President.

One of my first responsibilites was to organize the White House for efficiency.

I have read about "staff decision" but I have never understood exactly what was meant by the expression.

I have never known any successful executive who has depended upon the taking of a vote in any gathering to make a decision for him. The habit of depending upon an "Aulic Council"—or for that matter, a Cabinet—to direct the affairs of a great nation, or of calling a "council of war" by generals to make decisions which were either the province of commander-in-chief or were properly their own, went out of fashion long before most of us were born.

On a crucial question during the Civil War, Abraham Lincoln is said to have called for a vote around the Cabinet table. Every member voted no. "The ayes have it," Lincoln announced.

The presidency still works the same way today.

Soon after my inauguration, President Hoover had warned me to expect disappointments.

"In certain respects," he said, "you have probably the most difficult political problem ever encountered by a President. Some people will want you to lead them back at full speed to the 'good old days.' At the other extreme, some will want you to initiate welfare programs regardless of their wisdom or their effect on federal fiscal affairs and on the nation's economy." And then he concluded, "To go back is impossible, but many will not believe this, and will demand miracles of you. To allow present trends to go on is unwise: they will lead to disaster. All you can do is try to turn away gradually from the path leading to paternalism, until it takes a central course, and then stick with it. And both sides will dislike you."

For my part, I early embarked on a program of discussing issues, in a social atmosphere, with groups of congressmen and senators of both parties, in the hope that personal acquaintance would help smooth out difficulties inherent in partisanship.

Naturally, we all expected that the budget we inherited for fiscal year 1954 would once again be out of balance; and so it was, by nearly $10 billion. What we did not previously know was that our predecessors had piled on top of this mountainous debt additional COD purchases—largely in defense contracts—with no income whatsoever in sight to pay for them upon their arrival, over the next few years. These purchases totaled more than $80 billion—more than all the expenditures of the federal government put together from 1789 through World War I.

But I was determined, if humanly possible, to carry on the fight to conduct a revolution which would reverse the trend of the budgets of the past twenty years. It took us two years to do it, but we did achieve a balanced budget, while at the same time providing adequately for every essential function of government.

Despite difficulties, the Eighty-third Congress, under Republican leadership, had by adjournment day built a record that gave us hope for the future. Congress had, among other things, passed the tax extensions (which retained increased personal income and excess profits taxes passed during the Korean War in an effort to reduce the federal deficit), the Trade Agreements Act extension (which allowed the president to reduce tariffs in order to stimulate foreign trade), the Refugee Relief Act (which allowed for the admission of 215,000 refugees over three years, an effort to aid the large number of displaced Europeans after the war), a bill providing federal aid for school districts overloaded by nearby federal installations, and one sending emergency wheat to drought-stricken Pakistan.

Moreover, in eighty-three test votes on "Eisenhower issues" that year, seventy-four had turned out to be victories.

In the early postwar years Americans had gradually become aware of the danger to their freedom posed by international Communism. Even more slowly, perhaps because we did not like to admit it to ourselves, we came to realize that not all danger came from without—that there were dangers within as well. By the time of the 1952 election, sufficient evidence had piled up (the Rosenberg case was only one example) to induce the public to express its insistence that the government effectively tighten its regulations and rid the federal establishment of employees who were potential sources of danger to the national security.

Frequently during the political campaign, I had pledged to do just this.

Immediately after inauguration I set to work to close this gap in our defenses.

One case that attracted a great deal of public attention involved a brilliant scientist who had been a central figure in the development of the atomic bomb— Dr. J. Robert Oppenheimer.

The investigation (which produced three thousand pages of testimony) consisted of a thorough examination of all available records and a confidential hearing before a review panel before which forty witnesses appeared.

The examination ran several weeks, and the committee finally found, by a vote of two to one, that Dr. Oppenheimer was a security risk, though a loyal citizen. Dr. Oppenheimer's friends charged that the finding was based almost exclusively on the circumstances that Oppenheimer had opposed the development of the hydrogen bomb. Certainly I, and I am sure the members of the investigating committee of the AEC, gave no weight to this fact.

Years earlier an experience of my own had given me a striking example of the truth that conflicting judgments about the nation's security could be forcefully expressed without carrying the implication that either side deserved the charge of "security risk."

"As we heralded political victory in 1952," President Eisenhower once wrote (in *Mandate for Change*), "it was a far different world from the day in 1945 when we had announced the military victory over the Nazis. The world was caught up in a grim long-range struggle between former associated powers. The main characteristic of the seven years between VE Day and the day I was elected President had been a steady consolidation of two power blocs facing each other across the globe, the danger vastly multiplied by a growing arsenal of enormously destructive weapons on both sides."

The incident took place in 1945 when Secretary of War Henry L. Stimson, visiting my headquarters in Germany, informed me that our government was preparing to drop an atomic bomb on Japan. I was one of those who felt that there were a number of cogent reasons to question the wisdom of such an act.

During his recitation of the relevant facts, I had been conscious of a feeling of depression and so I voiced to him my grave misgivings, first on the basis of my belief that Japan was already defeated and that dropping the bomb was completely unnecessary, and secondly because I thought that our country should avoid shocking world opinion by use of a weapon whose employment was, I thought, no longer mandatory as a measure to save American lives. It was my belief that Japan was, at that very moment, seeking some way to surrender with a minimum loss of "face." The Secretary was deeply perturbed by my attitude, almost angrily refuting the reasons I gave for my quick conclusions.

But in spite of his instant rejection of my opinion, it never occurred to Secretary Stimson to question my loyalty to America, or for me to think that anyone else would or could do so. In the same way I refused to accept any implication that Dr. Oppenheimer was disloyal to America or was a security risk merely because he had opposed the development of a weapon many hundreds of times more terrifying than anything we had then produced.

It was entirely on other evidence, including Dr. Oppenheimer's own testimony, that I concurred in the recommendations of the investigation committee and approved the vote of the Atomic Energy Commission to deny re-instatement of his security clearance, the majority of whom cited "fundamental defects in his character," instanced by what the committee regarded as repeated falsehoods to security officers about Communists whom he knew.

During the course of 1953–54, 8008 cases of security risks were identified by properly appointed boards. As a result, 3002 were dismissed as security risks, and 5006 resigned before their cases were acted upon.

The problem of security in government was troublesome and was exaggerated by the extravagant and often baseless charges made against many individuals and groups by Senator Joseph R. McCarthy, Chairman of the Permanent Investigations Subcommittee of the Senate Committee on Governmental Operations.

Protected as he was by congressional immunity, anyone could be irresponsibly attacked. Strong resentment against McCarthyism developed among the educators, the press, and the clergy—indeed, among all informed groups. The question was often—and justifiably—asked, "Who is safe?" It could not be expected that my relations with Senator McCarthy would be cordial. As time

went on, he began to include my associates and me in his innuendoes and sometimes in his all-out attacks.

Some of my good friends and most trusted advisers would, periodically, become infuriated at his irresponsible actions and urge me to censure him publicly
in the strongest possible language in the hope of destroying his political position
and his capacity to distort the American ideal before the world. I even had
letters from Americans arguing that, as President, I should "fire McCarthy"—
a circumstance that made me wonder wryly, at times, how much the average
citizen really knows about the institutions and composition of his government.

If I were to attack Senator McCarthy, even though every personal instinct
so prompted me, I would greatly enhance his publicity value without achieving
any constructive purpose.

Television and radio increased his audiences. Cameras and klieg lights were
installed in the Senate committee room where he held hearings, a circumstance
which helped still more to sustain public interest in his appearances and incited
him to become even more extreme in his accusations.

At one point, Senator McCarthy insisted that the government get rid of all
the books in our overseas libraries that he decided were subversive and un-
American. Informed of this while on a visit ot Dartmouth College, I seized the
opportunity in an impromptu talk.

> Don't join the book burners. Don't think you are going to conceal faults
> by concealing evidence that they ever existed. Don't be afraid to go in your
> library and read every book, as long as that document does not offend our
> own ideas of decency. That should be the only censorship.
>
> How will we defeat Communism unless we know what it is, and what it
> teaches, and why does it have such an appeal for men, why are so many
> people swearing allegiance to it? It is almost a religion, albeit one of the
> nether regions.
>
> And we have got to fight it with something better, not try to conceal the
> thinking of our own people. They are part of America. And even if they
> think ideas that are contrary to ours, their right to say them, their right to
> record them, and their right to have them at places where they are accessible
> to others is unquestioned, or it isn't America.

McCarthy's last and most ambitious attack was on the Army. Fed up with
the continual harassment from the McCarthy subcommittee, Army Secretary
Robert T. Stevens, determined to make public a memorandum of facts, which
had been in preparation for two months.

McCarthy said he would testify under oath in the case, with another senator presiding. The Army-McCarthy hearings were launched. The hearings began on April 22, and as a result of the rules on cross-examination and the fact that the proceedings were televised, the public was subjected to more of an extravaganza than a dignified committee hearing. The questions themselves were soon lost in a welter of personalities and emotion. In the whole sorry mess of thirty-six sessions, stretching over some fifty-seven days, the television audience was absorbed in such details as innumerable points of order, cropped photographs, wrangles over procedures, the authenticity of letters produced as evidence, the admissibility of monitored telephone calls, and finally a near fist fight.

By the second week in June it was obvious that the hearings were finally coming to an end. The Army had now been able to present its case; and it was apparent that McCarthy's influence was slipping badly.

But the senator's troubles were not to end there. On July 30 Senator Ralph Flanders (Republican, of Vermont) introduced Senate Resolution 301: "Resolved, that the conduct of the Senator from Wisconsin, Mr. McCarthy, is unbecoming a Member of the United States Senate, is contrary to Senatorial traditions, and tends to bring the Senate into disrepute, and such conduct is hereby condemned."

On the 10th of November, Senator McCarthy issued a statement that did much to damage his position. "I would have the American people recognize the fact that the Communist party has now extended its tentacles to the United States Senate. It has made a committee of the Senate its unwitting handmaiden."

The ensuing debate was characterized by parliamentary maneuvering and much argument. For a while it appeared that the vote would never come about, since McCarthy was hospitalized for days with a sore elbow.

However, on the 2nd of December the matter was brought to a final vote. Sixty-seven out of eighty-nine Senators voted to condemn McCarthy for conduct "contrary to senatorial traditions." Senator McCarthy finally made what had been termed his "break" with me—why it was called such at that late date I could not fathom. He claimed that the administration was soft on Communism and apologized for having supported me in 1952.

But one thing was apparent. By a combination of the Senate's vote and the loss of his committee chairmanship, the senator's power was ended. Senator McCarthy died an untimely and sad—even pathetic—death in 1957, but as a political force he was finished at the end of 1954.

A giant item on our agenda was one which for nearly a half-century, since the days of Theodore Roosevelt, had been considered an impossible dream, a law which would permit the United States to cooperate with Canada to deepen the St. Lawrence River. Such an accomplishment would permit seagoing ships to sail from the Atlantic more than two thousand miles through the Great Lakes to the heart of the Middle West.

I had long favored the construction of the St. Lawrence Seaway. As Chief of Staff of the Army from late 1945 to early 1948, I expressed the conviction that this waterway would strengthen the security of both countries. Now as President I had become convinced that the seaway would be, in addition, an economic asset to both nations. While certain interests, primarily Eastern seaports and the railways of that region, might suffer some disadvantages, I was persuaded that the over-all benefit to the nation would more than counterbalance any harm suffered. I insisted, however, that the law provide that the seaway, through tolls, eventually pay for itself.

In another major economic request, four days after my State of the Union message, I sent the Congress a special message outlining a break with the present agricultural law, inherited from the preceding administration.

In my 1954 Agricultural message I said that "special attention" would be given to "The problems peculiar to small farmers"—the million and a half with incomes of less than $1000 a year. There followed a year-long, nationwide study, with the result that in April of the next year the administration launched its Rural Development Program.

On the same day, January 11, 1954, I sent the Congress a message suggesting amendments to the Taft-Hartley Act.

My message recommended guaranteeing the right of the employee, when called on to strike, to vote by secret ballot under federal auspices for or against continuing the strike. It seemed to me that the government had been so preoccupied with authorizing, supporting, and protecting union organizations that it had ignored the need of assuring the individual union member a full and untrammeled right to a voice, by secret ballot, in any decision on a strike, which was, in effect, a decision on his own weekly paycheck.

During 1954 I made 232 specific requests for legislation to the Congress. I knew that the struggle for passage of a program of this magnitude would be continuous and arduous, for Republicans had in the Senate an even more precarious majority than in the previous year.

I was ready to do my part, I told the Republican leaders; they also had to do theirs. We should decide what we wanted to do, and then do it, despite all opposition. "This program," I said, "is better than anything the Democrats have ever offered. The Republican party can win solid support from the country if we all get to work and put the program through."

In May the administration's determination began to pay off: the Congress passed the St. Lawrence Seaway bill—a historic victory.

With the exception of the seaway bill and the Federal Aid Highway Act of 1954, which I had signed on May 6, and which provided the largest two-year sum—nearly $2 billion—ever invested up to that time to modernize the United States' highways, this congressional session had produced little by the middle of July. Then came the deluge.

In the 1954 session, as these pieces of legislation and many other minor ones became law, I also vetoed forty-two bills; not once did the Congress override. Though the Congress had rejected health reinsurance, Taft-Hartley revision, Hawaiian statehood, increased postal rates, and voting rights for eighteen-year-olds, it had approved thirteen of my nineteen major proposals. And of the entire 232 which I had requested, the Congress had approved 150, giving the administration an extraordinarily favorable record for that session. We had made this progress despite a slight recession.

In 1954 the seven-and-a-half-year-old war in Indochina came to the end—temporarily.

During the first forty years of the twentieth century the region was relatively quiescent. Then, when the Japanese entered World War II, their armies moved into the region and rapidly took over complete control, a condition which persisted until the final Japanese defeat in August 1945.

This was the signal for the French to come in again to reassert control. Shortly thereafter, trouble developed between the French and the natives, many of whom were tired of overlordships of all kinds and wanted independence. This unrest mushroomed into fighting that gradually grew more widespread in scope and intense in character. By 1950 France had strong Regular Army units deployed in the area and was doing its best to raise, equip, and train loyal native troops to assist in quelling the rebellion. The disaffected forces were led by a man, Ho Chi Minh, who had once, in 1946, been Premier of all Indochina, with the blessing of the French.

Ho Chi Minh was a hard-core Communist, while the Vietminh, the forces under his command, were supported by the Chinese Communists in the north. Although guerrilla fighting was sporadic, the French controlled the deltas and the cities and an area along the waist of Vietnam, whereas the back country was controlled mainly by the Vietminh.

In early 1951 the Indochina affair had come emphatically to my attention when I was Allied commander of the NATO troops with headquarters in Paris.

The NATO defense needed greater French participation, but this was largely denied because of France's losses and costs in the Indochina war. These losses and costs to the French might be lessened, I believed, if allies could carry part of the load in defending Indochina. Such a development would depend, of course, upon a clear appreciation throughout the Free World that the war was in no sense an effort on the part of the French to sustain their former domination over the area, but was in fact a clear case of freedom defending itself from Communist aggression. To bring about such an appreciation, there would have to be a definite and public pledge on the part of the French to accord independence and the right of self-determination as soon as military victory should be attained.

I repeatedly urged upon successive French governments the wisdom of publishing to the Free World and particularly to all Indo-China such an unequivocal commitment.

In the absence of such a statement, the war was naturally looked upon in most cases as a domestic difficulty between France and one part of her empire. This attitude precluded the possibility that other free nations could help in what the French themselves considered so much a family quarrel that it could not even be submitted to the United Nations for adjudication.

By the time I entered the presidency the French nation had become weary of the war, and their government—at least in official circles, if not publicly—was promising eventual self-rule and even independence to Indochina.

On November 20, French Union forces moved west from the Red River Delta in Tonkin and occupied an area ten miles from the border of Laos. This place was later to become a household word throughout the Free World: Dien Bien Phu.

It was difficult then—as it is now with the advantage of hindsight—to understand exactly why the French decided to send ten thousand crack troops into this position, strong as it was, whose only means of resupply was by air. I decided to argue against the move.

Whatever the reasons, the occupation of Dien Bien Phu caused little notice at the time, except to soldiers who were well acquainted with the almost invariable fate of troops invested in an isolated fortress. I instructed both the State and Defense Departments to communicate to their French counterparts my concern as to the move.

About a week later, reports came in that the French garrison at that important outpost was surrounded by approximately three Vietminh divisions—outnumbering the besieged forces by three to one.

I let it be known that I would never agree to send our ground troops as mere reinforcements for French units, to be used only as they saw fit. Part of my fundamental concept of the presidency is that we have a constitutional government and only when there is a sudden, unforeseen emergency should the President put us into de-facto war without congressional action.

I remarked that if the United States were, unilaterally, to permit its forces to be drawn into conflict in Indochina and in a succession of Asian wars, the end result would be to drain off our resources and to weaken our over-all defensive position. If we, without allies, should ever find ourselves fighting at various places all over the region, and if Red Chinese aggressive participation were clearly identified, then we could scarcely avoid, I said, considering the necessity of striking directly at the head instead of the tail of the snake, Red China itself.

On the 4th of April I made an effort to have the British join with us in organizing a regional grouping of the United States, France, and the Southeast Asian nations. I wrote to Winston Churchill:

> I believe that the best way to bring greater moral and material resources to the support of the French effort is through the establishment of a new, ad hoc grouping or coalition composed of nations which have a vital concern in the checking of Communist expansion in the area.
>
> If I may refer again to history; we failed to halt Hirohito, Mussolini and Hitler by not acting in unity and in time. That marked the beginning of many years of stark tragedy and desperate peril. May it not be that our nations have learned something from that lesson?...
>
> With warm regard,<br>IKE

His brief answer showed that the British had little enthusiasm for joining us in taking a firm position and it seemed clear that the Congress would not act favorably unless I could give assurances that the British would be by our side.

The days before the opening of the Geneva Conference on April 26 were tense.

The fears I had expressed long ago concerning the wisdom of the French taking up a fortress position at Dien Bien Phu were turning out to be grimly accurate. When a French diplomat had told me of their plans at the time, I said, "You cannot do this!"

"This will bring the enemy into the open," he said. "We cannot find them in the jungle, and this will draw them out where we can then win."

"The French know military history," I said. "They are smart enough to know the outcome of becoming firmly emplaced and then besieged in an exposed position with poor means of supply and reinforcements."

## Indochina

Unfamiliar names become household words.

"French forces moved west and occupied an area ten miles from the border of Laos: Dien Bien Phu. It was difficult then—as it is now—to understand exactly why the French decided to send ten thousand crack troops into this position, strong as it was, whose only means of resupply was by air. I instructed State and Defense to communicate to their French counterparts my concern...

"As I viewed the prospects of military intervention in the relative calm of early 1954, it seemed clear that if three basic requirements were fulfilled, the United States could properly and effectively render real help...The first requirement was a legal right under international law; second was a favorable climate of Free World opinion; and third, favorable action by the Congress..."

The atomic-powered submarine USS Nautilus is christened by Mrs. Dwight D. Eisenhower and enters the Thames River at Groton, Connecticut, January 31, 1954.

Never before had I been so sad to be so right.

A river which ran through the French position was flooding, cutting the position in half. Four thousand troops were left and only 450 additional men had been dropped in since April 25. On May 7 the fortress fell, the final position having been reduced to a size no larger than a baseball field.

On the 8th of May the French government submitted to the Geneva Conference a proposal for ending the hostilities in Indochina.

I approved instructions to the United States delegation. The United States would not associate itself with any proposal from any source for a cease fire which would take effect in advance of an acceptable armistice agreement, including international mechanisms for enforcement. We would, however, "concur in initiation of negotiations" for the armistice itself. In the meantime, we would encourage the French Union forces to continue the fight in Indochina while the conference progressed, would provide more aid, and would go on with our efforts "to organize and promptly activate a Southeast Asia regional grouping..." The negotiations were long and tedious, and every day the military situation worsened in Vietnam.

As the days wore on, with Communist stalling at Geneva, and more intense fighting in Indochina, certain issues began to be clarified. By this time it was generally accepted that partition would occur in Vietnam and possibly even in the other Associated States.

On the 12th of June, the Laniel government failed to gain a vote of confidence in the French Assembly by a vote of 306 to 293. France was without a leader and without a government.

We decided that it was best for the United States to break off major participation in the Geneva Conference. The days of keeping the Western powers bound to inaction by creating divisions of policy among them in a dragged-out conference were coming to an end.

On the 18th of June, Pierre Mendes-France took office as Premier of France on the strength of the pledge that he would secure a peace in Indochina by July 20.

On the morning of the deadline, July 20, Secretary John Foster Dulles, now in Washington, called to report on cables received from Geneva. The Russians were pressing for a conference resolution and for us to join in adopting all the provisos. We, of course, were refusing to participate in the resolution because of my determination to avoid signing anything that ceded territory to the communists but were authorizing Bedell to make a declaration that we would not use force to disturb the resolution reached.

The next day the declaration was signed, ending the war in Indochina temporarily.

It provided for international controls. Cambodia and Laos were to adopt measures permitting all citizens (including the Communist Pathet Lao forces in Laos) to take their place in the community, with local elections to take place in 1955. The settlement in Vietnam was recognized as a military—not a political or territorial—one. General elections in Vietnam, Laos, and Cambodia were to be held in July 1956, supervised by an international commission. There were to be no reprisals against people who had collaborated with any one of the parties during the war. French troops were to be withdrawn when the three governments of the Associated States requested it.

I am convinced that the French could not win the war because the internal political situation in Vietnam, weak and confused, badly weakened their military position. I have never talked or corresponded with a person knowledgeable in Indochinese affairs who did not agree that had elections been held as of the time of the fighting, possibly 80 per cent of the population would have voted for the Communist Ho Chi Minh as their leader rather than Chief of State Bao Dai. Indeed, the lack of leadership and drive on the part of Bao Dai was a factor in the feeling prevalent among Vietnamese that they had nothing to fight for. As one Frenchman said to me, "What Vietnam needs is another Syngman Rhee, regardless of all the difficulties the presence of such a personality would entail."

Willingness to fight for freedom, no matter where the battle may be, has always been a characteristic of our people, but the conditions then prevailing in Indochina were such as to make unilateral American intervention nothing less than sheer folly.

At about seven o'clock on the evening of September 3, 1954, the Army Signal Corps at the Summer White House in Denver brought me a message from Deputy Defense Secretary Robert B. Anderson, in Washington. At one forty-five that morning (Eastern Daylight time), the Chinese Communists had begun a heavy artillery shelling of Quemoy Island off the Chinese coast. Though the shelling had diminished at about four-twenty in the morning, it was still, at last reports, continuing.

The next report predicted the Communists would launch an assault against Quemoy Island. The Commander-in-Chief of the Pacific Fleet, Admiral Stump, alerted, was moving carriers into position, to give support or to undertake a rescue.

As a result of the Sino-Japanese War of 1894–95, China lost to Japan the important islands of Taiwan (Formosa) and the Pescadores, lying about a hundred miles off the Chinese coast. The Cairo Declaration of December 1943 announced that after World War II these islands would be returned to the "Republic of China." The Japanese peace treaty of 1951 ended Japanese sovereignty over the islands but did not formally cede them to "China," either Communist or Nationalist.

The Quemoy and Matsu groups, much smaller and much nearer the China coast, had always been under the control of the government on the Chinese mainland, until Chiang Kai-shek had fled to Formosa in 1949. Chiang still controlled them and was prepared to defend them with his full strength.

To Chiang and his people, Quemoy and Matsu would one day be stepping stones for the invasion of their homeland. This threat, angering and irritating the Communists, strengthened their resolve to drive the island's defenders into the sea.

In his New Year's message for 1954, Generalissimo Chiang Kai-shek had pledged an attack on the mainland "in the not distant future" and his Easter message had called for a "holy war" against the Communists.

Premier Chou En-lai, as if in reply, called for the "liberation of Formosa" —meaning its capture—and warned that his government would not tolerate interference from the United States or anybody else.

The temperature was rising. And on August 17 I got a news-conference question on it.

"Mr. President, there have been reports recently of a build-up of Chinese Communist strength across on the mainland from Formosa.

"What would happen, sir, if the Communists did attack Formosa in force?"

"In January or February of 1953 instructions went out to the Seventh Fleet ...regarding the defense of Formosa. Those orders are still in force. Therefore, I should assume what would happen is this: any invasion of Formosa would have to run over the Seventh Fleet."

On November 1, 1954, Communist planes bombed the Tachen Islands. The next day they shelled other small offshore islands and their build-up of troops continued. Then on November 23 Peiping Radio reported the verdict of a Communist court on thirteen Americans, eleven of them airmen in uniform. They had been shot down by the Red Chinese (who announced their capture on my first day in office). The court sentenced them to prison terms ranging from four years to life, for "espionage."

Senator William F. Knowland demanded that the United States Navy blockade the coast of China, with or without the assent of the United Nations, and thus force Red China to free the American prisoners. Three days earlier at a breakfast meeting I had warned the senator against any such rash step. As President, I of course experienced exactly the same resentments, anger, and frustration as anyone else when such a thing happened to another American, and my impulse, like his, was to lash out. But I knew such a response would be self-defeating.

"The hard way," I said, "is to have the courage to be patient." The United States would work tirelessly for the American prisoners' eventual release. But I rejected the strategy of a naval blockade.

With the beginning of the New Year, events in the Formosa Strait began to take a turn for the worse. Generalissimo Chiang Kai-shek's New Year's message for 1955 forecast war "at any time." The Chinese Communists stepped up construction of jet airfields opposite Formosa—airfields which, by the end of the spring, might permit them to gain air superiority over Quemoy and Matsu.

On January 18, nearly four thousand Chinese Communist troops, with heavy air bombardment and an amphibious attack, overwhelmed one thousand Nationalist guerillas and seized the island of Ichiang.

I approved the wording of a special message to the Congress asking for authority to use American armed force to protect Formosa and the Pescadores and related positions, if necessary to the defense of the principal islands. I believed the Korean War had resulted, partially at least, from the mistaken Communist notion that under no circumstances would the United States move to the assistance of the Korean Republic. I resolved that this time no uncertainty about our commitment to defend Formosa should invite a major Chinese Communist attack.

For three days, senators debated the resolution on the floor.

On January 28 the Senate passed the resolution eighty-three to three, and the next day I signed it.

Throughout, we kept our principal allies informed of the reasons for our actions. Early in February, for example, I wrote to Prime Minister Churchill:

"Whatever now is to happen, I know that nothing could be worse than global war.

"I do not believe that Russia wants war at this time—in fact, I do not believe that even if we became engaged in a serious fight along the coast of China, Russia would want to intervene with her own forces. She would, of course, pour supplies into China in an effort to exhaust us and certainly would exploit the opportunity to separate us from your country."

"Would the United States," a reporter asked me, "use tactical atomic weapons in a general war in Asia?" Against a strictly military target, I replied, the answer would be "yes." I hoped this answer would have some effect in persuading the Chinese Communists of our determination.

As I was about to go to the Executive Office Building for my press conference the next week, Jim Hagerty reported a frantic plea he had just received.

"Mr. President," he said, "some of the people in the State Department say that the Formosa Strait situation is so delicate that no matter what question you get on it, you shouldn't say anything at all."

I could see the point of this advice. But I didn't take it.

"Don't worry, Jim," I told him as we went out the door, "if that question comes up, I'll just confuse them."

Three days later, External Affairs Secretary Lester Pearson announced that Canada would not fight over the offshore islands, a remark which led to a pontifical summary by one columnist on the morning of March 25 that "all our Allies, except Generalissimo Chiang Kai-shek, regard this as the wrong war, at the wrong time, and at the wrong place." Evidently there are citizens of the Free World who can never be made to see that any retreat in the face of Communist aggression merely assures another attack.

Chou En-lai, it was reported, estimated that in a war with the United States, Red China might lose 100 million men and still have 450 million left—apparently believing that this would constitute victory for his side.

Secretary Dulles told congressmen on March 30 that the United States had no means of knowing how much the Russians supported the aggressive tactics of the Chinese. A war between the United States and China would require the Russians to increase immensely their deliveries of military equipment to their Chinese allies. On the other hand we should remember, the Secretary went on, that last winter Khrushchev, in a visit with Bulganin to Peiping, ringingly denounced the United States for interference in the Formosa dispute, insisting that Formosa be made part of Red China.

I said that such bluffing was not impressive.

By April 23 reports from the Asian-African conference at Bandung, representing more than half the world's population, quoted Premier Chou En-lai as saying that Red China had no intention of going to war with the United States, and that it was ready to negotiate with us over Formosa and the Far East.

On April 26 Secretary Dulles, in a news conference, indicated that the United States would be willing to talk with the Chinese Communists about a cease fire.

By May 22 the newspapers reported an informal cease fire on the Formosa

Strait: Communist vessels were declining to attack Nationalist ships; Communist MIGs were holding their fire against Nationalist patrol planes.

And although on the eve of the Geneva Summit Conference of July 1955 Anthony Eden still looked upon Quemoy and Matsu with alarm, on August 1 the eleven American airmen were released as the United States and Communist Chinese ambassadors began talks on the release of the remaining American civilians and "other practical matters."

During the months of crisis the administration had to contend with not only the threats of the Communists but also with varieties of advice from leaders in the Free World.

Looking at the spectrum from one extreme to the other, the administration heard the counsel of Attlee (liquidate Chiang), Eden (neutralize Quemoy and Matsu), Lehman and Morse and Kennedy (abandon Quemoy and Matsu), Lewis Douglas (avoid entry into a civil war, on legal principle), Radford (fight for the Tachens, bomb the mainland), Knowland (blockade the Chinese coast), and Rhee (join him and Chiang in a holy war of liberation).

The administration rejected all of these suggestions, threading its way, with watchfulness and determination, through narrow and dangerous waters. For nine months we moved through treacherous cross-currents with one channel leading to peace with honor and a hundred channels leading to war or appeasement.

Mao Tse-tung once expressed his strategy of war in just sixteen words: Enemy advances, we retreat; enemy halts, we harass; enemy tires, we attack; enemy retreats, we pursue.

In the Formosa Strait in 1955 we refused to retreat, and the enemy, true to his formula, for a while tried harassment but refused to attack. The crisis had cooled; it would not heat up again for three years.

The United States entered a new era. The slogan "Peace, Progress, and Prosperity," which was applied to the first-term years and was used in the campaign of 1956, seemed platitudinous. But compared with any years of the two preceding decades, these surely must have seemed miraculous to most Americans. Not in the lifetime of millions of our citizens—children, adolescents, and men and women entering adult life—had we previously had peace, progress, and prosperity all at one time.

From the second quarter of 1954 our gross national product went into a strong and steady ascent, quarter by quarter, from an annual rate of $359 billion to $409 billion by the end of 1955. And it kept on climbing. Between 1952 and

1956 the increase alone—nearly $70 billion—was an amount greater than the 1961 gross national product of France.

In the same period personal incomes of our people went up $55 billion, or 20 percent. The average weekly earnings of production workers in manufacturing went up by nearly the same rate. Contrary to the political charges of some of our opponents, the fact was that in the middle years of the 1950s the bottom income groups were becoming richer, the rich were paying record taxes, and many from both groups were joining the "middle class." We still had our impoverished and our wealthy, but the new prosperity was reducing the relative size of both groups. The middle class, as sociologists were pointing out, was becoming the widening band around the country. Between 1947 and 1957 the number of American families with incomes of $4000 or more had increased by more than 100 percent.

The battle for legislative action in 1955 was fought against the background of the quiet but immensely significant changes in our country, as well as the change that had occurred in November the year before—the transfer of the control of Congress from Republicans to Democrats.

In my January 1955 State of the Union message I referred to the divided control under which the government would have to operate and offered to meet the new Congress halfway. "We shall have much to do together," I said. "I am sure that we shall get it done."

Early in February I sent the Congress a long letter urging federal assistance for school construction. As a result of the burgeoning population, there existed an estimated deficit of more than 300,000 classrooms in our country. The current building rate, then 60,000 classrooms a year, was doing little more than keeping up with increasing student numbers. Millions of children were receiving substandard education because of unsanitary, overcrowded, and unsafe classrooms. In many places it was possible to provide for only part-time instruction.

Despite the need for classrooms, the Congress did nothing.

As it failed on schools that year, the Congress also failed on highways.

An Army convoy, with which I had traveled across the country back in 1919, had started me thinking about good, two-lane highways. A third of a century later, after becoming acquainted with the autobahns of modern Germany and the great assets those highways were, I decided, as President, to do something similar in the United States. On February 22, 1955, I sent Congress a special message urging "comprehensive and quick and forward-looking" action to improve the United States highway system.

A highway bill passed the Senate in 1955 but died in the House.

Between crises, there are the simple, eternal pleasures. Barbara Anne Eisenhower, three, and Dwight David Eisenhower II, four, in their White House camera debut.

And the President, bags a trout and nearly grills it in a pleased smile.

The failure of the Congress to enact the road program, Dr. Burns told the Cabinet in a report later that year, not only put the United States behind in its race against time to get the country's streets and roads and highways into shape for the torrents of traffic which would surely be bearing down upon them; it also denied the government an important economic tool.

The Congress had turned in a disappointing record. When that session ended, it had approved 96 out of 207 of my requests. At the final Legislative-leaders meeting on August 2, 1955, I said that I was determined to continue fighting on into the election year of 1956 for the measures the country needed. I was set on getting the road program.

On the night of September 23, 1955, I was struck with a coronary occlusion. Subconsciously, every healthy man thinks of serious illness as something that happens occasionally—but always to other people. But when, after spending a most uncomfortable night under sedation I awakened to the realization that I was in an oxygen tent with doctors and nurses in attendance, I had thrust upon me the unpleasant fact that I was, indeed, a sick man.

On Friday morning, September 23, I had departed shortly after eleven o'clock for the golf course at Cherry Hills, near Denver. We had hardly started playing when word came that Washington was calling on the telephone.

At the clubhouse I learned that Secretary Dulles wanted to talk to me, but by the time I could answer I was informed that the Secretary was en route to an engagement, and that he would call again in an hour.

At the appointed time I was back at the clubhouse only to be told there was difficulty on the lines. I would be notified as soon as the circuits were ready for us. When word again came that my call was waiting, I went back to the club-house once more and this time talked with the Secretary.

Because the morning's golf had been so badly broken up, we decided to remain at the club for lunch and play a few more holes in the afternoon. This was not a particularly ambitious program of physical activity. We were using golf carts, and the exercise, even at Denver's relatively high altitude, was by no means strenuous.

My choice for luncheon was probably not too wise. It consisted of a huge hamburger generously garnished with slices of Bermuda onion and accompanied by a pot of coffee.

Once again on the golf course I was called back to the telephone after the first hole with a message that the Secretary of State would like to speak to me. After a period of waiting I learned that he had not requested another conversation. Someone along the way had not realized that our business had been concluded. That latest call was in error.

My disposition deteriorated rapidly. I was made the more unhappy by an uneasiness that was developing in my stomach, due no doubt to my injudicious lunch.

One or two doctors have later hazarded a guess that even at that moment I was having heart difficulty, mistaking it for indigestion. We finished the nine holes and later in the afternoon I went to the home of Mrs. Doud (Mamie's mother), accompanied by George Allen.

As the dinner hour approached, George and I were in the basement billiard room knocking the balls about. We declined a drink on the grounds that we were tired and expected to go to bed early.

I went to bed at about 10 P.M. and slept. Some time later—roughly 1:30 A.M., I think—I awakened with a severe chest pain and thought immediately of my after-luncheon distress the previous noon. My wife heard me stirring about and asked whether I wanted anything. I replied that I was looking for the milk of magnesia again. Apparently she decided from the tone of my voice that something was seriously wrong; she got up at once to turn on the light to have a look at me. Then, she urged me to lie down and promptly called the White House physician, General Snyder.

General Snyder arrived shortly thereafter, and gave me some injections, one of which, I learned later, was morphine. This probably accounts for the hazy memory I had—and still have—of later events in the night. I do remember that one or two doctors came into my room and that later I was helped into a car and taken to a hospital. Then, I think, I slept; but never after that night did I feel any pain or any other symptom connected with the attack.

I followed the doctors' orders exactly, not because I was feeling any differently than the day before but because they said I had a coronary difficulty and should follow a specified routine.

Shortly after my doctors told me that I had suffered a heart attack, they and Jim Hagerty wanted to know my wishes about the kind and amount of information that should be given to the public. I had been one of those who during President Woodrow Wilson's long illness wondered why the public was kept so much in the dark about his real condition, and thought that the nation had a right to know exactly the status of the President's health. So now I had a quick reply. "Tell the truth, the whole truth; don't try to conceal anything."

Mamie occupied adjoining quarters. She took on a task which amazed me at the time and has amazed me ever since: Thousands of letters of sympathy and encouragement flowed in—letters and cables and gifts from all over the world; she answered every one individually.

Mamie, above all others, never accepted the assumption that I had incurred a disabling illness. She told our son John that she could not reconcile herself to the idea that efforts in behalf of what I believed in had come to an end. While solicitous above all for my health and welfare, she perhaps more than any other retained the conviction that my job as President was not yet finished.

As soon as I was allowed regular periods out of bed, I asked for my easel and paints and began to derive from them a great deal of enjoyment even if every canvas I attempted, except for one, was, by my orders, destroyed.

Tuesday, October 25, was a big day in my journey back to health. It was the first day I was allowed to take a few steps. Even more enjoyably, I was placed in a wheel chair and transported to the roof of the hospital, where for the first time in weeks I met my old friends, the members of the press who traveled with us regularly. As my uniform of the day—a gift from friends of the press—I wore a pair of flashy red pajamas with five stars inscribed above the left pocket and with lettering, for all to read, saying "Much Better, Thanks."

As the Eighty-fourth Congress assembled for its 2nd Session in January 1956, it seemed evident in Washington that we would be having a six-month-long political Donnybrook. With a presidential election approaching, with my own intentions in that election not yet formed, much less announced, and with numbers of controversial recommendations to be submitted by a Republican President to a Congress dominated by Democrats, partisan temperatures would inevitably run high.

To finance a sweeping new system of American highways, a presidential advisory committee, headed by General Lucius Clay, had recommended in 1955 that the federal government issue $20 billion worth of bonds at 3 percent. This proposal had run into a buzz saw on Capitol Hill; many senators and congressmen wanted the whole project paid for by appropriations out of the Treasury. Though I originally preferred a system of self-financing toll highways, and though I endorsed General Clay's recommendation, I grew restless with the quibbling over methods of financing. I wanted the job done.

This difference disposed of, the Federal Aid Highway Act, with strong bipartisan support, moved quickly through the Congress. On June 29 I signed it into law.

It was not only the most gigantic federal undertaking in road-building in the century and a half since the federal government got into this field (by improving the National Pike between Cumberland, Maryland, and Wheeling, West Virginia) it was the biggest peacetime construction project of any description ever undertaken by the United States or any other country.

The total pavement of the system would make a parking lot big enough to hold two thirds of all the automobiles in the United States. The amount of concrete poured to form these roadways would build eight Hoover Dams or six sidewalks to the moon. To build them, bulldozers and shovels would move enough dirt and rock to bury all of Connecticut two feet deep. More than any single action by the government since the end of the war, this one would change the face of America with straightaways, cloverleaf turns, bridges, and elongated parkways. Its impact on the American economy—the jobs it would produce in manufacturing and construction, the rural areas it would open up—was beyond calculation. It would, I thought, provide an extraordinary stimulus to the auto-mobile industry and trucking companies. And motorists by the millions would read a primary purpose in the signs that would sprout up alongside the pave-ment: "In the event of an enemy attack, this road will be closed..."

This great highway system will stand in part as a monument to the man in my Cabinet who headed the department responsible for it, and who himself spent long hours mapping out the program and battling it through the Congress— Secretary of Commerce Sinclair Weeks.

Another major program of the administration, started in 1956, will stand as a living memorial to another Cabinet member—Secretary of the Interior Douglas McKay, whose department worked out the most comprehensive plan in this country's history for repairing and improving our system of national parks. It was called "Mission 66."

Hopes for a school-construction bill in 1956 died a death that became inevi-table in that year when Congressman Adam Clayton Powell of New York added an amendment to a bill, denying school-construction funds to any state which refused to comply with the 1954 Supreme Court decision on segregation. In January, I had sent to the Congress a "revised and broadened program for Education." I proposed more than a billion dollars in federal grants, to be, matched by the states, for the neediest school districts over the next five years, and $750 million to purchase school-construction bonds. I opposed any attempt to tie an anti-segregation amendment to a school-construction bill, knowing the amendment would doom the bill to defeat. I was therefore gravely disappointed when the House added the Powell amendment. The bill itself authorized federal grants *not on the basis of need*—as I recommended—but rather on the basis of the states' school age population.

In 1956 the Congress not only failed to pass legislation to meet obvious needs. It also passed legislation which required a veto.

As in the years before, American agriculture suffered from food, fiber, and grain surpluses, stored in federal warehouses—put there as a result of legislation which set a floor under farm prices, a floor as high as most ceilings.

Nonetheless, the Congress that year passed a monstrosity of a farm bill, which while incorporating the recommended soil-bank plan, made the great error of going back to the 90 percent of parity price supports for the six basic crops. In effect it was less a piece of farm legislation than a private relief bill for politicians in that election year.

On April 16 I vetoed the bill.

The pitiful result of this state of affairs is that by and large it enriched those who needed no help and was almost useless to the "small farmers"—those who live and operate on the thin, ragged edge of poverty. The family that lives on a small farm, unable to afford advanced types of labor saving machinery, sells very little of its product, consuming much of it at home. Two million commercial farms sell 85 percent of our annual product; 3.5 million families living on small farms sell only 15 percent. These families, of course, provide a fertile field for political conniving, but they themselves seldom find enough fertility in their inadequate landholdings to make a decent living.

In the long run the agricultural industry must look to the open market, the still operative laws of supply and demand, for its salvation. Surpluses seem now to be a thing of the past.

Party loyalty is normally a weak influence indeed when compared to a congressman's desire to cast his vote for whatever he believes may help re-elect him. There were, however, legislators who voted their convictions, not their politics. For 1955–56 as a whole, the Eighty-fourth Congress supported our administration on roll-call test votes 72 percent of the time; the Republican-led Eighty-third Congress of 1953–54 had supported us 83 percent of the time.

The administration's record with both Democratic and Republican Congresses outranked the records of the postwar Democratic administrations, which for a single two-year term only had to work with a Congress controlled by the opposition party.

So we arrived at the end of the Eighty-fourth Congress. The actual adjournment of a session of Congress follows a prescribed ritual. The leaders of both houses fix the time of adjournment. Just before the critical hour, they approach the President and ask him whether he has any further business to place before them. This approach is sometimes made in person by a committee of each house. In recent years it became the fashion—a more convenient one—to make the contact by telephone, since the notification often takes place during the early morning hours.

As I went through this midnight ritual in 1956, I was, as usual, seated in a big chair at the end of the darkened West Hall of the White House, clad in bathrobe and slippers. Though the conversations were somewhat enlivened by jocular exchanges, a more serious thought was in my mind. Would I be present in Washington to carry it out again? Would the electorate want me for a 2nd term?

What about a second term? For me the matter had come up even before my nomination at Chicago in 1952.

I would be sixty-two years old if elected, I said, and this almost precluded any thought of my occupying the Presidency for eight years.

This determination to limit my political life to the four years ahead became so conscious an intent that, after election, I planned to include such an announcement in my Inaugural Address. Then I found that, the election having settled the immediate problem, my colleagues no longer accepted with tolerant smiles my ideas about re-election.

I wrote to Milton in December 1953 about a statement I saw in the paper one morning. One of my good political friends had said that of course the President would run for re-election in 1956—who ever heard of a President who didn't want a second term? Admitting that I could not talk publicly yet, I asked my brother's help: "If ever for a second time I should show any signs of yielding to persuasion, please call in the psychiatrist—or even better the sheriff...I feel there can be no showing made that my 'duty' extends beyond a one time performance."

The newspapers reported on a poll taken of 134 Republican governors, state chairmen, and national committeemen. More than half of them believed that I, if physically able, would head their ticket.

Milton, my son John, and my old friend George Allen all urged me to refuse to run. While each had slightly different reasons for his recommendations, they were unanimous in their belief that a release from governmental responsibilities would increase my longevity prospects. On the other hand, my wife insisted that this was a mistaken notion. She felt, and said, that it would be best for me to do exactly whatever seemed to engage my deepest interest. She thought idleness would be fatal for one of my temperament; consequently, she argued that I should listen to all my most trusted advisers, and then make my own decision. She said she was ready to accept and support me in that decision, no matter what its nature.

"I have reached a decision," I told the reporters on February 29. "Subject to the decision of the Republican National Convention," I said, "my answer will be positive."

I described my physical condition as accurately as I possibly could, explained what the doctors believed to be the prospects for my future activities, and then called attention to the record of the programs that had occupied our interest and attention for all the years of my Presidency. With this, my personal political Rubicon was crossed.

One week before the Republican convention opened, the Democratic party met in Chicago and again nominated Governor Stevenson as its candidate for President, this time naming Senator Estes Kefauver for the second spot.

Adlai Stevenson had been the first Democrat to announce his candidacy. Afterward, he had traveled a rocky road toward renomination.

Former President Truman, backing New York's Governor Averell Harriman, was alleging that Stevenson could not win because he was a tame campaigner—"too defeatist."

My view, at the time, was that a Democratic team of Senator Lyndon Johnson for President and Senator Hubert Humphrey or Senator John F. Kennedy for Vice President would have had better vote-getting power than the one named. Such a ticket would have appealed to both wings of their party, while, in addition, Lyndon Johnson's experience in the national legislature—especially his acknowledged skill in legislative maneuver and negotiation—would have had considerable appeal to voters.

Throughout the campaign, my confidence in the outcome did not waver. As the tempo of the campaigning increased, accusations were bandied back and forth by speakers for both parties. Some were complete distortions, others were witty. They did little to inform the nation but sometimes they amused it. One story was that a Republican asked a friend whom he was going to vote for. The man said he planned to vote for Adlai Stevenson. The Republican, upset, asked why. "Because," the man said, "I voted for Stevenson four years ago, and everything's been fine ever since."

"What are you going to do for a living if the President loses?" a reporter asked Jim Hagerty, my press secretary.

"The question," Jim answered, "is academic."

On the evening of November 6 the results were tabulated. Though the Republicans failed to regain control of either House of Congress, the national ticket swamped the Democratic nominees by 457 electoral votes to 73 and by a margin of more than nine million popular votes.

We carried forty-one states—all but Alabama, Arkansas, Georgia, Mississippi, Missouri, and North and South Carolina. For the first time in eighty years, Louisiana went Republican. For the first time since 1928, the Republican ticket carried the city of Chicago.

---

# PART FOUR

OCTOBER 20, 1956 was the start of the most crowded and demanding three weeks of my Presidency. The drama of those weeks is still so fresh in my memory that I can recite its principal events and our decisions with scarcely a pause. What follows is only a brief sample.

Shortly after two o'clock on the morning of October 20, Khrushchev, Molotov, Mikoyan, and Deputy Premier Lazar M. Kaganovich, then in Poland, boarded a plane at the Warsaw airport and flew home to Moscow. They had gone to Poland the day before reportedly to pressure the heads of the Polish Communist Party into retaining in the party leadership the Russian Marshal Konstantin Rokossovsky—Minister of Defense in the Polish government and a symbol of Soviet control. They had failed.

Khrushchev was furious: He is reported to have burst out. "If you don't obey we will crush you..." And he leveled the standard Communist charge: "We will never permit this country to be sold to the American imperialists."

The Poles refused to knuckle under; Khrushchev flew home. Gomulka, a Polish leader, said that his "people will not be pushed off the road of democratization."

That day, newspaper reports said, Soviet troops crossing the Polish border from East Germany ran into Polish gunfire.

The Polish unrest spread like a prairie fire. In Wroclaw, thousands of students paraded through the streets shouting, "Long live free Poland!" In Lodz, six thousand textile workers threatened to go on strike unless the Russian troops stationed in Poland were withdrawn. In Warsaw, students rallied under a banner reading "Long live friendship with the Soviet Union on the principles of equality!"

Stalin's statue, beheaded, pulled down as the Hungarian people raised their flag of red, white, and green.

The fire ignited in Poland brought a holocaust to Hungary. Against their Soviet masters, the Hungarian people had a long list of grievances. In the three years following the death of Stalin the Hungarian Communist Party had been the arena for a running intramural battle between the Stalinist Matyas Rakosi and the milder Imre Nagy. In 1953 Nagy became Premier. In 1955, Rakosi succeeded him, was ousted in 1956 but his replacement was another Stalinist, Erno Gero.

On October 23, young Communist demonstrators marched through the streets of Budapest shouting: "Down with Gero!" "We want Nagy!" "Out with the Russians!" They headed for Radio Budapest. There they paused outside and sent in a delegation asking the radio to broadcast their demands. Police put the delegates under arrest. The crowd, angered, moved to storm the station doors. The police fired. When the smoke cleared several demonstrators lay wounded, one dead.

Ten thousand Soviet troops, with eighty tanks, artillery, and armored cars rolled into Budapest to crush the "counterrevolutionary uprising." That afternoon, Budapest time, several hundred workers and students demonstrated peacefully in Parliament Square, demanding the ouster of Gero. The political police and Soviet tanks opened fire. The dead littered the square. Inflamed, mobs raced through the city, tore down Soviet flags, and smashed Soviet monuments.

On the 26th, Belgian diplomats who had fled from Budapest to Vienna were reporting that the rebels controlled all of Western Hungary; that Hungarian soldiers, who had torn the red stars from their caps, controlled the roads out of Budapest, and that "freedom stations" had begun broadcasting.

"Lay down your arms!" Imre Nagy urged over Radio Budapest, promising to establish a popular front government. The rebels refused.

On October 21 *Pravda* published an astonishing and seemingly contrite "Declaration by the Soviet Government on the Principles of Development and Further Strengthening of Friendship and Cooperation between the Soviet Union and Other Socialist States." It promised that the Soviet Government would withdraw its troops as soon as the Hungarian Government considered that withdrawal necessary.

"This utterance," Allen Dulles declared, "is one of the most significant to come out of the Soviet Union since the end of World War II."

"Yes," I replied, "if it is honest."

The Hungarian revolution was, at that moment, at its high-water mark. How cynical would their statement appear within a matter of days.

On Thursday, November 1, an eventful day, Imre Nagy informed the Soviet

Ambassador that Hungary was renouncing the Warsaw Pact (the Communist parallel to NATO), declaring its neutrality, and appealing to the United Nations for help in defense of that neutrality.

At 3:13 in the morning of November 4 the UN Security Council began a meeting in which the Soviet Union, using its veto for the seventy-ninth time, torpedoed an American resolution calling upon the Russian government at once to withdraw its forces from Hungary.

The Soviet Union promptly launched a major assault on Hungary; two hundred thousand troops and four thousand tanks reportedly moved into Budapest "to help the Hungarian people crush the black forces of reaction and counter-revolution." A new Communist government—the Hungarian Revolutionary Workers and Peasants Government—under the command of Janos Kadar came into existence. That one day, it was reported, there were fifty thousand Hungarians dead and wounded in the streets of Budapest.

At once I wrote to Bulganin: "I urge in the name of humanity and in the cause of peace that the Soviet Union take action to withdraw Soviet forces from Hungary immediately..."

The Hungarian uprising, from its beginning to its bloody suppression, inspired in our nation feelings of sympathy and admiration for the rebels, anger and disgust for their Soviet oppressors. No one shared these feelings more keenly than I; indeed, I still wonder what would have been my recommendation to the Congress and the American people had Hungary been accessible by sea or through the territory of allies who might have agreed to react positively to any attempt to help prevent the tragic fate of the Hungarian people.

Unless the major nations of Europe would, without delay, ally themselves spontaneously with us (an unimaginable prospect), we could do nothing. Sending United States troops alone into Hungary through hostile or neutral territory would have involved us in general war. Though the General Assembly passed a resolution calling upon the Soviets to withdraw their troops, it was obvious that no mandate for military action could or would be forthcoming. I realized that there was no use going further into this possibility.

So, as a single nation the United States did the only thing it could: We readied ourselves in every way possible to help the refugees fleeing from the criminal action of the Soviets, and did everything possible to condemn the aggression.

Late in November, in violation of a pledge of safe conduct, the Soviets seized Imre Nagy. In an exhibition of pure, barbaric vengeance, he was later tried in secret and executed. On December 1, I announced that the United States, under existing law, would offer asylum, as a start, to more than twenty-one thousand

Hungarian refugees—that we would bring to the United States with all possible speed refugees who sought asylum here; and that I would request emergency legislation to permit qualified refugees who accepted asylum to obtain permanent residence in the United States. By the end of the year 150,000 Hungarians had left their homeland.

Simultaneous with the Hungarian uprising, a crisis developed in the Middle East.

The Middle East is a land bridge connecting Europe, Asia, and Africa. Its soil has borne the travelers, merchants, and conquering armies of the centuries. Three of the world's religions were founded there—Judaism, Christianity, and Islam—and under its surface lie the world's largest-known oil reserves, the "black gold" of our machine age.

Jewish-Arab tensions, dormant for many years, broke out explosively after World War II and became inflamed by the war in 1949, during which the Arabs converged on Israel in an attempt to drive the new settlers into the sea. The Israeli defeated their neighbors in a series of limited actions. From 1949 onward, peace in the region has never been complete. Border incidents are common and boundaries, to this day (1966), are lined with pillboxes, machine guns, and watchful border guards.

In an early attempt to establish peace and preserve the status quo, three Western nations, Britain, France, and the United States, signed in May 1950, an agreement to act together to defeat any seizure of Middle East territory by force.

Egypt occupied a position of pivotal importance to the politics of the area, partly because the personality and views of Gamal Abdel Nasser appealed to Arabs everywhere who desired to unite in one great Arab nation. Moreover, Egypt had within its borders one invaluable tangible asset: the Suez Canal, Western Europe's lifeline to the East.

This canal was the most important waterway in the world and a highly profitable one.

The year 1952 marked the beginning of a long and difficult diplomatic negotiations between Egypt and Britain regarding the Suez Base, occupied ever since World War II by the British Army. These forces and their dependents were subjected to a relentless guerilla warfare; there was scarcely day or night that did not witness one or more murders in the garrison's population.

I believed that it would be undesirable and impracticable for the British to retain sizable forces permanently in the territory of a jealous and resentful government amid such an openly hostile population. Therefore, Secretary Dulles and I encouraged the British gradually to evacuate the eighty thousand troops still stationed there. Protracted negotiations were finally brought to a successful conclusion in 1954; the last soldier was scheduled to leave the base area in June of 1956.

Meanwhile a once small, threatening cloud was becoming larger and darkening the entire region; it was the growing closeness of relations between the ambitious Nasser and the Soviets. This development colored the negotiations that had been under way for some months between Nasser on the one side and the World Bank, Britain, and ourselves regarding plans for financing a huge dam on the Nile.

The prospective Aswan High Dam was a long-term pet of President Nasser, a gigantic power and irrigation project that would take nearly twenty years to construct and would cost over a billion dollars. By the middle of June my associates and I were becoming doubtful of the wisdom of United States participation in the Aswan Dam project. Nasser completely ignored the set of conditions that the World Bank, Britain and ourselves believed must be fulfilled by Egypt before construction could become feasible.

When Nasser received specific news of cancellation of our aid offer, he went into a rage. He made a vitriolic public attack on the United States on July 24. And on the 26th he proclaimed, in a three-hour harangue, the nationalization of the Suez Canal with all its properties and assets, ostensibly as a means of financing the Aswan Dam.

The fat was now really in the fire. Nasser had moved to take over in total the world's foremost public utility. Its loss—if it were to cease functioning—would seriously cripple Western Europe. To permit such an eventuality to occur was unthinkable.

The Egyptians argued that as long as international rights to the use of the canal, as listed in the Constantinople Treaty of 1888, were not interfered with, it was Egypt's right to operate and receive the proceeds from any utility within its national boundaries.

Deeply suspicious of Nasser's motives, France and Britain considered Suez as a symbol, a symbol of their interests and rights in the entire Middle East and Arab world; their reaction was not immediately predictable but it would require all we could do to keep the lid from blowing off. The weight of world opinion seemed to be that Nasser was within his rights in nationalizing the Canal Company.

In my telephonic and other communications with Prime Minister Eden I frequently expressed the opinion that the case as it stood did not warrant resort to military force.

I told Anthony that I doubted the validity of his argument that no one except the European technicians, then operating the Canal, were capable of doing so.

On Tuesday morning, July 31, Foster Dulles, came to my office to discuss a message from London of even more serious implications. In essence it stated that the British government had taken a firm decision to "break Nasser" and to initiate hostilities at an early date for the purpose.

It contemplated an action that, under existing circumstances, we would not support; and so informed our British friends.

I can scarcely describe the depth of the regret I felt in the need to take a view so diametrically opposed to that held by the British. Some in the British Cabinet were old friends of mine; indeed, several were comrades in the dramatic days of World War II and of the less exacting but still momentous times at NATO. I admired these men.... Yet I felt that in taking our own position we were standing firmly on principle and on the realities of the twentieth century.

My conviction was that the Western world had gotten into a lot of difficulty by selecting the wrong issue about which to be tough.

To choose a situation in which Nasser had legal and sovereign rights and in which world opinion was justifiably on his side was not in my opinion a good one on which to make a stand.

On October 15, Foster and several assistants came to see me about a new situation. The Israeli, for some reason we could not fathom, were mobilizing. High-flying reconnaissance planes revealed that the Israeli had *sixty* French Mystere airplanes, not twelve, as the French had reported to us. Obviously a blackout of communications had been imposed. From about this time on, we had the uneasy feeling that we were cut off from our allies.

On October 27, the State Department forwarded my cable to Ben-Gurion, expressing my "concern at reports of heavy mobilization on your side . . . I renew the plea . . . that there be no forceable initiative on the part of your Government which would endanger the peace . . ." On October 29 an attack did come. In the course of the night, the Israeli had knifed seventy-five miles into Egypt, arriving at a point only twenty-five miles east of Suez.

I decided that we should telephone Mr. J. E. Coulson, who, in the absence of the British Ambassador, was serving as *charge d'affaires,* ask him to come to the White House, and tell him what we planned to do.

" . . . The prestige of the United States and the British is involved in the developments in the Middle East," I said. "I feel it is incumbent upon both of us to redeem our word about supporting any victim of aggression.

"In view of information that has reached us concerning Mysteres and the number of messages between Paris and Israel in the last few days, I can only conclude that I do not understand what the French are doing."

"I do not know about the messages," Mr. Coulson interposed.

"If I have to call Congress in order to redeem our pledge," I went on, "I will do so. We will stick to our undertaking."

"Would the United States not first go to the Security Council?" Mr. Coulson asked.

"We plan to get to the United Nations the first thing in the morning—when the doors open," I replied, "before the U.S.S.R. gets there."

At 4:39 the next morning, a cable from David Ben-Gurion answered my messages. Nasser has "created a ring of steel" around Israel, Ben-Gurion said:

"With renewal of incursions into Israel territory by Egyptian gangs, my government would be failing its essential duty if it were not to take all necessary measures to ensure that declared Arab whim of eliminating Israel by force should not come about. My government has appealed to people of Israel to combine alertness with calm. I feel confident that with your vast military experience you appreciate to the full the crucial danger in which we find ourselves."

Mollet (of France) admitted afterward: "If your government was not informed of the final developments, the reason...was our fear that if we had consulted it, it would have prevented us from acting."

On October 31, Ambassador Lodge telephoned from the United Nations that there was enthusiastic and well-nigh unanimous approval of the policy we had adopted before that body—calling upon Israel and Egypt to cease fire, upon Israel to withdraw behind the armistice line, and upon all UN members to refrain from the use of force and from military, economic, and financial aid to Israel until it complied with this UN resolution.

Then, as dusk fell over Egypt, British planes based on Cyprus launched a bombing raid against Cairo, Alexandria, Port Said, and Ismailia. In the Suez Canal near Lake Timsah, the Egyptians quickly sunk a 320-foot-long ship, the AKKA, which more than two months before had been loaded with cement and rocks and towed to the spot for a voyage to the bottom should events so require. The Suez Canal was blocked. In the next few days the Egyptians were to send thirty-two ships to the floor of the Canal and blame all the sinkings on the British.

A President paints. Camp David, Maryland, August 1954. "I refuse to refer to my productions as paintings. They are daubs, born of my love of color, nothing else. I have tried more portraits than anything else. I've also burned more portraits than anything else."

And the family grows. In the Presidential lap, Susan. Beside him, Barbara, Barbara Anne, John, David, and Mamie Eisenhower.

In 1954, a settlement of Suez. In the storms that swirled around that troubled region, the government of Egypt got a new President, Gamal Abdel Nasser, and the British agreed to withdraw their troops.

To the Summit conference in Geneva in 1955, the President brought an open mind, cautious optimism, and the electrifying "Open Skies" disarmament plan. To the meeting the Soviets sent (left to right, front row) Nikita Khrushchev, First Secretary of the party; Premier Nikolai Bulganin, Foreign Minister V. M. Molotov. Behind Bulganin, in uniform, is Georgi Zhukov, then Defense Minister. Andrei Gromyko (left) shields his face from the sun, and beside him is Yakov A. Malik.

I then stated my belief in the United Nations as the soundest hope for peace. Though the society of nations had been slow to accept it, the truth was that:

"The peace we seek and need means much more than mere absence of war. It means the acceptance of law, and the fostering of justice, in all the world."

On the morning of November 2 the UN General Assembly approved the United States cease-fire resolution 64 to 5. Britain, France, Australia, New Zealand, and Israel opposed it;

Though Egypt announced its acceptance of the cease-fire resolution Anthony Eden refused to postpone his invasion: "If we draw back now" he said to me, "everything will go up in flames in the Middle East...We cannot have a military vacuum while a UN force is being constituted."

At eight o'clock in the morning of November 5, six hundred British paratroopers jumped on Gamil Airfield, to the west of Port Said on the Suez Canal. Five hundred French paratroopers dropped to the south of Port Said.

In the next hour or so, the Soviet Union broke silence. Loudspeaker vans in Port Said blared out the news that Russian help was on the way. At the same time Bulganin wrote to me proposing that the United States and the Soviet Union join forces, march into Egypt, and put an end to the fighting. "If this war is not stopped, it is fraught with danger and can grow into a Third World War," he added.

The White House statement called the Soviet plan for joint American-Soviet action "unthinkable," and warned that the entry of any new troops into the Middle East would oblige all members of the United Nations, *including the United States,* to take effective countermeasures.

In an immediate meeting in the White House Cabinet Room I suggested that the military services might soon call back personnel from leave, an action impossible to conceal and which would let the Russians know—without being provocative—that we could not be taken by surprise.

At the very moment we were meeting in the White House the British government was ordering a cease-fire, and I quickly telephoned Anthony Eden. I told him of our satisfaction that he found it possible to order the cease-fire.

"I hope that you will now go along with the United Nations resolutions without imposing any conditions," I said. "This I think would be highly advisable so as to deny Russia any opportunity to create trouble. The United Nations is making preparation for the concentration of a caretaking force."

Anthony felt that the size of that force would have to be considerable.

"I hope you [the Americans] will be there," he said. "Are we all going to go?"

"I would like to see none of the great nations in it," I replied. My thought was that if any of the large nations provided troop contingents the Soviets would try to provide the largest. I told Anthony we should put the matter in Mr. Hammarskjold's hands and say to him, "When we see you coming in with enough troops to take over, we'll leave."

If anyone then made an aggressive move, I said, the attack would be a challenge to the whole United Nations. This, I felt, no one would want to make.

The Prime Minister asked time to think this suggestion over and then referring to our election he asked: "How are things going with you?"

We had been giving all our thought to Hungary and the Middle East, I said. "I don't give a darn about the election, I guess it will be all right."

Later that afternoon Prime Minister St. Laurent of Canada called.

"Things are pretty encouraging," I told him. "Never have I seen action on the part of a government that excited me more than the rapid way you and your government moved into the breech with your proposal for a United Nations force to go to Suez. You did a magnificent job, and we admire it."

At two o'clock in the morning of November 7, Cairo time, fighting ended in the Middle East.

Looking backward to those days, it is easy to see that the British and French won battles but nothing else. Israel, also winning battles, succeeded in unblocking the Gulf of Aqaba and temporarily halting the raids across her borders.

Some critics have said that the United States should have sided with the British and French in the Middle East, that it was fatuous to lean so heavily on the United Nations. If we had taken this advice, where would it have led us? Would we now be, with them, an occupying power in a seething Arab world? If so, I am sure we would regret it.

On November 23 Winston Churchill wrote me a long letter urging that we leave to historians the arguments over recent events in the Middle East and that we take action in harmony to forestall a Soviet triumph there; it would be folly, he said, to let the great essentials be lost in bickerings, and to let misunderstanding make a gulf in the Anglo-American alliance.

I replied at once in a letter which closed:

"I hope that this one may be washed off the slate as soon as possible and we can then together adopt other means of achieving our legitimate objectives in the Mid-East. Nothing saddens me more than the thought that I and my old friends of years have met a problem concerning which we do not see eye to eye. I shall never be happy until our old time closeness has been restored."

One item in the budget that I was anxious to preserve in spite of my determination to minimize over-all expenditures was the appropriation for the United States Information Agency.

After World War II, our government was compelled to transform the Office of War Information into a permanent United States Information Agency whose sole and essential purpose was to let all the world know the truth and only the truth about our policies, plans, actions, and purposes. "Wars begin in the minds of men and in the minds of men the foundations of peace must be constructed."

To my associates and me, the Agency was a non-military arm of defense and a voice of our foreign policy, both of which would be helped by achieving genuine understanding among the peoples of the world. Unfortunately, however, the Agency had never been popular with the Congress.

In the January 1957 budget I had asked for $144 million for the USIA— $31 million more than the year before, but far less than I believed essential. Despite my urgent support of the Agency's important work, the House on April 17 refused.

From the ominous beginning, things grew steadily worse... Senator Lyndon Johnson already was talking about slicing the House's low figure of $105 million to $91 million, Mansfield to $70 million, and Fulbright to $55 million.

Senator Johnson left no doubt about his views: "There is not one scintilla of evidence in the more than twelve hundred pages of hearings which would justify the assertian by a judicious, prudent man that the $90 million we have recommended will be wisely spent."

Two weeks later Senate conferees agreed to raise the final figure to $96 million. I was disappointed by this irresponsible diminution of an agency on the front line in the cold war.

Another battle that enlivened and marred Executive-Legislative relations during the first session of the Eighty-fifth Congress involved school construction. At that time, the United States, according to the calculations of the Department of Health, Education, and Welfare, had a shortage of approximately 159,000 classrooms.

Early in 1957, therefore, I again sent to Capitol Hill a Special Message on Education, including a request for a four-year, $1.3 billion total program of federal grants to the states for school construction. This was to be an "emergency measure," to stimulate greater state and local efforts to meet needs.

At once the bill ran into crossfire.

On July 25 the House killed the educational bill, which as in 1956 carried an anti-segregation rider. This rider again consolidated the opposition. Ninety-seven Democrats and 111 Republicans had voted "aye"; 126 Democrats and 77 Republicans voted "no."

On August 21, I met with staff members for a briefing.

"What might you say," one asked, "about the accomplishments of the Congress so far in this session?"

"Nothing printable" was my reply.

The Congress had, by adjournment day, chopped nearly five billion from the budget I had sent up in January. The biggest reductions were in defense: for the entire military budget, I had requested 36.1 billion dollars; the Congress appropriated 33.7 billion dollars. Few congressmen who voted for these cuts were anxious to recall them one month later when the first Russian Sputnik was launched.

At the close of the session, I received the traditional phone call from the Majority and Minority Leaders. "Mr. President," said Senator Johnson, "I'll bet you're just as happy to see us go as we are to go."

In fervent assent, I wished them all a speedy trip home.

The 1957 session marked the low point in effective cooperation between the administration and the Congress.

But as the first session of the Eighty-fifth Congress passed into history unmourned by me, I could, however, point to one real accomplishment: enactment of the first piece of civil rights legislation since 1875.

On May 17, 1954, the United States Supreme Court, in a unanimous opinion, made one of the most historic judgments of its existence. It reversed the 1896 Plessy v. Ferguson decision, which had put the Court's approval on "separate but equal" public educational facilities for children of the white and Negro races.

The 14th Amendment to the Constitution, the Court said in 1954, guarantees equal protection of the laws to all citizens. Can separate facilities, it asked, be in fact equal? It decided not: segregating children, the Court concluded, "generates a feeling of inferiority as to their status in the community that may affect their hearts and minds in a way unlikely ever to be undone."

After the ruling, I refused to say whether I either approved or disapproved of it. The Court's judgment was law, I said, and I would abide by it. This determination was one of principle. I believed that if I should express, publicly, either approval or disapproval of a Supreme Court decision in one case, I would be obliged to do so in many, if not all, cases. Inevitably I would eventually be drawn into a public statement of disagreement with some decision, creating a suspicion that my vigor of enforcement would, in such cases, be in doubt. Moreover, to indulge in a practice of approving or criticizing Court decisions could tend to lower the dignity of government, and would, in the long run, be hurtful. In this case I definitely agreed with the unanimous decision.

As soon as the decision was handed down, I called the District of Columbia Commissioners and told them that the District should take the lead in desegregating its schools as an example to the entire country. By the opening of the fall term in September of that same year, the policy of nonsegregation had gone into effect in Washington, with no violence.

In March of 1956 I wrote to the evangelist Dr. Billy Graham urging him to influence southern ministers to strive for calm rather than to inflame popular opinion—to stress the progress already made, even before the 1954 Court decision. And I added that "I shall always, as a matter of conviction and as a champion of real, as opposed to spurious, progress, remain a moderate in this regard."

Civil rights supporters, I told the legislative leaders on April 17, 1956, seemed never to consider that although the federal government had, in the past, used troops on a number of occasions to enforce the laws, troops could not force local officials to operate the schools; private schools could be set up, and Negroes, as well as many others, would get no education at all. These words proved grimly prophetic.

I determined to seek an effective method for separating truth from falsehood in the whole troubled area. So, in my 1956 State of the Union message, I said that it was disturbing that in some localities there is evidence

> that Negro citizens are being deprived of their right to vote and are like-
> wise being subjected to unwarranted economic pressures. I recommend that
> the substance of these charges be thoroughly examined by a bipartisan com-
> mission created by the Congress.

After considerable discussion, in which the entire Cabinet participated, my civil rights recommendations went to the Congress. These were a four-point program, calling for a new bipartisan civil rights commission, a civil rights division under a new Assistant Attorney General in the Department of Justice, new laws to aid in enforcing voting rights, and amendments to existing laws to permit the federal government to seek in civil courts preventive relief in civil rights cases. At the time, these proposals were little less than revolutionary.

The Eisenhower farm at Gettysburg, Pennsylvania. (Building in left, background, is the barn.)

"Mamie had found the place she wanted. She started off by deciding to restore the old farmhouse...I had an engineering survey made and found, much to Mamie's dismay, that she could not really re-build. The logs were worm-eaten, about two hundred years old. There was nothing to do but tear the place down. So anxious was she to retain even a fragment of the original that when she found one portion of the wall and a Dutch oven in which no logs had been used, she built a complete house around them."

David Eisenhower gets off a shot while his grandfather helps with a little body English and, perhaps, a hoot and a holler. Fraser, Colorado, 1955.

On the sundeck outside his room at Fitzsimons Army Hospital, Denver, the President greets the press after his first heart attack. October 1955.

The opposition massed. On July 13, eighty-three southern representatives—four of them were Republicans—signed a manifesto against the administration bill, urging all members of the Senate and House "to join with us in the employment of every available legal and parliamentary weapon to defeat this sinister and iniquitous proposal."

The opposition forces proved to be too powerful in 1956, for although the bill passed the House, it died in the Senate Judiciary Committee.

In the State of the Union message on January 10, 1957, I submitted to the Congress a succinct and uncomplicated civil rights request: enact the program I had proposed for 1956.

Incidentally, a few Southerners in the Congress, some of them my personal friends, privately told me that in the matter of voting rights they agreed on the justice of and the need for my stand. But their declarations were accompanied by the statement, "Officially and publicly, I must be, in my state, against every kind of proposal on civil rights of whatever nature."

On July 16 the Senate agreed to take up the House bill. Senator Russell announced that the southern forces were "prepared to expend the greatest effort ever made in history to prevent passage of this bill in its present form." That same day I issued a statement approving the purposes of the bill as it came from the House and urging the Senate, "in whatever clarification it may determine to make," to "keep the measure an effective piece of legislation to carry out these...objectives."

After a month of intense debate, and despite several disappointing cuts and amendments, the bill finally became law.

Thus the United States had its first Civil Rights Act in eighty-two years.

But there was little time for rejoicing or relaxation. Four days after the Senate approved the compromise, the Governor of Arkansas, Orval Faubus, called out units of the Arkansas National Guard and ordered them to take up positions outside Central High School in Little Rock to "preserve peace and good order" and, incidentally, to keep Negro students from passing through the doors to take their seats on their first day in school in classrooms formerly all white.

In response to Faubus' request for my assurance of understanding and cooperation, I said, "The only assurance I can give you is that the Federal Constitution will be upheld by me by every legal means at my command."

The Little Rock school board, apparently fearful of an impending crisis, asked Judge Davies of the District Court to set aside his order for immediate integration. The judge refused.

On September 9 the district court asked the United States to enter the case and to file a petition for an injunction against the Arkansas Governor. The court set September 20 as the date for its hearing on the legality of his action.

The United States government and the Governor of Arkansas were now heading toward a collision.

I said that if Governor Faubus wanted to have an honest discussion, I would see him. The Democratic congressman who represented the Little Rock district, Brooks Hays, had, at my insistence, persuaded Faubus to agree that in wording his wire requesting a meeting he would say, "It is certainly my intention to comply with the order... by the District Court." But when the wire arrived, it read, "It is certainly my desire to comply with the order... *consistent with my responsibilities under the Constitution of the United States and that of Arkansas.*" This significant change made by Faubus supported Attorney General Brownell's skepticism that any good could come out of a meeting with him.

On the morning of Saturday, September 14, Faubus arrived at Newport. He talked alone with me for about twenty minutes.

"I believe," I told him, "that when you go home, you should not necessarily withdraw the National Guard troops. Just change their orders to say that since you have been assured that the federal government is not trying to do anything that has not been already agreed to by the school board and directed by the courts, the Guard should continue to preserve order but allow the Negro children to attend Central High School." He was due to appear the following Friday, the 20th, before the Court to determine whether an injunction was to be issued.

"In any event," I said, "you should take this action promptly. Then the Justice Department can go to the court and ask that you not be brought into court."

Finally I told him that I did not believe it was beneficial to anybody to have a trial of strength between the President and a Governor.

Overseas, the mouthpieces of Soviet propaganda in Russia and Europe were blaring out that "anti-Negro violence" in Little Rock was being "committed with the clear connivance of the United States government..."

The morning of Monday, September 23, arrived. From all over Little Rock, a mob of more than a thousand angry and determined whites, stirred up by recent events and Governor Faubus, converged on Central High School, determined to keep out the Negro students who were due to enter. Eight Negro children arrived, however, and somehow slipped in unseen through a side door. For three hours the mob rioted outside. They brushed aside the local police. Then, on an order from Little Rock's Mayor Mann, the police removed the Negro children from the school.

The issue had now become clear both in fact and in law.

Cruel mob force had frustrated the execution of an order of a United States court, and the governor of the state was sitting by, refusing to lift a finger to support the local authorities.

There was only one justification for the use of troops; to uphold the law. Though Faubus denied it, I, as President of the United States, now had that justification and the clear obligation to act.

A frantic wire arrived from Mayor Mann:

"The immediate need for federal troops is urgent. The mob is much larger in numbers at 8 A.M. than at any time yesterday. People are converging on the scene from all directions and engaging in fisticuffs and other acts of violence. Situation is out of control and police cannot disperse the mob..."

Shortly after twelve noon on September 24 I telephoned the Attorney General that I was about to sign an Executive Order (10730) which would federalize the Arkansas National Guard and send regular federal troops into Little Rock. At 12:15 I did so.

That afternoon five hundred paratroopers of the 101st Airborne Division, from nearby Fort Campbell, Kentucky, arrived in Little Rock; another five hundred moved in later the same day.

My action caused, as expected, loud protests, mostly politically inspired, throughout the south. Governor Faubus was perhaps the most restrained: "I believe he showed bad judgment." Senator Lyndon Johnson contributed: "There should be no troops from either side patrolling our school campuses." Senator Eastland was perhaps the most doom-laden: "The President's move," he said, "was an attempt to destroy the social order of the South"; and Senator Olin Johnston's was surely the bravest: "If I were a governor and he came in, I'd give him a fight such as he's never been in before."

By the next morning, however, violence had ended. Two men tried to keep the troops from dispersing spectators around Central High School; one was clubbed, and another was struck in the arm by the point of a bayonet. This was the entire casualty list. But nine Negro students entered the high school doors.

What Little Rock was to law in the United States, Suez was to law among the nations; an example of the United States government's staking its majesty and its power on a principle of justice—a principle greater and higher than the particular interests of the individuals who clashed in the crisis. Both events, however tragic and unnecessary they may have been, have left to history a demonstration of a profound regard for that supreme law whose voice is the

"The twin problems of Hungary and Suez now became more acute and created an anomalous situation. In Europe we were aligned with Britain and France in our opposition to the brutal Soviet invasion of Hungary; in the Middle East we were against the entry of British-French armed forces in Egypt.

Egyptian prisoners under French guard. Suez.

Hungarian freedom fighters.

Sunken ships blocking entrance to the Suez Canal at Port Said.

"harmony of the world"—a law to which, in the words of Richard Hooker, all men owe "homage, the very least as feeling her care, and the greatest as not exempted from her power."

In late January 1958 Egypt's President Nasser—whose exact political leanings were still something of a mystery—announced that Egypt and Syria planned to unite, forming a new nation, the United Arab Republic. The other Arab nations viewed the development with real anxiety.

In that same spring serious trouble began to break out in Lebanon.

The pro-Western orientation of President Chamoun's government, while gratifying and helpful, had its dangers in that it accented the cleavage within his own country.

Nasser worked hard to aggravate these internal difficulties. If he was not a Communist, he certainly succeeded in making us very suspicious of him.

There had been increasing numbers of border crossings between Lebanon and Syria by Arab nationalists, and it seemed likely that Lebanon occupied a place on Colonel Nasser's timetable as nation to be brought under his influence.

Then in late April matters came to a head. The trigger for the crisis was a rumor, well-substantiated, that President Chamoun had given his assent to a movement to amend the Lebanese constitution, with the purpose of achieving for himself an unprecedented second term in office.

Rebellion, smoldering for some weeks, finally broke out in early May in an armed uprising in Beirut.

On the 22nd of May President Chamoun requested an urgent meeting of the United Nations Security Council to consider his complaint that Egypt and Syria had been instigating the revolt and arming the rebels. There was no doubt in our minds of the truth of the charge. Arrogant and aggressive, the rebels seemed to be trying to cut the northern half of Lebanon from the southern half, as a preliminary to gaining control of the whole.

On Monday morning, July 14, 1958, I was astounded by news of a coup in Baghdad, Iraq, against the Hashemite monarchy. This was the country that we were counting on heavily as a bulwark of stability and progress in the region. The army, apparently with mob participation, had moved upon the royal palace and had murdered Crown Prince Abdul Illah. The fate of King Faisal and Premier Nusi as Said...was in serious doubt.

The time had come to act. I turned to Secretary Dulles; "Foster, give us your analysis of an American intervention in Lebanon. What would the Russians do?"

"Obviously, the decision to send troops to Lebanon was not one to be taken lightly...the problem was to select the least objectionable of several courses of action.

"I directed that the landing take place at 3 p.m.

"On October 25, 1958, the final withdrawal of United States troops took place, almost without public notice. This lack of attention contrasted vividly with attitudes in the early days of our intervention when some international critics were crying that America's purpose was to establish a permanent and imperialistic foothold in the Middle East."

He replied, "The Russians will probably make threatening gestures—toward Turkey and Iran especially—but will not act unless they believe the results of a general war would be favorable to them." Foster did not believe the Soviets would put this to the test because of their respect for our power.

The present case, from a legal viewpoint, was far different from that of the British-French attack on Egypt. Our intervention would be a response to a proper request from a legally constituted government and in accordance with the principles stated in the Middle East Doctrine.

I directed that the landing take place the next afternoon, at 3 P.M. Lebanon time.

On the military side, the news during the day of July 15 was good. In fact, the Lebanese along the beaches welcomed our troops.

I instructed General Nathan Twining to be prepared to employ, subject to my personal approval, whatever means might become necessary to prevent any

unfriendly forces from moving into Kuwait. In the state of tension then existing, these measures would probably bring us no closer to general war than
we were already.

During all this time we were in finger-tip communication with Prime Minister
Macmillan. In the two days following the landings, the British Cabinet discussed
the possibilities of further action in the Middle East. On July 17 that government decided, in compliance with King Hussein's plea, to send twenty-two
hundred British paratroopers (into Jordan) to bolster his shaky regime. The
British were undoubtedly influenced by reports of a dangerous plot against the
King's life.

All these detailed concerns were dwarfed by the fears that gripped the rest
of the world over what the Soviet reaction might be to the United States and
British interventions. Personally I had always discounted the probability of
the Soviets doing anything as "reaction." Communists do little on impulse;
rather their aggressive moves are the result of deliberate decision. They staged
extensive military maneuvers in the south of Russia, but confined their external
moves to the diplomatic.

The situation began to stabilize itself by the end of July. Special presidential
elections were successfully carried out in Lebanon.

When the UN General Assembly convened, it seemed wise for me to request
the opportunity to address it. I hoped it might be possible to establish a constructive atmosphere conducive to real results.

We made up a list of six items important to peace in the Middle East. The
first two, as might be expected, involved the preservation of peace in Lebanon
and in Jordan.

The resolution the United Nations General Assembly passed on August 21
was instituted by the Arabs themselves. It pledged non-interference among the
Arab states in each others' affairs and instructed Secretary-General Hammarskjold to make practical arrangements leading to the withdrawal of the
West's troops from Lebanon and Jordan.

Fundamentally, this action in the United Nations terminated the Lebanon
crisis, although American troops were to stay there for another two months.

Apart from the successful outcome of the intervention to save Lebanon, I
believe that one additional benefit to the West, was a definite change in Nasser's
attitude toward the United States.

The Suez incident, and our long negotiations to reach a satisfactory solution
to all the problems arising out of it had led him into the egregious error of
doubting America's firmness in carrying out her pledges.

Queen Elizabeth arrives for a visit.

Pro-Castro pickets march in front of the White House, "urging the United States to prevent the use of U. S. arms against Castro and his followers," said a news agency caption.

In our action and the Kremlin's cautious reaction he found much food for thought, it would appear; certainly he had his complacency as to America's helplessness completely shattered.

On the military side the Lebanon operation demonstrated the ability of the United States to react swiftly with conventional armed forces to meet small-scale, or "brush fire" situations.

The Lebanon operation was not to be compared with the serious fighting of the Korean War. But such operations had convinced me that if, "small wars" were to break out in several places in the world simultaneously, then we would *not* fight on the enemy's terms and be limited to his choice of weapons. We would hold the Kremlin—or Peking—responsible for their actions and would act accordingly.

These facts were not secret; they were well-advertised. The Communists had come to be aware of our attitude and there was reason to think that they respected it.

At 7:30 on the evening of Friday, October 4, 1957, at the Tyrratam Range in Kazakhstan, the Soviet Union fired into orbit the world's first man-made satellite. It carried a new name into the language—"Sputnik," Russian for "traveling companion."

This feat precipitated a wave of apprehension throughout the Free World. People now recalled with concern that only a few weeks earlier the Soviet Union had claimed the world's first successful test of a multi-stage ICBM—a shot which, the Russians said, demonstrated that they could fire a missile "into any part of the world."

Most surprising of all, however, was the intensity of the public concern. Soviet space ambitions had been no secret. The New York Times, on October 1, 1957, carried on its front page an article headlined "Light May Flash in Soviet's 'Moon'"; the story caused little stir. Yet three days later, when the "moon" became a fact, its light was blinding. Politicians declared themselves "shocked." They purported to read in the Sputnik success alarming evidence that the Soviet Union was now not only first in space, but far ahead in guided missiles.

Why, such critics demanded, were we not the first to place a satellite in space?

One answer, which the political opposition soon realized and understandably soft-pedaled, was supplied by one of America's foremost missile experts. *"The United States,"* Dr. Wernher von Braun said, *"had no ballistic missile program worth mentioning between 1945 and 1951.* Those six years, during which the

Russians obviously laid the groundwork for their large rocket program, are irretrievably lost...our present dilemma is not due to the fact that we are not working hard enough now, but that we did not work hard enough during the first six to ten years after the war."

In February of 1947, when I was serving as Chief of Staff of the Army, I had reported at a hearing before the House Military Appropriations Subcommittee that "in the field of guided missiles, electronics and supersonic aircraft we have no more than scratched the surface of possibilities which we must explore in order to keep abreast of the rest of the world. Neglect to do so could bring our country to ruin and defeat in an appallingly few hours."

However, the responsible political authorities, preoccupied in those years with the reduction of military force and expenditures, failed to put more than token effort into the development of the ballistic missile.

Deeply concerned in 1953 at the previous lack of attention given to missile development, my administration quickly turned to outstanding scientists and engineers to determine the feasibility of developing effective weapons of this character.

The Air Force reshaped its program and began to accelerate work on an ICBM. By early 1955 its Atlas project was mushrooming.

On the morning of October 9, 1957, at a news conference, I congratulated Soviet scientists on putting a satellite into orbit. I reminded the reporters that merging our scientific satellite effort with our military programs "could have produced an orbiting United States satellite before now, but to the detriment of scientific goals and military progress." Therefore, I concluded, though Sputnik proved that the Russians have a "very powerful thrust in their rocketry," so far as security was concerned, the new satellite did "not raise my apprehensions."

Then on November 2 the world received word that the Soviet Union had launched its second satellite—an eleven-hundred-pound vehicle with an air-conditioned compartment containing a dog, named "Laika" or "Limonchek" ("Little Lemon"). This time there was no hysteria. By a strange but compassionate turn, public opinion seemed to resent the sending of a dog to certain death—a resentment that the Soviet propagandists tried to assuage, after its death, by announcing that he had been comfortable to the end.

On the morning of November 7 newspapers carried Khrushchev's boastful prediction of a Soviet victory over the United States in the building of heavy industry and the production of consumer goods. That evening, from my office in the White House, I delivered the first of a series of nationwide talks on science and defense. This was no exercise in positive thinking based on hopes alone. We had much about which to be confident. The talk bristled with specifics.

The United States, I said, could practically annihilate the war-making capability of any other nation. Ever since our adoption of the so-called "New Look" in military preparation, and especially after the 1954–55 reports of our scientific panels, soaring imagination, skill, and energy had gone into our missile programs. American submarines were carrying missiles with nuclear warheads. One of our submarines had cruised under the Arctic ice cap for more than five days. We had dispersed our stock of nuclear weapons to assure that, if we were attacked, ample quantities would be available for instant retaliation.

"As of today the over-all military strength of the Free World is distinctly greater than that of the Communist countries."

Concluding, I said that although for that night's purposes I was stressing science and defense, we were not forgetting that there was more to science than its function in defense. The peaceful contributions of science, to healing, to enriching life, to freeing the spirit—these "are the most important products of the conquest of nature's secrets." And the spiritual powers of a nation—its religious faith, its capacity for intelligent sacrifice—these were the most important stones in any defense structure.

By early 1958 the time had clearly arrived for another step in streamlining our military establishment and for moving forward in science with speed, not haste. During the ensuing congressional session these efforts produced gratifying results:

(1) To strengthen American education, particularly in science, mathematics, and foreign languages, the Congress passed the administration's National Defense Education Bill.

(2) Despite entrenched opposition on Capitol Hill, we recommended and obtained new legislation to reduce interservice rivalries and to strengthen the control of the President and the Secretary of Defense in strategic planning and operations.

(3) Obtaining needed laws for intensifying research and development for both peaceful and military purposes, we established a new space agency, NASA, under civilian authority, and orbited a succession of satellites.

No one can contemplate the rapidity of scientific advance during recent decades and the consequent vast changes in our social order without pausing to speculate on the actual and as yet unimagined accomplishments, and their several effects, certain to confront mankind in the next half-century.

For three thousand years—from the time of Rameses II to that of Napoleon—

man's means of transportation and communication changed little. By land, he depended upon the horse as his most useful aid in moving from place to place, and for transmitting messages. Sea routes were utilized only by the sailing ship. Air travel was unknown.

But within 150 years after Napoleon's Waterloo, the sailing ship, except for sport, has practically disappeared and the horse in all civilized countries is experiencing the same fate. Their places have been filled with jet planes and atomic power.

Today the guided missile is reinforcing, and gradually supplanting the airplane as an engine of war. Manned satellites about the earth will soon be almost commonplace.

The curve of change bends ever-steeply upward; almost every day brings us news of a new scientific advance in pure research, in engineering, in medicine, in the products and services presented to man for his use. With scientific advances rushing forward at an incredible speed, what is going to be the effect on humans?

One plausible conclusion is that we—especially of the Western world—will lose something of our spirit of nationalism, possibly too rapidly for our own good. We must realize that few of us, because of our sketchy information about others, can think globally. Our outlook on the times in which we live is certain to be colored by national history, traditions, customs, and aspirations.

We must constantly study ourselves, both individually and as a society, and do so with as much care and thoughfulness as we do when bringing into man's service every significant invention or discovery. As we achieve new understandings of elements and forces that for ages past have been believed impervious to change, we must be watchful lest we weaken the vitality of the human spirit and the devotion to moral principle that are mankind's most priceless possessions.

In early August 1958, while the Lebanon issue was being debated in the United Nations, the Communists made their next provocative move. This time they stepped up their belligerencies against islands off the Chinese mainland, the Quemoy and Matsu groups. The Red Chinese had not seriously challenged these Chinese Nationalist-held islands since the crisis four years before that had brought on our Far East Resolution of January 1955.

Why, we wondered, were they choosing this moment to stir up trouble in the Far East? Was Khrushchev still trying to hold Mao back, as some believed, or was he urging him on? For my part, I was quite sure that, to disturb and divide the Free World, Khrushchev would never fail to suggest dark and dangerous possibilities whenever he had an excuse.

One possibility we considered was that he may have been rankled because we had ignored his threats on Lebanon, and had concluded that a reopening of the offshore island issue might divert the attention of the world from Lebanon to the Far East and show that the Communists were still on the offensive.

Chiang Kai-shek had helped complicate the problem. Ignoring our military advice, he had for many months been adding personnel to the Quemoy and Matsu garrisons, thus moving more of his available forces forward, nearer the mainland. By the summer of 1958, a hundred thousand men—a third of his total ground army—were stationed on those two tiny island groups. From a sensible military viewpoint, those little islands should have been defended only as outposts, with the permissible minimum in personnel strength. However, Chiang had always insisted that the loss of the offshore islands would inevitably mean the loss of Formosa itself.

The Communists continued to fire about eight thousand rounds a day, causing no extensive physical damage to the fortifications, but inflicting casualties among both the military and the civilian populations. Quemoy was strafed and the Reds sent out fighter planes in strength. In addition the Communists set up a blockade which for two weeks prevented the Nationalists from convoying supplies to the islands.

All United States forces in the area were placed on a "readiness alert," prepared for immediate war operations. United States forces were directed to be ready to escort Nationalist Chinese resupply vessels to the offshore islands.

In my televised report to the nation on September 11, I spoke of the bombardment, of the Chinese Communist naval craft which were trying to break up the supply of Quemoy, of the fact that over one thousand people had been killed or wounded, in large part civilians. I recalled that in 1955 the Reds had broken off their attack on the offshore islands when we moved to support Free China. We had hoped they would act peacefully but now that they were.not, we were bound by our treaties, and our principles, and authorized to act by the Formosa Resolution. I announced that there would be no retreat. The security of the western Pacific was essential but we were acting not just to save the islands, but to demonstrate that force may not be used for aggressive purposes in the modern world. "There is not going to be any appeasement," I said, and "I believe there is not going to be any war."

On October 5 the Communist Chinese, apparently admitting the failure of their efforts to subdue Quemoy by artillery fire, turned back to psychological warfare to try to split us from our ally. Their Defense Minister announced that Communist guns would cease firing for a week on Quemoy supply convoys if

United States vessels went back to normal patrolling of the Strait.

It was apparent that the Chinese Reds did not choose to precipitate a major war. So I made another attempt to convince the Generalissimo of the wisdom of reducing his garrisons on the islands. He finally did reduce them somewhat.

The Chinese Communists now suddenly announced that they would fire on Nationalist convoys only on odd days of the month, and would permit the Chinese Nationalists to resupply the offshore island garrisons on even-numbered days. I wondered if we were in a Gilbert and Sullivan war. In any event the Nationalists could easily build up any level of supply desired by simply shipping in all they desired every other day.

While saying nothing to Chiang directly, I expressed to our military authorities the hope that he would continue to resupply on any day of his own choosing, to test the true intentions of the Communists. The shelling was costing them much more in expensive ammunition than it was accomplishing in material damage to the Nationalists. However, as a concession to the "terms" of this weird little war, the United States would not engage in any convoying operations unless the Chinese Communists attempted to interfere with the supply program on the even-numbered days in international waters.

Thus the crisis passed. The supply situation on the offshore islands was solved. The Chinese Communists, after issuing an astronomical number of "serious warnings" to the United States, gradually seemed to lose interest in Quemoy and Matsu and, except upon unusual or ceremonial occasions, ceased firing.


On the morning of Monday, November 25, I went to Washington National Airport to extend a ceremonial greeting to the Moroccan King, Mohammed V, who was arriving for a state visit.

Afterward, I went back to the White House for a short midday rest.

Following a light lunch, I walked to my office to resume work for the afternoon.

At the desk I found papers waiting for signature. As I picked up a pen to begin, I experienced a strange feeling of dizziness. Since the sensation lasted only a moment, I reached for another paper. Suddenly I became frustrated. It was difficult for me to take hold of the first paper on the pile. This finally accomplished, I found that the words on it seemed literally to run off the top of the page.

Now more than a little bewildered, I dropped the pen. Failing in two or three attempts to pick it up, I decided to get to my feet, and at once found I had to catch hold of my chair for stability.

I sat down quickly and rang for my secretary. As Mrs. Whitman came to my desk I tried to explain my difficulty—and then came another puzzling experience: I could not express what I wanted to say. Words—but not the ones I wanted—came to my tongue. It was impossible for me to express any coherent thought whatsoever. I began to feel truly helpless.

Actually my performance must have been worse than I suspected, for Mrs. Whitman, after urging me to go home and unable to make any sense out of my words—which I was fully aware were nothing but gibberish—became thoroughly alarmed and called for General Goodpaster.

I responded without protest to Goodpaster's grasp of my arm and his urgent, "Mr. President, I think we should get you to bed."

Sometime later there arrived the inevitable medical consultants.... By this time I could communicate a little, but only a little. The doctors, following a lengthy examination, arrived at a tentative conclusion.

I had suffered, they said, a minor "spasm"—I am not sure whether they referred to a nerve or a small blood vessel. In any event the result was, according to their explanation, a temporary interruption in communication between my mental "dictionary" and the thought I wished to express. Thus, when I sought for a word there was no way of finding the right one; so far as vocabulary was concerned I had a loss of memory. The doctors said I had improved even during the period of their visit, and predicted a full recovery in a matter of days, possibly of hours.

On Mamie fell the burden of entertaining that evening the King of Morocco. I was told that she, and Vice-President Nixon who sat at my place, carried off the affair with skill and aplomb.

Gradually, memory of words returned; the doctors pronounced me 95 percent recovered and said that before long I should be completely cured.

In this prediction they were not wholly accurate. From that time onward I have frequently experienced difficulty in prompt utterance of the word I seek. Even today, occasionally, I reverse syllables in a long word and at times am compelled to speak slowly and cautiously if I am to enunciate correctly.

By the time I came back to work a new argument broke out over my health and planned activities. Sometime earlier I had decided to go to the NATO meeting scheduled for December, only a matter of days after my illness. Doctors, friends, family, and associates protested but now, able to talk, I was determined to have my way—and for a good reason.

This particular illness was of a kind that could, if it became severe, create a situation in which the patient might be partially incapable of analyzing difficult problems and of making reasonable decisions concerning them. Possibly he could become unable to express his thoughts—in the case of the President, be unable even to express a decision to resign. Some believed that a situation of this sort may have happened during the Wilson Administration. I was going to make sure it would not happen in my case.

The test I now set for myself was that of going through with my plan of proceeding to Paris and participating in the NATO conference.

The NATO meeting was a success.

When we were back in Washington my doctor, General Snyder, turned to me to say, "You are much better than when we set out on the journey."

As he spoke, I realized that I already had abandoned any doubt concerning my physical capacity to continue my duties; during the remaining three years of my Presidency no question of the kind again occurred to me.

The year 1958 brought an economic recession which, for the most part, repeated the story of the 1954 recession: a dip in the economy, frenzied Democratic calls for action, the administration's determination not to panic, and the economy's gradual emergence from difficulty.

In January 1958, one of my most highly valued consultants, Dr. Arthur F. Burns, wrote to me about a meeting of the American Economic Association. He reported on the "gloom of the academic fraternity about our economic prospects. If there was an optimist in the crowd, he kept his counsel."

In a later meeting with members of the executive committee of the AFL-CIO, we went over one sobering statistic after another. Their single suggstion was posed as a question: "Why don't you act now?" Others had been insisting on quick Executive actions.

In reply I reminisced a bit: "You know, the same thing happened in the war. Whenever a crisis occurred, some interested but excitable people began screaming for action. And when they did, I had only one answer, 'I guess I'm just too stubborn to act until all necessary facts are in.'"

The story broke the ice at that particular meeting. But it did not stop the calls for crash federal action to bail the country out of its troubles.

For example, early in the 1958 session, the Congress passed a stupid bill— I choose the adjective carefully—authorizing appropriations for rivers, harbors, and flood control projects. It authorized fourteen projects in which local participation did not measure up to the possible local benefits. In another group were four projects on which adequate reports did not even exist. Worse, it authorized three projects on which Corps of Engineers reports did exist, but they were all negative because the projects made no economic sense whatever.

"I cannot overstate my opposition to this kind of waste of public funds," I said, and on April 15 I vetoed the bill.

In another attempt to appear to be taking "vigorous action" against the recession, many members of the Congress voted for Joint Resolution 162, which would freeze farm price supports for the year.

I vetoed the bill, saying that it was one which would pile up more farm products in government warehouses, restrict the growth of markets, and postpone the day when agriculture could be released from the straitjacket of controls.

As evidence of specific government action which could effect good results quickly, I announced that I had directed the Postmaster General to submit to the Congress a $2 billion program to modernize Post Office buildings and equipment—a program which could put men to work quickly in big cities where many of the unemployed lived.

By the end of February we felt certain the economic decline was "bottoming out." We watched and waited.

Fortuitously, there was warm encouragement several weeks later from an unusual corner. I had an interesting talk at the White House with Ludwig Erhard, the West German Vice Chancellor and Minister of Economics. His words came as welcome relief to alarm bells I had been hearing. "I would not really worry about the American economy. Because of Sputniks and fear of other developments in the uneasy world, your recession may have psychological causes which will disappear as public apprehensions lessen. I believe with you that the federal government should not start too early to intervene directly in economic affairs but should continue to reassure the public as to its own security as well as to the basic soundness of the economy." And, as he once before had said to me. "Inflation is always a greater enemy to a nation than deflation."

The weeks rolled by and several of my leading economic advisers came to the conclusion that the administration should urge the Congress to cut taxes. However, I still refused to advocate a tax cut without more evidence that it would help rather than hurt.

As in 1954, the clouds of pessimism gradually began to roll back. The Gross National Product, in the second quarter of 1958, was on its way upward again.

The storm was over.

Though the year 1958 was characterized by controversy it was, happily, not exclusively so. There was significant achievements, some in quiet corners of government.

For one thing, it was a year in which, after previous attempts had failed, we approved the admission of a new state, Alaska, to the Union, setting the stage for admission of a second new state, Hawaii, the following year.

On Monday, November 10, 1958, Soviet Premier Khrushchev declared his intention of signing at an early date a "peace treaty" with East Germany, thus— he contended—terminating Allied rights in West Berlin. With this pronouncement he transformed the city of Berlin, which had remained relatively quiet for more than nine years, into a tinderbox.

Since Berlin lay within the Soviet Zone in East Germany, the Western sector of that city was dependent for access on narrow corridors some 110 miles long through East German territory, completely controlled by the Soviets.

Khrushchev did not at first threaten drastic action, such as the blockade of 1948. Instead he called on the Western nations to begin negotiations with the East German government toward a complete withdrawal of Allied forces from the city. The Soviet Union said it intended to transfer all its administrative functions in the city to the East Germans; but politically we would not, under any circumstances, do business with the East German mock government.

When the news of Khrushchev's statement first broke, there was no reason for an immediate public reply by the United States government; too much eagerness to counter Khrushchev's statement would give the impression that our government was edgy.

On Friday, November 14, four days after the initial announcement, the Soviets detained three United States Army trucks for 8½ hours at a checkpoint on the Autobahn just outside Berlin.

There matters stood until the 27th of November, when my son John arrived in Augusta with an extensive summary of current State Department, CIA, and military reports. Together, the reports stated that none of the Western governments or any member thereof advocated pulling out of Berlin.

Foster had more to report. The State Department had just received a note from Moscow that seemed to defer any move on Khrushchev's part for six months, during which time negotiations over Berlin should take place. Khrushchev had also proposed that West Berlin become a "free city" under the United Nations, and that all occupying powers' military forces withdraw from Berlin.

If an agreement to this effect could not be reached at the end of six months, Khrushchev concluded, the Soviets would go ahead with their program.

Now at the end of 1958, with the threat suspended for the moment, we began to plan the United States' response.

Foster Dulles and I put less credibility in Khrushchev's threat to move in

Senate leaders and Cabinet officers listen to the State of the Union message, January 9, 1959. (Left to right) Senator Everett Dirksen, Ill., minority leader; Secretary of State John Foster Dulles; Treasury Secretary Robert Anderson; Secretary of Defense Neil McElroy; Attorney General William Rogers. Behind them, Senate majority leader Lyndon Johnson.

The blooming Eisenhowers at the Brown Palace Hotel, Denver. May 1959.

the following May than he possibly expected. But every tick of the clock brought us nearer to the moment when we had to be ready to meet him head on, if necessary. Though six months can sometimes seem like an age, there was little enough time to perfect contingency planning with our allies.

The soundest basis for our remaining in Berlin, I felt, was our solemn obligation expressed to the two million Germans of West Berlin and to the entire world to stand by a city that had freely chosen to stay with the West and the cause of freedom. If our word to them would be broken, then no one in the world could have confidence in any pledge we made.

While giving Khrushchev every opportunity to be sensible, we were determined that he should have no reason to question our readiness and capacity to defend our rights. "In this gamble," I said, "we are not going to be betting white chips, building up the pot gradually and fearfully. Khrushchev should know that when we decide to act, our whole stack will be in the pot."

I had a forty-five minute conversation with Mr. Anastas I. Mikoyan, one of Khrushchev's deputies and an expert on trade affairs. I hoped that he was prepared to talk constructively. I was disappointed to find no evidence whatsoever of a softening of the Soviet attitude.

In late January I called a meeting of Defense and State Department officials to discuss Berlin developments. It would not be easy to explain to the public why a nation would risk war over an issue so seemingly slight as the nationality of the man who stamps the papers as a convoy proceeds through a checkpoint. The central point was that all rights the allies had in Berlin were brought about by agreement with the Soviet government, not with the puppets they had installed in a fragmented part of Germany. There would be no way in which we could hold the East Germans responsible for carrying out Soviet promises made years before.

One purpose of the meeting would be to provide a means by which Khrushchev could, without losing face, modify his position regarding Berlin. We stood firm in saying that we would deal only with the Soviets; not with a puppet satellite, and we'd defend our treaty rights in Berlin. Possibly we were risking the very fate of civilization on the premise that the Soviets would back down from the deadline when confronted by force. Yet this, to my mind, was not capricious gambling, for if we were not willing to take this risk, we would be certain to lose. Our approach was cautious, controlled, and I was confident it was correct. We were trying to give the Soviets every opportunity to be reasonable without humiliation but we were keeping our powder dry.

During the following sixteen weeks, Premier Khrushchev executed a remarkable diplomatic retreat. So skillful and subtle was each step backward that its significance was hardly noticed and for this reason the retreat, although absolute, caused scarcely any loss in Khrushchev's public standing. The Western governments deliberately encouraged this evolution.

However, a number of legislators continued to express anxiety about the adequacy of our Armed Forces. I insisted that if we were to respond with frantic haste to every annoying threat of the Soviets we would merely be dancing to the tune they called, with the result that they could destroy effective planning on our part and push us toward bankruptcy. "We are going to live with this type of crisis for years." I warned, "and our great problem will be to prevent the Communists from throwing us off balance."

Foster asked our critics why we spent $40 billion a year or more to create deterrent and defensive power. "If appeasement and partial surrender are to be our attitude," Foster said, "we had better save our money." He admitted that we could not prevent Khrushchev from strutting across the stage and making grandiloquent speeches; but we could avoid the impression that whenever he sounded conciliatory we would rejoice, and whenever he sounded threatening we would become "fearful as though he were the Lord of Creation."

On March 30 Khrushchev accepted the Western proposal (for talks to begin on May 11, 1959).

Unfortunately, soon after the foreign ministers conference began, it became obvious that little or no progress was to be expected. Gromyko, in the formal meetings, maintained his tiresome attitude of intransigence.

For two weeks the talks remained in a practical deadlock and so produced no surprises. The one potentially striking news story occasioned almost no comment. As the pages of the calendar turned and the clock ticked the seconds away, May 27 approached and finally arrived. This was the date which Soviet Premier Khrushchev some six months earlier had declared he would turn over to East Germany control of access to Berlin. It was the ultimatum that, only a few months before, many had feared would bring up the curtain of World War III. The day came and went—a day lost in history.

But for the Free World the day brought no cause for elation. The Berlin situation would continue to be a challenge. And on May 27 the four foreign ministers, including Gromyko, entered an airplane for a transatlantic journey to Washington, D.C. The occasion for their coming was, for me and one American family in particular, an event of almost unspeakable sadness: the funeral of John Foster Dulles.

On Sunday, May 24, 1959, it was my sad duty to write an announcement which began:

"John Foster Dulles is dead.

"A lifetime of labor for world peace has ended. His countrymen and all who believe in justice and the rule of law grieve at the passing from the earthly scene of one of the truly great men of our time."

During 1958 and 1959 and with the election of 1960 rumbling beyond the horizon, Republicans and Democrats fought with more than normal intensity. Two main engagements were the congressional elections of 1958 and the battle of the budget of 1959.

On October 20 in Los Angeles, I delivered what some writers called the most unvarnished political speech of my career: The Democratic party, I said, "is not one—but two—political parties with the same name. They unite only once every two years—to wage political campaigns.

> "This year in Congress...One after another administration bills were mangled and mushroomed...
>
> "...And only sturdy Republician resistance in Congress and my vetoes blocked over $5 billion of this spending. And I remind you—these federal billions are your money—your own money. Either they come out of your paycheck through higher taxes, or your pocket is picked by inflation."

It was a futile effort. The Republicans suffered a resounding defeat. When the votes were counted in November 1958, Democrats outnumbered Republicans in both Senate and House by nearly two to one. With these results came a dubious distinction: I became the first President in American history to face three successive Congresses in which the opposition had majorities in both houses. The voters, I said, had obviously cast their ballots for people whom "...I would class among the spenders....And I promise this: for the next two years, the Lord sparing me, I am going to fight this as hard as I know how."

"Every sort of foolish proposal will be advanced in the name of national security and the 'poor' fellow," I told the legislative leaders at our first meeting on January 13. "We've got to convince Americans that thrift is not a bad word."

The fight revolved around the fiscal year 1960 budget which I submitted to the Congress in January of 1959—a budget balanced at $77 billion.

I knew we could not expect to win it completely. As in the struggle over

"Though John Foster Dulles was a man of great intellect and stature, he was a perfect advocate not of the perfect or the theoretical best but of the possible. He was called legalistic, arrogant, sanctimonious, and arbitrary —but such descriptions never occurred to those who knew Foster as I did.

"Foster's favorite time for coming to my office was toward evening, around six o'clock. We would lean back in our chairs and talk about the world drama we saw unfolding...

"At the end of a talk about our form of government, he got up, went to the door and just before leaving turned and chuckled: 'Well, it's served us pretty well for two centuries. I guess it will keep on doing so'."

defense reorganization the year before, I wrote to hundreds of friends asking them to do what they could to persuade the Congress to hold the lid on federal spending.

I concluded that the Democrats' idea of cutting the budget—which would admittedly be helpful in avoiding inflation—was to slice primarily into foreign aid, never a politically popular cause, and then to keep on seeking larger appropriations for domestic purposes with scant thought of priority.

There was, in the end, only one way to win: to alert the country to the dangers of cheap money, to turn a bright spotlight on the Congress and, in view of the scarcity of Republican members, to get enough Democratic votes to defeat the outlandish proposals brought forward by those who believe that bigger appropriations mean always a better America.

We did not have to wait long for a test. At the legislative leaders' meeting on February 3, I warned we were facing our first crucial vote—on a Democratic proposal to expand the administration's program for federally financed housing.

The Republicans, united, soon showed what they could do; together with conservative Democrats, they voted down a proposal to provide an exorbitant $450 million a year for the next four fiscal years. Later in the year, when both chambers of the Congress had enacted a housing bill, its cost was still out of bounds, and I vetoed it. On August 12 the Senate supported my veto. Three weeks later, the Congress sent me another housing bill, one that was still too big. I vetoed it. And once again the Senate failed to override.

In voting patterns like these throughout the session, again and again the thin line held. Only once that year did the Congress override my veto. As a result of our economy we actually completed fiscal year '60 with a surplus of more than a billion dollars.

Even more significant than this fiscal victory, however, was the victory in public education evidenced by the grass roots support that turned the tide. Out of the jaws of a political defeat we had snatched at least a partial victory for common sense.

During the summer of 1959, foreign ministers met at Geneva in an attempt to bring Soviet and Western thinking closer over such issues as Berlin. The hope was that almost any initial success at Geneva could lay the groundwork for a future summit meeting. As negotiations at Geneva gradually proved to be fruitless, so did expectations for a formal summit meeting.

An effort related at least distantly to East-West summits was that of encouraging exchanges of visits between United States and Soviet officials at all levels in the hope that such exchanges might lift the Iron Curtain somewhat. It was to help gain acceptance for this idea in the U.S.S.R. that Vice-President Nixon flew to Moscow that summer. Accompanied by my brother, Milton, he went to officiate at the opening of the United States Exhibition there.

I had long advocated—and still advocate today—direct people-to-people exchange as one fine, progressive step toward peace in the world. In September of 1956 I initiated a broad-scale People-to-People program—an effort to stimulate private citizens in many fields (the arts, education, athletics, law, medicine, business), to organize themselves to reach across the seas and national boundaries to their counterparts in other lands.

In 1958 I studied and worked on a proposal (which I never got to make) for a massive exchange of undergraduates by the United States and the Soviet Union—an exchange which, far outstripping the handful we normally send and receive each year, could come to a total of as high as ten thousand.

I was getting tired of dealing with a Communist generation set in their prejudices. One day a new crop would wield the power in the Soviet Union, and it was this generation I was trying to reach.

The most important exchange, however, was a visit from Khrushchev to the United States scheduled for September.

I held a press conference on the forthcoming visit of Premier Khrushchev, nearly a month away, and my possible return trip to Russia.

Peter Lisagor of the Chicago *Daily News* asked:

"Mr. President...part of the criticism is that your visit to Russia somehow or other will erode the presidential prestige to a ceremonial visit of that kind. Would you care to comment on that?"

"I get a little bit weary," I observed, "about people who say, 'Well, this would be a terrible blow to presidential prestige,' or any other prestige. We are talking about the human race and what's going to happen to it."

I once told the legislative leaders, I wanted to make "one great personal effort, before leaving office, to soften up the Soviet leader even a little bit. Except for the Austrian peace treaty," I said, "we haven't made a chip in the granite in seven years."

Shortly after noon on September 15 I met the Chairman at Andrews Air Force Base.

Khrushchev at once presented me with a gift, a model of the spherical projectile called Lunik II, which had been used in the recent Soviet moon shot. This seemed, at first, a strange gift, but it then occurred to me that quite possibly the man was completely sincere. I accepted it, of course, with all the grace I could command.

The Chairman said that he had come to the United States empowered to talk in the broadest terms, his purpose to find agreement on many things. The Soviet Union, he said, did not want war and furthermore he believed that we realized this fact. I agreed that there was no future in mutual suicide, but remarked that the attitudes shown at the latest meeting of the foreign ministers gave a contrary impression. Mr. Khrushchev stressed that his purpose was to try to establish trust between us, a trust based on acceptance of each other's existence; as to the differences between us, which we both recognized, he said, "let history decide."

He said, "I am surprised to find on arriving here that people in the United States welcome us with such tolerance and obvious friendliness." Then he added, "In the Soviet Union there would have been no welcome whatsoever if I had, in advance, publicly spoken against the visitor."

"That is the basic difference," I said, "between our two systems."

Khrushchev was obviously much concerned about the extent of the newspaper and television coverage that would be given to his speeches while he was in the United States. He alleged that our publicity media had not covered his side of things adequately. To this I replied that our press, radio, and television companies were free to report what they regarded as news, or to decline to disseminate any story that had, in their opinion, little news value. I said that his utterances would be reported according to this kind of editorial judgment, not mine. Despite my insistence, he refused to believe that we have in this country a free press, without governmental censorship. He said, "Of course, the American government gets printed what it wants printed and is able to suppress what it does not want printed."

At that moment the two of us went to the White House lawn to begin a helicopter ride around the city. One of the suggestions I had made, long before the Chairman's arrival, was an offer to arrange such a tour. To this he had sent a courteous but firm refusal on the ground that he disliked that sort of machine. But while riding with him from the airport that morning I deliberately expressed my regret that he could not join me on this kind of sightseeing, for I had found them convenient and always interesting.

"Oh," he replied, "if you are to be in the same helicopter, of course I will go!"

He openly expressed his admiration for the helicopter itself, and later gave an order for the purchase of three of them for his own use, specifying that each should be identical with the one in which we were then riding. The next morning Chairman Khrushchev and his family left Washington for a ten-day tour around our country.

On the afternoon of his return to Washington he came again to my White House office. Without delay we boarded a helicopter on the lawn for the trip to Camp David. We arrived at 6 P.M. and went to the cottage named "Aspen," where the Chairman and I, with a couple of others, were housed.

Khrushchev mentioned my former counterpart in Berlin, Marshal Zhukov, who was reportedly involved in an attempted coup in 1957 to supplant the Chairman. Here, for the only time in the conversation, Khrushchev developed a twinkle in his eye. He merely remarked, rather parenthetically, "Your old friend Zhukov is all right. Don't worry about him. He's down in the Ukraine fishing—and like all generals he is probably writing his memoirs."

In our more serious private conversations the Chairman told me that he had decided to abandon all development of naval equipment except submarines and possibly some destroyers.

In reply I said that we were, as he well knew, developing a fleet of atomic submarines including the Polaris type. Indeed, my naval aide brought a model of the Polaris submarine (it was procurable in toy stores everywhere) to give to the Chairman as a memento of his visit. In addition I told him that while we were busy developing an atomic submarine fleet, we were alive to the dangers to us posed by any powerful hostile submarine force. We were giving close attention to the problems of contacting and destroying such vessels in the event of an emergency. To this he simply said, "Of course—I understand."

Aside from these private talks, our sessions naturally dealt with subjects of interest to one or both of our nations. Frequently he interspersed his expositions with comments on his two-week tour around America. Obviously he had, as Cabot Lodge had reported, gained some comprehension of the privileges of a free press, and of the workings of our federated system of government. When he learned, for example, that the President of the United States has no control over the Mayor of Los Angeles, he said, "Now I begin to understand some of the problems of President Eisenhower."

When I again called his attention to our magnificent highways and the automobiles that crowded them—as I had done on our helicopter trip around Washington ten days earlier—he now had a ready answer. He said that in his country there was little need for this type of road because the Soviet people lived close together, did not care for automobiles, had slight interest in driving around the countryside on a Sunday afternoon, and rarely changed their residences from one city to another. To this he added to my amusement: "Your people do not seem to like the place where they live and always want to be on the move going someplace else."

Chairman Khrushchev comes to Camp David. At one point he remarked: "Your old friend Zhukov is all right. Don't worry about him. He's down in the Ukraine fishing—and like all generals he is probably writing his memoirs."

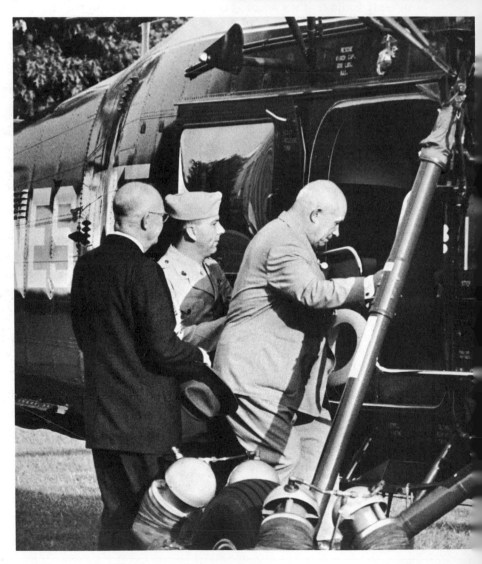

At first Khrushchev suspiciously refused to fly in a helicopter for sightseeing over Washington. Then, when he learned that the President planned to go along, he changed his mind.

The Khrushchevs and the Eisenhowers gather for dinner at the Soviet Embassy. From left, Chairman Khrushchev, Mamie Eisenhower, Mrs. Khrushchev, President Eisenhower, Barbara Eisenhower, Major John Eisenhower.

One question that produced a real argument was his conviction that we should quickly have a four-power "summit." I replied that, like mountain summits, political summits are normally barren, but that, under proper circumstances, I would have no particular objections to such a meeting. I would never go to it as long as there existed the faintest semblance of an ultimatum by his government respecting its purpose to make a peace treaty with East Germany and, according to him, to terminate the rights and privileges of the allies in Berlin.

He talked about Germany and Berlin without rancor, but obviously felt he had committed himself so firmly that he saw no way to retreat immediately from his position. However, the Chairman finally said he recognized my determination in this matter and said he would take steps publicly to remove any suggestion of a time limit within which he would sign a Soviet-East German peace treaty, thus making the future of Berlin a proper subject for negotiation, not one for unilateral action.

Khrushchev said he would not want his concession to appear in a joint communique at the end of our meeting.

"This ends the whole affair," I said, "and I will go neither to a summit nor to Russia."

But he quickly interposed to say that before he could publicize such a statement he needed an opportunity to explain to the members of his own government the reasons that led him to his decision.

This I accepted.

As Khrushchev left the United States, we thought he had come to realize that he had a bear by the tail on the Berlin issue, and was relieved at having found a way out with reasonable dignity. I am sure he was pleasantly surprised with the degree of consideration with which he was treated in the United States.

At any rate he had gone in good spirits. He himself later talked much about "the Spirit of Camp David."

As always, we would have to wait for deeds to determine the sincerity of Soviet words.


War is stupid, cruel, and costly. Yet wars have persisted. In the name of self-defense, nations have paid the human price and, spurred on by fear and competition, have continued to accept the burdens of armaments, the size and cost of which grow ever more fantastic.

With the desire for peace so universally and deeply felt, the obvious question is, "Why do wars occur?" The answer is not to be found in peoples themselves (save where they have been deliberately misled), but in the blind arrogance and conflicting ambitions of governments, especially those whose philosophy is essentially hostile to others and whose objective is nakedly imperialistic.

But hope is more difficult to kill than men, and humanity is not ready spinelessly to accept the cynical conclusion that war is certain to recur, that the law of the jungle must forever be the rule of life.

Men have begun to realize that the best interest of all, no matter how mutually hostile their ideologies, might be served by agreeing upon *controlled* reductions of armaments.

From the very beginning of my administration, we sought creative proposals that might, if accepted by others, lead to progress. For eight years the effort was unremitting. No matter how deeply preoccupied my associates and I became with other urgent situations, never for a day was there absent from our minds and organized work the search for some kind of agreement that would mark a first, even if only a small, step toward a satisfactory disarmament plan.

In the end our accomplishments were meager, almost negligible. Except for the considerable accomplishment of the founding of the IAEA, following my Atoms-for-Peace speech before the United Nations in December of 1953, the most significant, possibly the only, achievement of the entire effort was the wider education of all civilized peoples in the growing need for disarmament and the reasons for our failure to achieve tangible results.

That failure can be explained in one sentence: It was the adamant insistence of the Communists on maintaining a closed society. Their obdurate attitude was based on fear—fear that once they lifted the Iron Curtain their own people, discovering the goodness and richness of life in freedom, might repudiate Communism itself, and, learning of the sincerely peaceful intentions of free peoples who had been proclaimed to them as deadly enemies, would soon reject the Communist goal of world domination.

Since an acceptable treaty for controlled disarmament was not realized, we continued to build an overpowering military establishment as the only feasible defense against the menace and probings of international Communism and as the indispensable platform from which to continue negotiations for a peaceful world.

In September 1959, I began seriously to consider the feasibility of a personal visit to the Mediterranean area and the Middle East. As my second term of office was more than half over, I reflected on a fact in American history: a President's influence on domestic affairs is assumed to wane in the last days of his administration. The thought of marking time waiting for January 20, 1961, did not appeal to me, particularly since my health was good and even seemed to be improving. How, I wondered, could I make the best use of this remaining time for the benefit of the United States?

I realized that internationally I enjoyed a measure of good will, or at least, a wide acquaintanceship, garnered during my many years abroad, performing duties assigned by our government. This might be put to some use.

Presidents did not ordinarily travel far and wide. My own hope, in the event I undertook such an ambitious and somewhat dramatic venture, unprecedented in peacetime, would be to assure all the people I could reach of the sincerity of our search for peace and our desire to be helpful. I wanted to try to raise the morale of struggling and underprivileged peoples, to enhance confidence in the value of friendship with the United States, and to give them assurance of their own security and chances for progress.

After considerable study in Washington and consultation with the appropriate embassies, the route was laid out. First stop, Rome, Italy. From there we were to go to Ankara, Turkey; Karachi, Pakistan; Kabul, Afghanistan; New Delhi, India; Teheran, Iran; Athens, Greece; Tunis, Tunisia; Paris, France; Madrid, Spain; Casablanca, Morocco; and back home.

Sunday was the final day of our stay in "sunny Italy" but our first of sunshine. In the apartment of His Holiness Pope John XXIII on the second floor of the Vatican, I visited for approximately an hour with this remarkable person. Bright and active at the age of seventy-eight, he had the vivacity and zest of a far younger man. The conversation included reminiscences, observations on the cold war, some of our hopes for the future, and cheerful banter about our respective careers and present positions. Before Pope John's elevation to the papacy we had met in Paris where he was in the diplomatic service. We talked of those days. "You were a general and became President," he said jokingly, "and I was a sergeant and became Pope." He said that he almost had not made sergeant and if he hadn't, he might never have become Pope.

On the way out of the Pope's apartment I noted, with some amazement, that the United States Army had penetrated even the Vatican. Nonchalantly sitting on a table in the anteroom was a member of the Signal Corps, equipped with a telephone, ready to connect me instantly with any spot that could be reached by American communications.

We arrived in India a half hour late. I was relieved to learn, however, that our tardiness had been fortunate, since a severe traffic jam on the roads from

New Delhi to the airport delayed Mr. Nehru's arrival beyond the time scheduled for our landing.

The airport ceremonies that evening took place in an almost eerie setting. Darkness was approaching and, save for the spaces cleared for the ceremonies, every square foot of the broad field was jammed with people.

The motorcade had not even left the airfield before it became obvious that anything resembling a timetable had to be discarded.

The whole teeming, boisterous, confused, happy crowd outdid in size anything I had ever seen, including those of the victory celebrations in the great cities of America and Europe. The pace of the motorcade necessarily became so slow that enthusiastic well-wishers could approach the car from the rear and fill it with garlands of flowers, especially marigolds, heaping them upon us.

The Prime Minister finally took a hand himself. When travel remained at a standstill, he dismounted and forced his way to the front of the car. Using the stick he always carried, Nehru began laying about him. He tried to whip the blocking crowd toward one side or the other. This was lively non-violence but the Prime Minister could no more get the attention of even those he was striking than I could get his. His presence in the crowd was almost unnoticed. It did not take him long to recognize the futility of trying to control the almost hysterical fervor, however, and he crawled resignedly on an escorting jeep, stalled only three feet ahead of my car. At long last, with the help of police reserves, the jam loosened. We were allowed, slowly, to proceed.

Mr. Nehru said this was the largest demonstration he had seen since Independence Day eleven years before. He was obviously delighted.

In Teheran, the Shah of Iran and I went through welcoming ceremonies in bitterly cold weather. The trip from the airfield to the Marble Palace was neither long nor strenuous, but it brought another new experience. As in Ankara, arches had been constructed at intervals, to span the highway along which we traveled. But as we approached the first of these arches, I found that the entire road for something like a hundred yards on each direction was carpeted by beautiful Persian rugs. Somewhat taken aback, I exclaimed to the Shah, "I assure Your Majesty that in America we show far more respect for Persian rugs than you do."

"In the 'old days,' " he replied casually, "the entire road to the Palace would have been covered, rather than merely at each of the arches."

Our last stop was in Morocco. There we were met by King Mohammed V, who had visited Washington two years earlier. Among the crowds along the road to Casablanca were Berber tribesmen, who had received word unofficially

A televised talk at No. 10 Downing Street with Prime Minister Harold Macmillan. (There was some fear that the floor might not be able to sustain the weight of the heavy TV equipment. DDE commented about the possibility of the floor giving way during the telecast: "It might have been curious, with both principles falling out of sight of the viewing public while expressing confidence in the future.")

As a lame duck President, DDE said, he was determined to be neither lame nor a sitting duck. After a lengthy trip in an unprecedented attempt at personal diplomacy, he concluded that the eleven-nation trip to Europe and the Middle East was worth the effort. "Their faces are interestingly different and their lands exotic, but their fate and ours are one." Right, Paris 1959.

Ankara, Turkey.

With Pope John XXIII. Sharing in the laughter are Lieutenant Colonel Vernon Walters and the President's daughter-in-law, Barbara Eisenhower.

In India.

And then home again...

that some kind of a celebration was in the offing. Without the knowledge of the Moroccan government, these hardy warriors, with their antique muzzle-loading rifles and their flowing robes, lined the route of the motorcade to fire salutes, one-handed, straight into the air. I think the Secret Service agents were not so fearful that a tribesman might deliberately take aim and shoot, but the possibility did occur to them that one of the old weapons might explode alongside our car. Having been accustomed, as a boy, to muzzle-loaders and black powder—the same used by the Berbers—I knew that the agents needed to have no fear of an explosion from the size of the charges they were using. These tribesmen were just as conscious of the cost of powder as I had had to be sixty years earlier.

Flying home, we crossed the Atlantic and landed at Washington on December 22, at 11:30 P.M. local time after a 21½ hour day. Mamie was there to greet us, along with the Nixons and members of the Cabinet. We were truly happy to see them.

As Mamie and I drove down Pennsylvania Avenue, approaching the White House, we found hundreds of sparkler-carrying well-wishers filling Lafayette Square with a dazzling midnight illumination. It was a unique reception and, because of the cold and the lateness of the hour, one that we deeply appreciated.

When we reached the second floor of the White House I saw a startling formation.

Seated around a table in the West Hall were my friends, General Gruenther, Bill Robinson, George Allen, and Slats Slater, all engaged in what appeared to be a routine bridge game. As we came in, Al Gruenther turned around slightly, said "Hi," turned back to his bridge hand, and said, "I double."

George looked up long enough to ask, "What's new?"

Another asked, "Just in?"

But despite their best efforts at indifference, they had succeeded in displaying a welcome sight to a tired and glad-to-be-home traveler.

For myself, I had no doubt that the trip was worth the effort it required. By no means does such a conclusion imply that an American President should spend a large portion of his time traveling the earth. But when any future Executive may find the circumstances favorable for undertaking a similar journey, then whatever trouble and inconvenience he might be subjected to in visiting the less well-known parts of the world will be repaid many times over. He will be showered with kindnesses and courtesis to the point of exhaustion, but he will be rewarded richly by the eagerness of whole populations to learn about America, and by his better understanding of the peoples he, directly or indirectly, as head of the strongest nation on earth, is destined to serve.

Their faces are interestingly different and their lands exotic, but their fate and ours are one.

In November of 1959 trouble blazed in Panama: a mob of Panamanians, stirred up over the sovereignty issue, as well as the old issue of allegedly unfair rates of pay for native workers in the Canal Zone (and mistakenly believing that the United States made huge profits from the Canal), attempted to "invade" the Zone. There were elements of justice in the Panamanian complaints, and we had been working on a nine-point program for the Zone, including a low-cost housing project and revised wage rates. But before the program could be started, the mob marched. After calm returned, parts of the program gradually went into effect.

Prior to this incident, in May 1958, a worse explosion had occurred, during the Latin American trip of Vice-President and Mrs. Nixon. On May 8, a mob at San Marco University in Lima, Peru, shoved, stoned, and booed the Vice-President and his party. The events of that week in May 1958 brought home to all of us the clear truth that, as the Vice-President reported at the end of his trip, "The threat of Communism in Latin America is greater than ever before."

This threat, though none of us knew it at the time, was to be thrust into the open first, not on the Latin American mainland, but on the island of Cuba. There a bearded young man named Fidel Castro had succeeded in gathering together a band of about a thousand guerrillas in the Escambray Mountains, a force promising to throw out the self-enriching and corrupt dictator, Fulgencio Batista, and end the suppressions and brutalities of his police state.

We would not take sides or intervene, I told a news conference on November 5, 1958, except to protect American citizens in Cuba. A month later Castro launched a major attack against Santa Clara, the capital of Las Villas Province in central Cuba. Batista's local forces, unable to defeat Castro, decided to join him. Obviously Castro had won the emotional and now the significant material support of the Cuban people.

"Communists and other extreme radicals appear to have penetrated the Castro movement," Allen Dulles said. "If Castro takes over, they will probably participate in the government." When I heard this estimate, I was provoked that such a conclusion had not been given earlier.

One of my advisers recommended that the United States should now back Batista as the lesser of two evils. I rejected that course. If Castro turned out to be as bad as our intelligence now suggested, our only hope, if any, lay with some kind of non-dictatorial "third force," neither Castroite nor Batistiano.

In any event, by early 1960 there was no longer any doubt in the administration that "something would have to be done"—the questions were what, when, and under what circumstances? We knew that precipitate, unilateral action could easily be fatal to our hopes of strengthening the Western Hemisphere's Organization of American States for dealing with international problems of common interest. For one thing, we did know: Fidel Castro was a hero to the masses in many Latin American nations. They saw him as a champion of the downtrodden and the enemy of the privileged who, in most of their countries, controlled both wealth and governments. His crimes and wrongdoings that so repelled the more informed peoples of the continent had little effect on the young, the peons, the underprivileged, and all others who wanted to see the example of revolution followed in their own nations.

Given these problems and the need for collective action to solve them, I decided by early 1960 that, among other things, the time had arrived for a presidential journey to South America.

At seven-thirty on the morning of Washington's Birthday, 1960, I took off, with a considerable party, from snow-covered Washington, D.C., for Ramey Air Force Base in Puerto Rico. When we landed there, in its sunshine with the temperature in the eighties, we were embarked on a fifteen-thousand-mile trip which would take us to the four southernmost countries of Latin America. Our first stop was Brasilia, the new inland capital of Brazil.

Entering Rio de Janeiro the next day, we met crowds of spectacular size, estimated by the police at a million. Along a five-mile motorcade route, which took an hour to travel, people jammed the roadways and streets and filled office windows. Along the way I heard one band after another play "God Bless America," but it was less comforting to see a sign proclaiming: WE LIKE IKE; WE LIKE FIDEL TOO.

After a visit to São Paulo and the flight to Buenos Aires, I flew south for a brief visit to the seaside resort of Mar del Plata, where a million Argentinians warmly greeted the combined Argentine-U.S. party. As we prepared to leave from the Mar del Plata airport, President Arturo Frondizi expressed his enthusiasm for the beautiful presidential aircraft. I knew, of course, about the Latin American tradition that whenever a guest admires an object, the host must give it to him. Unhappily, however, the plane was not mine to give away.

Next we went to Bariloche, a famous resort in the south. The next morning after a farewell to President Frondizi, we vaulted the Andes and came down in the third country of our visit, Chile, to be greeted by its intelligent and impressive President, Jorge Alessandri.

**Signatures in the Cold War.** Japanese Prime Minister Kishi and Secretary of State Christian Herter simultaneously sign a security treaty.

Anastas Mikoyan and Fidel Castro sign a pact for Soviet sugar purchases and assistance, including a hundred million dollar credit.

While there, I received a long letter from the President of the Federation of Students of Chile, an organization claiming a membership of twenty-five thousand drawn from the country's seven major universities. The letter came right to the point: "Has the United States become a satisfied nation, one which fights for the maintenance of the prevailing order in the world and in Latin America? This dangerous image is becoming accepted more every day. If this is true, we must respectfully say to you that the United States will have little or nothing to offer the younger generation and the immense multitude of the poor, who compose 90 percent of the Latin American population. And we will have little or nothing to expect from the guidance and genius of North America...

I could not at that time reveal what was shaping up in my mind—that the private and public capital which had flowed bounteously into Latin America had failed to benefit the masses, that the demand for social justice was still rising. But upon my return home I determined to begin planning, and the plans would culminate eventually in historic measures designed to bring about social reforms for the benefit of all the people of Latin America.

Leaving Chile we flew back to Uruguay, landing at its capital, Montevideo. From there we started for Puerto Rico, again a long trip enlivened by the loss of an engine over the Amazon jungle that forced us to transfer to our follow-up plane when we landed at Paramaribo, Surinam. As in other cities we found some dissidents, people who were adopting Castro as their idol. As in other places I had to make speeches, always emphasizing U.S. readiness to help those nations that showed a determination to advance the welfare of the masses and the energy to help themselves.

I was fatigued. As I wrote Prime Minister Macmillan later that month: "...Frankly, no prior tour of mine in the past fifteen years has been so (physically) tiring as the one I (have just) completed in South America. The combination of dust, crowded days, and summer heat persuaded me that I'm not as young as I was when we were together in Algiers."

On the trip I had made thirty-seven addresses and toasts, including two nationwide telecasts. The effort had not been unproductive, at least as seen by our journalists. At the end of the trip, Tad Szulc, a New York Times reporter who had gone along, wrote that: "relations between the United States and South American lands appeared today to stand on the highest plateau since the end of World War II..." The expedition, at least in the eyes of the press, was a real success.

When the Soviets rejected my Open Skies proposal in 1955, a proposal to initiate mutual aerial inspection of the Soviet Union and the United States in order to guard against the possibilities of surprise attack, I decided that more intelligence about their war-making capabilities was a necessity. So I directed that we would begin aerial reconnaissance, making use of the then relatively invulnerable, high-flying U-2 aircraft. It had been making some weather flights, but from 1956 onward its basic mission was to provide us with current information on the status of the Soviet missile and armaments programs.

Proof of the plane's capacity to produce photography of excellent definition was striking. I was shown photographs, taken from an altitude of seventy thousand feet, of some of our important cities. On these we could easily count the automobiles on the streets and even the lines marking the parking areas for individual cars. There was no doubt about the quality of the information to be obtained.

An important characteristic of the plane was its fragile construction, with an assumption (insisted upon by the CIA and the Joint Chiefs and frequently reported to me) that in the event of mishap the plane would disintegrate and the pilot would almost certainly perish.

On the afternoon of May 1, 1960, General Goodpaster telephoned me: "One of our reconnaissance planes," he said, "on a scheduled flight from its base in Adana, Turkey, is overdue and possibly lost." I knew instantly that this was one of our U-2 planes, probably over Russia. Both the State Department and the CIA advised immediate release of the always ready "cover story" which was based on the theory of the destruction of the plane and the death of the pilot. I demurred but in view of the need for speed if the whole story was to be at all credible, agreed to let the story be used. Early the next morning Goodpaster came into my office, his face an etching of bad news. He plunged to the point at once. "Mr. President, I have received word from the CIA that the U-2 reconnaissance plane I mentioned yesterday is still missing. The pilot reported an engine flameout at a position about thirteen hundred miles inside Russia and has not been heard from since. With the amount of fuel he had on board, there is not a chance of his still being aloft."

Nearly two days after Goodpaster's first report went by without a word reaching me from any source as to the fate of the missing pilot. Then, on May 5, while I was attending a meeting of the National Security Council, we learned of the Soviet reaction. The text arrived just as the meeting ended.

The two Presidents do a little cannon-climbing on the Gettysburg battlefield. April 24, 1960.

Vice-President Nixon makes a trip to Russia—and engages in an informal, rough and tumble debate as they tour U.S. exhibition. Here, a pause for the interpreter.

"My acknowledgment of responsibility" for the U-2 missions "was practically unprecedented in history but so were the circumstances . . . When the world can entertain not the slightest doubt of the facts there is no point in trying to evade the issue."

Khrushchev had announced the shooting down of a United States reconnaissance plane that had penetrated deep into Soviet territory. The theory that Khrushchev would never admit such an occurrence was demolished.

On the afternoon of May 6, Mr. Khrushchev, appearing before the Supreme Soviet once more, announced the unbelievable.

The uninjured pilot of our reconnaissance plane, along with much of his equipment intact, was in Soviet hands. Francis Gary Powers, the pilot, had confessed to those aspects of the flight that were obvious from the evidence and thus the world was aware that his mission had been to penetrate deeply into the Soviet Union. Pictures of Powers were made public and parts of the reconnaissance airplane were put on display.

In the diplomatic field it was routine practice to deny responsibility for an embarrassing occurrence when there is even a 1 percent chance of being believed, but when the world can entertain not the slightest doubt of the facts there is no point in trying to evade the issue.

My acknowledgment of responsibility for espionage activities was practically unprecedented, but so were the circumstances.

"We will now just have to endure the storm," I said, with everyone fully realizing that it was I personally—and rightly so—who would do the enduring.

In the midst of all this turbulence, it was necessary to avoid losing sight of the next immediate issue: the effect of the U-2 on prospects for success at the forthcoming summit meeting in Paris. I promptly told Prime Minister Macmillan that there was no possibility that I would apologize for acts that I thought necessary to the security of the United States, particularly in view of the proof in our hands of persistent and flagrant espionage activities in our nation by numbers of Soviet agents.

The real issue at stake was not the fact that both sides conducted intelligence activities, but rather that the conduct and announced intentions of the Communists created the necessity for such clandestine maneuvers. As a consequence, the West—more specifically the United States as the major military power of the West—had to maintain constantly the capacity to detect any possible prelude to an infinitely more destructive Pearl Harbor.

The summit meeting convened on May 16. President de Gaulle, presiding, had not even finished calling the meeting to order before Khrushchev was on his feet, red-faced, loudly demanding the right to speak. General de Gaulle looked rather quizzically at me and upon my nod to him, turned to Khrushchev and said this would be quite satisfactory.

The chairman of the Soviet delegation then launched on a long diatribe, speaking from a prepared text. He went on into a much longer dissertation on the reasons it had now become necessary for him to revoke the invitation that he had previously extended to me to visit the Soviet Union later in the spring.

The length of his explanation and the emphasis he gave to this subject clearly indicated that he was determined to keep me out of Russia. His document was repetitious, and at one point he became so vehement that I could not help grinning. He happened to notice this, and thereafter kept his eyes glued to the text of his speech.

The Paris meeting was the last time I saw Khrushchev in person. In a way I was sorry this was so. There was no denying that he was an interesting man. Of course he stood for everything in government that, to me, was unacceptable, even abominable. He was shrewd, tough, and coldly deliberate, even when he was pretending to be consumed with anger. Certainly he was ruthless. In personal conversations he was blunt but witty; he laughed often and seemed devoted to his family. The Khrushchev of the tea table was scarcely recognizable to one who knew him at the conference table.

Regarding the U-2 program itself, I know of no decision that I would make differently, given the same set of facts as they confronted us at the time.

When I have been questioned about the wisdom of the U-2 flights, I have replied with a question of my own: "Would you be ready to give back all of the information we secured from our U-2 flights over Russia if there had been no disaster to one of our planes in Russia?"

I never received an affirmative response.

From the breakup of the Paris meeting in May 1960, to the end of my administration, the Soviets indulged in an intensified campaign of vituperation and false charges. The peaceful line was gone; in its place was a Kremlin attitude reminiscent of the days of Stalin.

Their professed explanation, the one Mr. Khrushchev would have liked us to believe, of course, was that the Chairman had become indignant at the "impudence" of the United States in conducting air reconnaissance over his land in mid-1960. This was ridiculous: Khrushchev had known of many earlier U-2 flights. He had long been well aware, also, that we had volumes of evidence on Soviet espionage in our nation and had apprehended their spies in our territory regularly. This knowledge had not deterred him, in apparent good will, from coming to the United States, visiting at Camp David, and arguing for a summit conference.

The cancellation of Khrushchev's invitation to visit the Soviet Union caused a revision in my plans for going to Japan. Originally I had expected, after traveling in the Soviet Union for several days, to fly eastward across Siberia and arrive in Tokyo on June 19. I saw no reason to change this arrival date in Tokyo, but the extra time now available made it possible to accept a long-standing invitation to revisit the Philippines, Korea, and Formosa. Immediately upon my return from Europe on May 20, intensive planning was started for what quickly became a tour of several bastions of the Free World in the Far East.

But the Communists, having canceled the trip to the Soviet Union, set about to disrupt this one also. In Japan, with its stray Communist elements and its far left Socialist party, the Communists wielded a strong influence with a consequent ability to stage public disturbances.

Japan was not properly equipped to handle this kind of difficulty. The reason largely stemmed from her extreme pacifism. The only nation to have suffered atomic attacks on civilian populations and determined to prevent a resurgence of Samurai dictatorship, she had disarmed to an extent that not even billy clubs were provided her police forces. The police were thus completely unable to control large and unruly mobs. Moreover, while Communist elements began urging violence to prevent my entry into their country, the U-2 incident was intensively advertised as warlike aggression against the Soviets and increased the apprehension of the populace.

The Communist tactic in Japan was fundamental: their propaganda set out to create in the public mind a direct link between my visit and the forthcoming ratification of the new Japanese-American Security Treaty. This treaty, a revision of the agreement of 1952, obligated the United States more definitely to participate in the defense of Japan and increased Japanese rights as partners in this effort. Socialist opposition to the treaty had been felt as early as November of the previous year.

One of the most indelible memories I have of the many journeys into other countries is that of the people I saw—masses of glowing faces, friendly shouts, songs, gaily printed placards, and homemade signs of welcome. Their message, I felt, was one of kinship with the United States. No matter what the color of the skin, the shape of the eyes, the character of the costume, all were met for one purpose: to show, in this rather vicarious way, their favorable conception of American freedom, American purpose, and American aspirations for all men.

With the Republican convention had named a national ticket, my responsibility for determining the character and tone of Republican national campaigns naturally fell to other hands.

"Thus we see as our goal, not a superstate above all nations, but a world community embracing them all, rooted in law and justice and enhancing the potentialities and common purposes of all peoples."

"Khrushchev continued his bad manners to the last. He stood up and began interrupting an address by Prime Minister Macmillan. Harold handled the situation calmly. With immense dignity, British reserve in its finest flower, he simply paused long enough to ask for a translation of Khrushchev's insults. Khrushchev later removed his shoe and brandished it at the other delegates."

Early in August the Vice-President and I agreed that I could do the most good by making a number of speeches around the country, before non-partisan audiences, in support of principles that had guided my administration. I believed with him that these would help the ticket more at the moment than partisan speeches by me under political sponsorship. No one wanted to see us win the election more than I. As I told Ben Fairless in a telephone conversation on August 19: "I'm going to make eight to ten appearances during the campaign. Motorcades kill me, but I'm going to do them to try to arouse enthusiasm." I said I would do any honorable thing to avoid turning the country over to the "big spending" type of Democrats.

Nixon's campaign was interrupted at its outset by circumstances beyond his control. Congress consumed tedious weeks in winding up its business, and Dick himself was confined for a painful period in Walter Reed Army Hospital. He had to cancel planned visits but on Monday, September 12, I saw him and Cabot off for the big weeks of the campaign. That they had a tough job ahead of them was evidenced by a Gallup Poll report on this question: "Which party would you like to see win the congressional elections in your state?" The Democrats were favored by 58 percent, the Republicans by 42 percent.

Election Day was November 8.

That night I watched the returns with John and Barbara and a friend of theirs, Dorothy Daniel. By 11 o'clock, when I went to bed, the results were not encouraging. The next morning, though the election had turned from an initial landslide into a horse race, no one held out much hope for the Republicans. At 12:25 in the afternoon the Vice-President telephoned me from his headquarters at the Ambassador Hotel in Los Angeles.

"I still think we'll take California, Minnesota, and Illinois by the time the absentee ballots come in," he said. "But even so, we won't have enough. Therefore," he added, "I have conceded the election." (He had earlier refused to do so because of the inconclusiveness of the returns the night before.)

"I ran 7 percent ahead of the other Republican candidates," he said. "Kennedy ran a little more than that behind other Democratic candidates." The final result, indeed showed how close the Vice-President had come to winning. Trailing by only 113,000 votes, he and Cabot Lodge polled 49.5 percent of the total, against 49.7 percent for Kennedy and Johnson. A switch of fewer than 12,000 votes in five states would have reversed the result.

Later the Vice-President recalled that during that conversation he had never heard me sound more depressed. He was right. As I wrote to a friend several weeks later, when I heard the outcome, I felt as though "I had been hit in the solar plexus with a ball bat—" as though eight years of work had been for naught.

Five neutralist countries hold a summit during the UN meeting in September, 1960. From left, Prime Minister Jawaharlal Nehru of India, President Kwame Nkrumah of Ghana, President Gamal Abdel Nasser of United Arab Republic, President Sukarno of Indonesia, and President Tito of Yugoslavia.

President Eisenhower greets President-elect John F. Kennedy. "I must confess to considerable gratification in this visit with the young man who was to be my successor. He conducted himself with unusual good taste. Resisting any temptation to flood the White House with his own retinue, he came riding in the back seat of an automobile by himself."

A final Christmas in the White House. An American family gathers to exchange gifts and wish peace to the world.

After the White House years, President Kennedy invites his predecessor to Camp David for talks on the explosive Cuban missile situation. April 22, 1961.

On December 6, Senator Kennedy came to the White House, at my invitation, for a discussion on the transfer of responsibilities.

While meetings such as this can rarely serve as an indication of the future, I must confess to considerable gratification in this visit with the young man who was to be my successor. Throughout the entire program he conducted himself with unusual good taste. Resisting any temptation to flood the White House with his own retinue, he came riding in the back seat of an automobile by himself. In our conversations I was struck by his pleasing personality, his concentrated interest, and his receptiveness.

The life of my administration was now measured in hours, and on the evening of January 17 I spoke in farewell to the American people:

"Three days from now, after half a century in the service of our country, I shall lay down the responsibilities of office as, in traditional and solemn ceremony, the authority of the presidency is vested in my successor.

"This evening I come to you with a message of leave-taking and farewell, and to share a few final thoughts with you, my countrymen.

"Like every other citizen, I wish the new President, and all who will labor with him, Godspeed. I pray that the coming years will be blessed with peace and prosperity for all."

The idea, then, of making a final address as President to the nation seemed to call on me to warn the nation of a danger and to include a sobering message in what might otherwise have been a farewell of pleasantries.

The most quoted section of the speech came in these paragraphs:

Until the latest of our world conflicts, American makers of plowshares could, with time and as required, make swords as well. But now we can no longer risk emergency improvisation of national defense; we have been compelled to create a permanent armaments industry of vast proportions. Added to this, three and a half million men and women are directly engaged in the defense establishment. We annually spend on military security more than the net income of all United States corporations.

This conjunction of an immense military establishment and a large arms industry is new in the American experience. The total influence—economic, political, even spiritual—is felt in every city, every state house, every office of the federal government. We recognize the imperative need for this development. Yet we must not fail to comprehend its grave implications. Our toil, resources, and livelihood are all involved; so is the very structure of our society.

In a series of televised post-Presidential talks, Walter Cronkite, CBS correspondent, draws out of his subject thoughtful and reflective views on the Presidency and the times in which we live.

In the councils of government we must guard against the acquisition of unwarranted influence, whether sought or unsought, by the military-industrial complex. The potential for the disastrous rise of misplaced power exists and will persist.

We must never let the weight of this combination endanger our liberties or democratic processes. We should take nothing for granted. Only an alert and knowledgeable citizenry can compel the proper meshing of the huge industrial and military machinery of defense with our peaceful methods and goals, so that security and liberty may prosper together.

The next morning I held my final news conference as President. In the last question a reporter asked: "...would you sum up for us your idea of what kind of a United States you would like your grandchildren to live in?"

I said I hoped that they might live "in a peaceful world...enjoying all of the privileges and carrying forward all the responsibilites envisioned for the good citizen of the United States, and this means among other things the effort always to raise the standards of our people in their spiritual, intellectual, (and)

In a revisit to Normandy, two decades after the invasion, the architect of victory offered personal recollections and reflections. And in the "Afterthoughts" of his *Waging Peace*, he wrote: "As I look over my shoulder, the landscape of memory is dominated by the ridges and peaks of crises, which almost conceal the peaceful pastoral plains between them. But there were calm and happy hours..."

economic strength. That's what I would like to see them have."

The evening of January 19, 1961, saw a deluge of snow dumped on Washington. Early in the evening Secretary of Defense Thomas S. Gates called to say he was turning out all possible troops from Fort Belvoir, Fort Myer, and other locations to assist the overwhelmed authorities in Washington to clear the streets and make the 1961 inauguration possible without delay.

On January 20, I attended the inauguration ceremonies of John F. Kennedy.

After the now President Kennedy had repeated the traditional, "So help me God," Mamie and I, making our way toward a side exit, made a fantastic discovery. We were free—as only private citizens in a democratic nation can be free. This time as we left the Capitol, we were not solemnly accompanied by escorting committees of the Senate and the House or surrounded by the always loyal and helpful members of the Secret Service. Quietly avoiding the general flow of the crowd, we made our own way to a waiting car.

Later, we followed the route, now grown familiar to us, through the suburbs of northwest Washington, past Rockville, Frederick, Thurmont....We talked of our years in the White House, which had been our home for a longer time than any other place in our forty-four years of married life and would always hold for us a wealth of pleasant memories. During those years three of our grandchildren left babyhood behind and learned to swim and ride and began their formal education. The youngest was born in Walter Reed Army Hospital and christened in the lovely Blue Room of the White House. We formed many new and enduring friendships, and every day we learned something new about our country and its people, and the great world about us.

As we rolled through the countryside, we found that many of our fellow citizens had learned of our planned route and paused along the way to wave a friendly greeting. Approaching Emmitsburg, we were saluted by the students and the sisters of St. Joseph College. Much had happened since that day, over five years before, when the college had paid us a similar compliment as Mamie and I were driving to Gettysburg for convalescence from my heart attack. Mamie was particularly excited, the more so because she was an honorary doctor of the college. On this day, standing in the fresh, deep snow, all the lovely young girls in their caps and gowns and the faculty of sisters lined the road to welcome us back to the region where we were establishing our new home.

And so we came to Gettysburg and to the farm we had bought eleven years earlier, where we expected to spend the remainder of our lives.